The Beaverkill

The Beaverkill

The History of a River and Its People

Ed Van Put

Lyons & Burford, Publishers

Lyons & Burford, Publishers
31 West 21 Street
New York, New York 10010

Printed in the United States of America

10 9 8 7 6 5 4 3 2 1

Design by Lynne Amft

Maps © by Michael Musto

LIBRARY OF CONGRESS CATALOGING-IN-PUBLICATION DATA

Van Put, Ed.
The Beaverkill / Ed Van Put.
p.   cm.
Includes bibliographical references and index.
ISBN 1-55821-475-5
1. Trout fishing—New York (State)—Beaver Kill (Ulster County and Delaware County) 2. Beaver Kill (Ulster County and Delaware County, N.Y.) I. Title.
SH688.U6V36 1996
799.1'755—DC20   96-22398   CIP

To my wife Judy O'Brien

Contents

Acknowledgments

A great deal of the information gathered for this book was obtained from the weekly newspapers published in the small hamlets of the Catskills and the larger communities along its borders. Newspapers were found in regional libraries, either in their original form, bound into yearly volumes, or on microfilm. In a few instances volumes were available through newspapers that are still publishing, or individuals who owned collections.

Further research was collected through an invaluable service known as inter-library loan. Rare books, antiquated periodicals, and newspaper microfilm became available close at hand, through local libraries.

Early on, I had the good fortune to meet Catskill historian Alf Evers at the Kingston Area Library, and while our encounters were brief, his advice on research was extremely helpful. He once stated that a good librarian could be of great assistance, and I was fortunate in finding several. A special debt of gratitude is owed to the librarians of Livingston Manor, Walton, and Delhi.

It took more than ten years to collect *Beaverkill* material, and I am eternally indebted to my wife Judy for getting involved with my project. Searching old newspapers and periodicals is tedious, difficult, time-consuming work. There are no shortcuts. Countless hours are often spent with no useful data gathered. She became a persistent and reliable researcher, sharing in the elation that comes with finding or discovering "new" information.

My gratitude is extended to the following individuals who made my work easier by giving advice and direction, or who allowed access to their photographs, libraries, files, records, and collections: Charlotte Steenrod, Judie Darbee Vinceguerra, Delbert Van Etten, Irene Barnhart, Evelyn Gerow, Dr. Paul D'Amico, Jim Elliott, Julie Allen, George Fulton, Joan and Lee Wulff, the Balsam Lake Club, Joe Purcell, Steve Starrantino, and the Historical Societies of Greene and Sullivan Counties.

Old photographs are difficult to obtain, and I am grateful to Doug Bury, Bob and Alice Jacobson, Jack Niflot, Jean Boyd, Emerson Bouton, Mary Dette Clark, Ray Pomeroy, Sherry Bellows, Timothy Foote, Patricia M. Sherwood, and Francis Davis for their contributions.

I also owe a special thank you to Joe Horak, who over the years allowed me the use of the copy machines at his law office in Livingston Manor.

Introduction

John Merwin

Great waters only occasionally breed great books. Ed Van Put's *The Beaverkill* is a wonderful example of both, bringing two hundred years of angling tradition to life in one grand, sparkling riffle.

Fly fishing for trout is a sport in which basic equipment, more abstract but no less important than hard-core items such as rods and flies, is tradition. The mere act of grasping a fly rod creates a kinship spanning the centuries back to Walton and beyond, a donning of history's cloak that can immediately make a cold rain just a little warmer by adding a sense of belonging. Theodore Gordon fished the same pool, for example, as did Lee Wulff. As do I. And so it is that we all belong, one way or another, to the Beaverkill, a modest river in New York's Catskills with a very immodest history.

There are, as Van Put points out, other American trout streams that might be prettier; other rivers that may offer more and larger trout. But there are none with stronger and more diverse traditions. As a touchstone of American angling, the Beaverkill is in a class by itself.

This is partly an accident of geography. American fly fishing developed rapidly within fledgling cities such as Philadelphia, New York, and Boston as colonization progressed through the late 1700s. But by 1800, the best of this urban sport was gone, and anglers started to look for fishing beyond the city limits. Although travel wasn't easy, areas such as Pennsylvania's Poconos and New York's Catskills were attainable with effort and so became trout-fishing meccas well before the Civil War.

It's important to realize that American fly fishing wasn't "born" in any one of these places at the expense of another, despite modern boosterism and the claims of numerous chambers of commerce. Things just aren't that simple, and fly fishing for North American trout evolved in various ways simultaneously from Virginia north to Montreal and beyond during the early 1800s. And as it happens, fly fishing itself was "born" in none of these places, but was—and is—an immigrant, brought in baggage to the New World from western Europe along with Grandma's silver spoons and Grandpa's clock. But partly because of its proximity to New York City and other early population centers—and partly just because it's a good trout stream—the Beaverkill's layers of angling history are unusually thick: two centuries' worth of lore, legend, and anecdote, which in a sport that venerates tradition has made the Beaverkill a shrine.

The roots of all those stories, the actual history within the legends, are hard to find. Typically, local histories are the most difficult to assemble; everybody knows when a war started, for example, but an old fish hatchery or nineteenth-century boardinghouse once popular with fishermen is much harder to pin down. The answers are often found in the dusty, bound volumes of forgotten weekly newspapers like the old Kingston (NY) *Argus* or Ellenville, New York's former *Journal*. Historical societies are also a help, although knowledge here is bought slowly—scrapbook by cardboard box by tattered diary. Van Put's extraordinary effort in these obscure arenas enriches every page of this book, bringing the Beaverkill's story to life not just in legend, but in carefully assembled and often colorful fact.

It's tempting to say that Ed Van Put is uniquely qualified to have written this book, but that's only partly true. Certainly he knows the river itself as few others do, having lived and fished along it for more than twenty-five years. Then, too, his perspective is acute, deriving from a career as a New York State fisheries technician dealing with the acquisition of public fishing rights along the Beaverkill and other area waters. As a trout fisherman, he's widely known as one of the most skilled anglers in a valley filled with fishermen. Any or all of these things might have made a Beaverkill book in the usual sense of an author's qualifications, but Ed—to his undying credit—chose to take an extra giant step.

A series of steps, actually, through—at last count—the dusty records of four New York counties, the archives of fourteen regional libraries, old volumes from thirty-seven different regional newspapers, countless old books, state and federal reports, plus numerous personal interviews over the years with both anglers still living as I write, and those recently passed beyond. Through all of that essential yet dreary homework over endless hours, Van Put wrote his book along a road that's increasingly less traveled these days: one dedicated to doing it right and to getting it right, too.

It is that uncommon effort that has produced this richly uncommon book—a genuinely definitive and thoroughly enjoyable record of America's best-known trout stream.

Maps of the Watershed

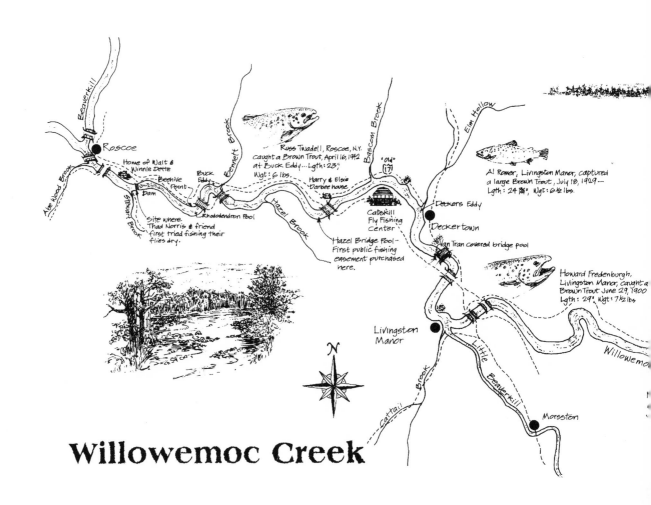

Beaverkill

Alder Wood Brook

Roscoe

Home of Walt & Winnie Dette

Beehive Point

Stewart Brook

Dam

Site where Thad Norris & friend first tried fishing their flies dry.

Buck Eddy

Beaverbrook

Bennett Brook

Rhododendron Pool

Hazel Brook

Russ Twadell, Roscoe, N.Y. caught a Brown Trout, April 16, 1942 at Buck Eddy...Lgth: 23" Wgt: 6 lbs.

Harry & Elsie Darbee house

Catskill Fly Fishing Center

Hazel Bridge Pool — First public fishing easement purchased here.

Biscom Brook

"old" 17

Elm Hollow

Al Rower, Livingston Manor, captured a large Brown Trout, July 18, 1929 — Lgth: 24¾", Wgt: 6½ lbs.

Deckers Eddy

Deckertown

Van Tran covered bridge pool

Howard Fredenburgh, Livingston Manor, caught a Brown Trout June 29, 1900 Lgth: 29", Wgt: 7½ lbs

Livingston Manor

Little Beaverkill

Willowemoc

Cattail Brook

Morsston

N

Willowemoc Creek

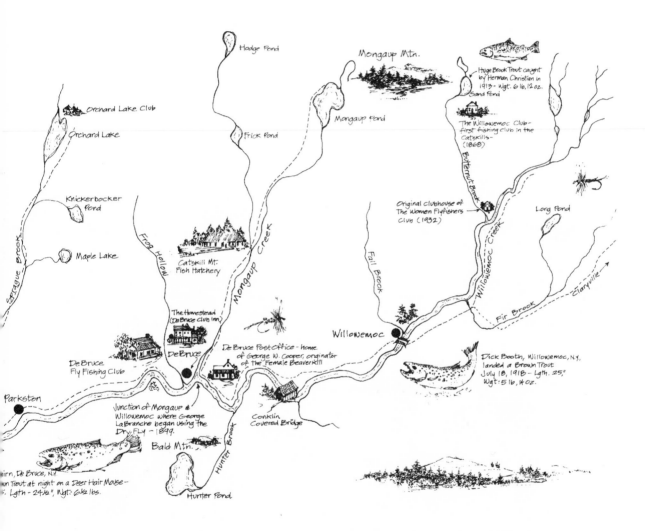

Hodge Pond

Mongaup Mtn.

Huge Brook Trout caught by Herman Christian in 1913 - Wgt. 6 lb, 12 oz.

Sand Pond

The Willowemoc Club - first fishing club in the Catskills - (1868)

Orchard Lake Club

Orchard Lake

Frick Pond

Mongaup Pond

Original clubhouse of The Women Flyfishers Club (1932)

Long Pond

Knickerbocker Pond

Butternut Brook

Frog Hollow

Maple Lake

Catskill Mt. Fish Hatchery

Mongaup Creek

Fall Brook

Willowemoc Creek

Fir Brook

Claryville

Sprague Brook

The Homestead (De Bruce Club Inn)

De Bruce

De Bruce Post Office - home of George W. Cooper, originator of the "Female Beaverkill"

Willowemoc

Dick Booth, Willowemoc, N.Y., landed a Brown Trout July 18, 1918 - Lgth. 25", Wgt: 5 lb, 14 oz.

De Bruce Fly Fishing Club

Parkston

Junction of Mongaup & Willowemoc where George LaBranche began using the Dry Fly - 1899.

Conklin Covered Bridge

Bald Mtn.

Hunter Brook

irn, De Bruce, N.Y.

wn Trout at night on a Deer Hair Mouse - . Lgth - 24½", Wgt: 6½ lbs.

Hunter Pond

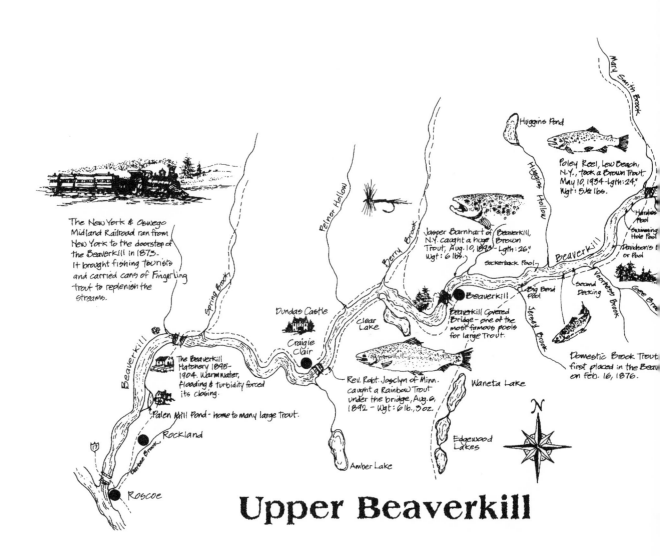

The New York & Oswego Midland Railroad ran from New York to the doorstep of the Beaverkill in 1875. It brought fishing tourists and carried cans of Fingerling trout to replenish the streams.

The Beaverkill Hatchery 1895-1904. Warm water, flooding & turbidity forced its closing.

Palen Mill Pond - home to many large Trout.

Beaverkill

Pardee Brook

Rockland

Roscoe

Spring Brook

Pelnor Hollow

Dundas Castle

Craigie Clair

Clear Lake

Berry Brook

Rev. Robt. Josclyn of Minn. caught a Rainbow Trout under the bridge, Aug. 6, 1892 - Wgt: 6 lb., 3 oz.

Amber Lake

Waneta Lake

Edgewood Lakes

Mary Smith Brook

Huggins Pond

Huggins Hollow

Poley Reel, Lew Beach, N.Y., took a Brown Trout, May 10, 1954 - Lgth: 24", Wgt: 5½ lbs.

Jasper Barnhart of Beaverkill, N.Y. caught a huge Brown Trout, Aug. 10, 1895 - Lgth: 26", Wgt: 6 lbs.

Snackerback Pool

Beaverkill

Big Bend Pool

Beaverkill Covered Bridge - one of the most famous pools for large Trout.

Hardscrabble Pool

Swimming Hole Pool

Davidson's Rip or Pool

Second Decking

Voorhees Brook

Cave Brook

Shin Creek Brook

Domestic Brook Trout first placed in the Beaverkill on Feb. 16, 1876.

N

Upper Beaverkill

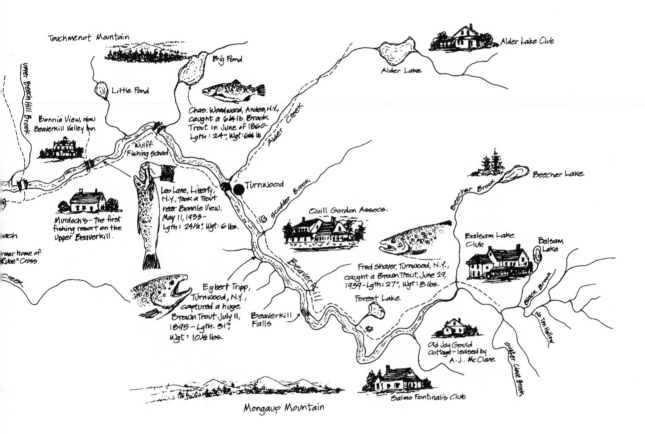

Touchmenot Mountain

Big Pond

Little Pond

Upper Beech Hill Brook

Bonnie View, now
Beaverkill Valley Inn

Wulff
Fishing School

Murdoch's- The first
fishing resort on the
Upper Beaverkill.

Former home of
"Rube" Cross

Creek

Chas. Woodward, Andes, N.Y.,
caught a 6¼ lb. Brook
Trout in June of 1860-
Lgth: 24"; Wgt: 6¼ lb

Leo Lane, Liberty,
N.Y., took a Trout
near Bonnie View,
May 11, 1933-
Lgth: 24½"; Wgt: 6 lbs.

Turnwood

Scudder Brook

Alder Creek

Alder Lake

Alder Lake Club

Quill Gordon Assocs.

Beecher Brook

Beecher Lake

Balsam Lake
Club

Balsam
Lake

Fred Shaver, Turnwood, N.Y.,
caught a Brown Trout, June 29,
1939-Lgth: 27"; Wgt: 8 lbs.

Egbert Tripp,
Turnwood, N.Y.,
captured a huge
Brown Trout July 11,
1895 - Lgth: 31";
Wgt: 10½ lbs.

Beaverkill
Falls

Beaverkill R.

Forest Lake

Black Brook

No Ten Hollow

Old Jay Gould
Cottage - leased by
A.J. McClane

Quaker Clove Brook

Salmo Fontinalis Club

Mongaup Mountain

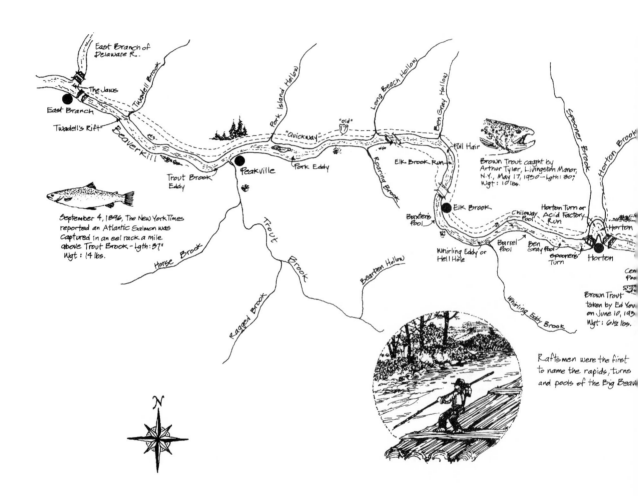

East Branch of
Delaware R.

The Jaws

East Branch

Twadell's Rift

Twadell Brook

Beaverkill

Trout Brook
Eddy

Peakville

Pork Island Hollow

"Quickway"

Pork Eddy

"old"

Roaring Brook

Long Beach Hollow

Ben Gray Hollow

Elk Brook Run

Pull Hair

Baxter's
Pool

Elk Brook

Whirling Eddy or
Hell Hole

Barrel
Pool

Chilaway
Pool

Horton Turn or
Acid Factory
Run

Ben
Gray Flat
Spooner's
Turn

Spooner Brook

Horton Brook

Horton

Horton

Cem
Poo

September 4, 1896, The New York Times
reported an Atlantic Salmon was
captured in an eel rack a mile
above Trout Brook – Lgth: 37"
Wgt: 14 lbs.

Horse Brook

Trout
Brook

Ragged Brook

Bearpen Hollow

Whirling Eddy Brook

Brown Trout caught by
Arthur Tyler, Livingston Manor,
N.Y., May 17, 1950 – Lgth: 30;
Wgt: 10 lbs.

Brown Trout
taken by Ed You
on June 10, 193
Wgt: 6½ lbs.

Raftsmen were the first
to name the rapids, turns
and pools of the Big Beav

Big or Lower Beaverkill

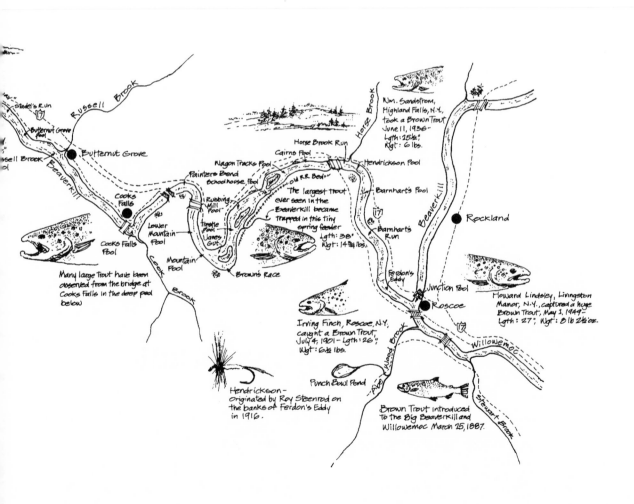

Stadel's Run

Russell Brook

Butternut Grove Pool

Russell Brook

Beaverkill

Butternut Grove

Cooks Falls

Cooks Falls Pool

Lower Mountain Pool

Cooks Brook

Mountain Pool

Many large Trout have been observed from the bridge at Cooks Falls in the deep pool below

Horse Brook

Wm. Sandstrom, Highland Falls, N.Y., took a Brown Trout June 11, 1936 - Lgth: 25½" Wgt: 6 lbs.

Horse Brook Run

Cairns Pool

Wagon Tracks Pool

Painters Bend

School house Pool

Rubbing Mill Pool

Throttle Pool

Lanes Gut

Old RR Bed

The largest trout ever seen in the Beaverkill became trapped in this tiny spring feeder Lgth: 38" Wgt: 14¾ lbs.

Hendrickson Pool

Barnhart's Pool

Barnhart's Run

Brown's Race

Ferdon's Eddy

Junction Pool

Roscoe

Beaverkill

Rockland

Howard Lindsley, Livingston Manor, N.Y., captured a huge Brown Trout, May 1, 1949 - Lgth: 27"; Wgt: 8 lb 2½ oz.

Irving Finch, Roscoe, N.Y., caught a Brown Trout, July 4, 1901 - Lgth: 26" Wgt: 6½ lbs.

Hendrickson - originated by Roy Steenrod on the banks of Ferdon's Eddy in 1916.

Punch Bowl Pond

Little Beaver Kill

Willowemoc

Stewart Brook

Brown Trout introduced to the Big Beaverkill and Willowemoc March 25, 1887.

Part

I

1

America's Stream

To a great many fly fishers, the Beaverkill is the standard by which all other trout streams are judged. It is first and oldest in reputation.

Heralded as the cradle of fly fishing in America, the Beaverkill is known all over the world, wherever men and women fly fish for trout. Even before sporting periodicals and angling books began recording the history of American fly fishing, the Beaverkill's fame was well established. Steeped in tradition and lore, the stream was the favorite of many of our earliest and most gifted anglers.

Down through the decades, countless men have learned the art of fly fishing along its banks, and bonded with the Beaverkill. Many became regulars, forming a brotherhood that not only fished its waters but acted as guardians, preserving its fisheries and protecting the stream from would-be despoilers.

Angling writers, too, have enjoyed an intimate relationship with the stream, and its reputation has been furthered not by one but by every generation of our best-known and most talented fishing journalists. The Beaverkill, with its storied pools such as Barnhart's, Hendrickson's, and Cairns, is as familiar to fly fishermen as Brahms, Bach, and Beethoven are to music lovers. And just as football fans view the Dallas Cowboys as "America's team," trout-fishing enthusiasts look upon the Beaverkill as "America's stream."

Perhaps there are streams that have more natural beauty—there are those where the trout grow larger and are more abundant—but the Beaverkill is revered by fly fishermen, in much the same manner as Cooperstown is revered by baseball fans. To wade and cast a fly in waters where fly-fishing immortals have before them can be likened to taking the mound at Fenway, or roaming center field at Yankee Stadium.

Fly fishers come from across the land, as if on a pilgrimage: to walk the well-worn streamside paths; to fish and stand in the pools and shadows of the legendary anglers. Corey Ford, in a fine article titled, appropriately, "The Best-Loved Trout Stream of Them All," expressed these thoughts as well as anyone:

> Watch your backcast; the ghosts of a hundred departed anglers are standing behind you. That pool you are entering was once the favorite fishing hole of John Taintor Foote. Ted Townsend used to perch atop that very rock on which you are standing now. Perhaps Theodore Gordon dropped his first Quill over that small dark eddy where you have just cast your fly. . . .
>
> A trout stream is more than the fish in it. A great trout stream like the Beaverkill is a legend, a fly book filled with memories, a part of the lives of all the devoted anglers, living or dead, who ever held a taut line in its current.

The source of the Beaverkill is found deep in the forest of the Catskill Mountains, far from any road, in a narrow, rocky ravine between the mountains Graham and Doubletop. The elevation is 2,900 feet, and even though there is very little soil, beech, birch, and maple dominate the landscape; their roots reach down, through, and over an indefinite number of gray-colored rocks that clog the narrow pass.

Though all of the rocks are of varying grayish hues, some are obvious in that they wear robes of bright green moss, marking a barely discernible stream flow. Water as clear as the finest crystal seeps under these mossy rocks, nourishing their velvety emerald clusters—this is where the celebrated Beaverkill is born, and its growth begins.

At first the water appears motionless, lying in a series of diminutive shallow pools. But gravity forces it along, forming a tiny rill that takes on the appearance of a pristine mountain spring. The spring runs only a few hundred feet before flowing into an ancient beaver meadow, where pools and riffles are formed and the cold, clean, well-oxygenated water becomes the home of native brook trout.

The source of the Beaverkill, between the mountains Graham and Doubletop.

© Ed Van Put

Traveling down through the forest, the stream receives additional water from every hollow and glen, from other springs and tributary feeders. The waters flow in a general westerly direction, and by the time the Beaverkill reaches Alder Creek, a dozen miles later, it widens, and the mountain stream has become a little river. It continues westerly until reaching the base of Touchmenot Mountain, where it turns southwesterly and flows, uninterrupted, an additional fourteen miles to where its waters join Willowemoc Creek.

This uniting with the Willowemoc doubles the Beaverkill's size, turning it into a large river. Its pools are large and deep, its riffle areas lengthy; before meeting with the East Branch of the Delaware River, the Beaverkill widens to over two hundred feet. The stream's gradient changes dramatically over the last fifteen miles, from a drop of fifty-six feet per mile to approximately nineteen feet per mile.

The lower Beaverkill becomes so wide that even the tallest, most mature trees are unable to adequately shade it from bright sunlight, which warms its waters. Water temperatures at times rise above those preferred by trout, and in years of drought, flows are greatly reduced. There is only one small cold-water tributary in the first five miles of the lower river.

The Beaverkill trout fishery is largely dependent on upstream environmental conditions—notably, the clean, cold water that flows through and over semipermeable soils on steep forested slopes, abundant summer precipitation, and gradient sufficient to keep the water moving and oxygenated.

Countless springs, numerous lakes and ponds, and more than a hundred tributaries contribute to the flow of the Beaverkill. The drainage area covers approximately 292 square miles and includes eighty-six classified trout streams that, in addition to providing cold water, serve as spawning grounds for mature trout and nursery habitat for trout fry.

The Beaverkill valley is narrow and steep-sided throughout its length; floodplains are relatively narrow, and mountain slopes often come right down to the water's edge. Flat- or bottomland is scarce. Mountainsides are densely forested with beech, birch, maple, and, as is often the case in northern hardwood forests, hemlock.

© Judy Van Put

A small beaver dam across the headwaters of the Beaverkill. The stream derived its name from the numerous beaver colonies settlers found along the headwaters.

The streambed of the Beaverkill and its tributaries is composed of sand, gravel, fragmented rock, boulders, and bedrock. Some of the best trout habitat is formed where the stream flows over or against bedrock. Water cascading over solid rock creates plunge pools that are deep, fairly stable, and picturesque. This bedrock is of sedimentary origin, and geologists believe that the mountainous region known as the Catskills was formed from the eroding soils of much larger mountains, located in what is now New England and southeastern New York.

Hundreds of millions of years ago, streams flowing from these mountains carried soil, sand, and gravel into a vast inland sea, which covered western New York, Pennsylvania, and parts of the Mississippi valley.

This eroding material deposited into a great sinking delta, or alluvial fan. Eventually, as the mountains were worn low, deposits into the delta halted, and rock strata were formed. The strata, piled layer upon layer, accumulated to a thickness of several thousand feet. About 225 million years ago, the delta was uplifted far above sea level to form a plateau. In time, the plateau took on a mountainous form, as it was dissected into deep valleys by weathering, stream erosion, and the breakdown of the flat-lying rocks.

A further event in creating the physiography of the Catskills occurred approximately twenty thousand to fifty thousand years ago, when the mountains were completely covered by glaciers. The glaciers reworked the soil, scattering rocks of all sizes and shapes through it. When the ice moved over the landscape, it scraped off the loose soil, sandstone, and rocks, and carried everything in, on, and under the ice. As the ice melted, glacial drift piled up at the ice borders was either carried away by streams coming off the melting ice or spread out as a sheet of till. This glacial till covers much of the region and is composed of an unsorted mixture of clay, sand, silt, and rock fragments of various sizes.

The present form of the mountains is mainly due to the continuing actions of the many streams, which cut narrow valleys into the landscape. All Catskill streams are basically unstable; the glacial till that is found in the area forms fragile banks and forever-changing streambeds. Understandably, banks composed of clay, sand, and unsorted gravel form a loose, erodible soil and collapse quite readily. Streams are steep-gradient, and runoff from rains and melting snow is rapid. Streams rise quickly and overflow their banks often. Flooding is a common occurrence, and erosion is evident on all streams.

2

"The People at the Rising of the Sun"

Following deglaciation, an arctic-alpine flora first covered the region. In time, animals such as mammoths and caribou found their way into the area, and approximately thirteen thousand years ago, Paleo-Indians, the first humans to inhabit the Catskills, roamed the valleys in search of these large animals, armed with little more than spears. These Indians grew no crops; their existence depended on gathering whatever wild foods were available, hunting, and fishing.

In time, milder climate allowed the arctic-alpine flora to be replaced by a boreal forest of red spruce, balsam fir, paper birch, and mountain ash. From the south, a northern hardwood forest of beech, birch, maple, and hemlock ascended the mountain slopes and slowly took over, in varying degrees, the boreal forest. (Although hemlock is not a hardwood, it is often associated with this type of forest.)

This largely deciduous forest was very similar to the woodlands of the Catskills today. It provided excellent habitat for deer, bear, and a variety of small mammals and birds, especially wild pigeons. Abundant wildlife and seasonal runs of shad formed a food supply for Archaic Indians, who lived in the region until approximately three thousand years ago. At that time, these Indians were replaced by the Woodland Indians, who used bows and arrows instead of spears and, in addition to hunting and fishing, grew crops of corn, beans, and pumpkins along the lowlands bordering the larger streams and rivers.

These were the Indians that Belgian, Dutch, and English settlers encountered when they came to the region. To the English they were known as Delawares, from the name of their principal river; to the French they were Loups, meaning "Wolves"; to other Indian tribes or nations they were known as Wapanachki, or "The People at the Rising of the Sun"—Eastlanders.[1] They, however, preferred to call themselves Lenape or Lenni-Lenape *(Lay nee Lay-na pay),* equivalent to "Real Men" or "Original People."[2] The Lenni-Lenape were said to be honored with the title of "Grandfather" by the nearly forty tribes that descended from them. Being of Algonquian stock, they spoke that language; and, according to their tradition and oral history handed down by their ancestors, they came from the west many centuries ago.[3]

When the first Europeans visited the waters of the nearby Hudson, the Lenni-Lenape inhabited the land extending from the Catskill Mountains south to the Potomac, occupying all of the region watered by the Delaware, Hudson, Potomac, and Susquehanna Rivers. They were composed of three principal tribes: the Unami, or "Turtle"; the Unalachto, or "Turkey"; and the Minsi, or "Wolf." Minsi also means "People of the Stony Country" or "Mountaineers," and these Indians of the Minsi, or wolf, tribe were the ones who chose to live along the rivers of the Catskills.[4]

Tribes were often subdivided into groups, which took their names from the places where they lived. Families whose dwellings and cultivated fields were near a river or stream often bore the name of that waterway: for example, the Esopus, Navisings (Neversink), Papagonk (East Branch Delaware), and the Whelenaughwemack, which is what the Indians called the Beaverkill.[5]

The Lenni-Lenape were river Indians who depended on agriculture, hunting, and fishing. While they pursued game, trapped, and traveled watercourses throughout the Catskills, they did not settle in the narrow valleys of the higher elevations. The Lenni-Lenape preferred to live in semipermanent villages along the lower, larger stream or river sections, where travel by canoe was possible and fields could be cultivated in the floodplains. Because of the narrowness of the valley, there were few sites along the Beaverkill that met the needs of the Indians. They were, however, reported to have lived along the flats at what today is called Rockland; at the mouth of Russell Brook (Cooks Falls); and at the mouth of the Beaverkill (the hamlet of East Branch).

It was shad, not trout, that attracted the Indians to the waters of the Beaverkill. Each spring, these anadromous fish traveled hundreds of miles upstream to spawn, just as they do today. Great

[1]Ruttenber, *The Indian Tribes of Hudson's River,* p. 45.
[2]Hodge, *Handbook of American Indians North of Mexico,* p. 385.
[3]Ruttenber, *The Indian Tribes of Hudson's River,* p. 45.
[4]Brinton, *The Lenape and Their Legends,* p. 36.
[5]Murray, *Centennial History of Delaware County, N.Y., 1797–1897,* p. 310.

© Judy Van Put

schools of shad ran up the branches of the Delaware and the Beaverkill and provided an abundant food supply for the Lenni-Lenape.

By piling stones from the stream bottom, Indians constructed walls from bank to bank in the shape of a large V, with a narrow opening in the middle. Here, the fish could be forced or driven into a net and speared or taken by pinching, a method in which a split stick was used to pin the fish to the stream bottom. The Indians also made brushwood mats, which they moved along like seines to drive shad and other fish into shallow areas. There the fish were taken by hand or with dip nets. Shad were cured by drying in the sun or over fires; they were ground and packed in skins for later use; some were even used as fertilizer.

An interesting method used by the Indians to capture trout involved the bark from the root of the walnut tree. The bark was crushed to a pulp to obtain the juices. This extract was then poured in the riffles at the head of a pool, and when it mixed with the water and was ingested, it drugged and stupefied the trout, causing them to come to the surface, where they were easily collected.

Apparently, the use of poison was a popular method in harvesting fish from rivers and streams, especially during periods of low flows. Woodland Indians were known to use

> the root of a plant called devil's shoestring *(Viburnum alnifolium),* although turnip root and poke berry were also used. Devil's shoestring was a common plant growing on the sandy ridges bordering many eastern streams. Several large posts were driven into the stream bed, their tops extending just above the water's surface. The roots that had been gathered were then pulverized with a wooden maul on the tops of the posts. As the mashed roots fell into the water, they exuded their toxins, and the affected fish weakly finned on the surface, gasping for air. Women and children braved the irritating effect the substance had on their skin and waded downstream to gather the fish.[6]

Riverside settlements were usually small and rarely permanent; when the soil became less productive after years of use, or when nature did not keep up with the needs of the Indians, they moved on to other areas where fish and wildlife were plentiful.

Of the various groups of Lenni-Lenape that inhabited the area, the Esopus, who resided near present-day Kingston and lower Rondout Creek, were the most numerous. They were of the Minsi, or wolf, tribe and claimed almost the entire Catskill region stretching from the Hudson to the Delaware as their hunting grounds.

Contact with the Esopus by European traders probably occurred as early as 1609, when Henry Hudson sailed the *Half Moon* up the Hudson River.[7] Over the next few years, explorers and fur traders visited the region, and in 1614, they started small settlements at Fort Nassau (Albany) and Manhattan Island (New York). In 1650, a settlement began at Catskill, and in 1652, another was started along the flats of Esopus Creek at Esopus (Kingston).[8]

In the years that followed, these principal settlements of New York depended greatly on trade with the Indians of the Catskills; and Kingston was the hub for these exchanges: "At this point the three valleys of the Esopus, Rondout and Wallkill converge. Down all these valleys came Indians in the spring with furs and skins to meet the Albany traders."[9]

----

[6]Irwin, *Hunters of the Eastern Forest,* p. 48.
[7]Evers, *The Catskills: From Wilderness to Woodstock,* p. 10.
[8]Fried, *The Early History Of Kingston and Ulster County, New York,* p. xxiv.
[9]Brink, *Olde Ulster,* Vol. IV, p. 116.

Furs, especially the highly prized beaver pelts, were traded for brass kettles, steel knives, blankets, firearms, and other items never before seen by the Esopus. Eager for manufactured goods, the Indians quickly decimated the beaver population. They hunted and trapped the animal until it could no longer be found in the Catskills. Even though unlawful, traders often gave the Indians alcohol to get the better of them in a trade. The resulting intoxication caused some of the first conflicts between the Esopus and early Dutch settlers.

As the number of settlers increased, greater pressure was placed on the Indians to sell, or convey, their land. The Dutch wished to grow their own crops on the tilled fields used by the Indians, whom they referred to as Kaalebakkers, or "Barebacks." To the Indians, land had no value; the custom of owning or having dominion over the land through words on paper was incomprehensible. The Esopus had no written language, and in their world the land could not be reduced to a private possession. Though not always understood by the Indians, land purchases by the Dutch began in 1652. At that time, European and Indian began living alongside one another—two cultures with vastly different values and philosophies that did not, and could not, live peacefully side by side.

> When there was an abundance with the Indian, they feasted; when scarcity, they starved. They were improvident. When they were in need they saw no reason why they should not help themselves from the stores of provisions of the whites. This the whites resisted. Red men were willing to share their abundance when there was aplenty. If his family were hungry, why should not a red man kill the fat porker of his white neighbor, which he found feasting upon the acorns in the forest? If that white man neighbor were out of food, would the Indian not throw into his white brother's door half of the deer which he had killed on his last hunt?[10]

It was not long before the friction between the two races grew and turned to war. In 1659, and again in 1663, armed conflicts were fought, and the Indians suffered many more casualties than the settlers. In addition, hundreds more died from epidemics of smallpox, measles, and other diseases not known to the Esopus. Slowly, steadily, the settlers drove the remaining Indians off the desirable, tillable river bottomlands and forced them into the more inhospitable mountainous areas of the Catskills, where they had previously only hunted and fished, living in huts or shelters built for temporary occupancy.

---

[10]Brink, *Olde Ulster,* Vol. I, p. 98.

Some Indians settled along the Papagonk (East Branch) and its tributaries, such as the Whelenaughwemack (Beaverkill), or alongside lakes and ponds. Some went farther west and lived along the Susquehanna River, and still others migrated into Ohio, Indiana, Missouri, and Kansas. Those who stayed wandered about the Catskills, clinging to a way of life they had known for generations.

The last of the Indian lands, their ancient hunting and fishing grounds, would also be taken, incredibly, by a single land transaction with a merchant-trader from Kingston. When New York was under Dutch control, the government, at times, would grant land in the colony without the formality of buying the land from the Indians. However, when the English took possession of the Dutch holdings in 1665, they insisted on first extinguishing the aboriginal title. It was customary to apply to the governor for leave to purchase; if this was granted, the next step was to secure a deed from the Indians. After a survey, the attorney general was then directed to prepare a draft of a patent, which then went before the governor for approval. In a few cases, grants of land were made directly by the Crown.

On March 22, 1707, Johannis Hardenbergh purchased an immense parcel of land of almost two million acres from Nanisinos, "an Indian of the Esopus Indians, and rightful owner and proprietor of several parts of land in the County of Ulster."[11] On April 20, 1708, Queen Anne granted a patent to Johannis Hardenbergh and six others for the land Hardenbergh had acquired from the Indians. This land included virtually all of the Catskill Mountains, as well as the remaining lands owned by the Esopus.

This immense forest of mountains and valleys remained a wilderness, as long as it was not divided. When surveyors tried to measure the land, they were met by Indians who were unfriendly and antagonistic, who tried to turn them back, stole their instruments, and hampered the completion of the survey. For years, the boundaries of the Hardenbergh Patent were disputed by the Esopus.

In 1726, Hardenbergh persuaded a group of Indians to sign a statement saying that he had paid them for their rights to the land inside the patent. Twenty years later, in 1746, he again rounded up Indian claimants, and for the sum of three hundred pounds acquired the signatures or marks of more than thirty Indians on a new deed for the lands he believed were already a part of the patent. This deed included the phrase "together with all Creeks, Rivers, Brooks, Waters, Ponds, Meadows, Reed Lands, Swamps, Woods, Underwoods, Fishing, Fowling and all the benefits, profits and emoluments."[12]

---

[11]Brink, *Olde Ulster,* Vol. IV, p. 131.
[12]Liber EE, Ulster County Clerk's Office, p. 61.

As early as 1743, there were a few scattered settlers living among the Indians; they lived along the Papagonk (East Branch), north of the Beaverkill, and in the nearby Lackawack and Neversink valleys. For the most part, the lands of the patent and the Catskills remained unchanged, and the Indians continued to live in the mountains very much as they had in the past.

Their population, however, was decreasing; and by the start of the Revolutionary War, the number of Indians living in and about the region was very small. On June 1, 1774, Lieutenant Governor Cadwallader Colden wrote the Earl of Dartmouth:

> The Indians who formerly possessed that part of the Province which lies below Albany are now reduced to a small number, and are in general, so scattered and dispersed, and so addicted to wandering, that no certain account can be obtained of them. They are remnants of the tribes; Montocks and others of Long Island—Wappingers of Dutchess County—Esopus, Papagunk, etc., in Ulster County, and a few Skachticokes. These tribes have generally been denominated River Indians, and consist of about three hundred Fighting Men. They speak a language radically the same, and are understood by the Delawares, being originally of the same race.[13]

Near the end of the war, new roads and trails into the region were being constructed, and additional settlers created increasing problems for the Indians. By the conclusion of the Revolutionary War, in 1783, only a thin scattering of Indian people was left. The Lenni-Lenape retreated to the west, the same direction from which their ancestors had come so many centuries ago. They left behind their names for rivers, streams, mountains, and localities, and not much else. Theirs was a society that lived in harmony with the natural world. The differences between the Indians and the Europeans who came into their world are best explained by Dr. William A. Ritchie, state archaeologist, in an article titled "The Indian in His Environment." Dr. Ritchie indicates that the average Western man "suffers a cultural compulsive to 'improve' everything," therefore striving to attain a "technological domination of his environment." The Indian, on the other hand, happily adjusted himself harmoniously into the scheme of nature, learning the ecological relationships surrounding him: "It is probable that the Indian knew and loved the world of his environment in a way that few white men, reared in the competitive, exploitative and possessive traditions of Western civilization, can ever comprehend."[14]

The Lenni-Lenape left the environment of the region very much as they found it. The first major human disturbance to the wilderness of the Catskills began with the people who came after them.

---

[13]Brink, *Olde Ulster,* Vol. III, p. 323.
[14]Ritchie, *Conservationist,* Dec.–Jan. 1955–56, p. 23–27.

3

Whelenaughwemack, Pioneers, and Rafting Days

In 1751, the Hardenbergh Patent was surveyed and divided among its shareholders into fifty-two "Great Lots"; and while some of these lands were further subdivided and sold, the Catskills remained a wild, rugged, unbroken forest.

Colonists built their homes and farms on the fringe of the mountains, and even though within sight of them every day, they made no attempt to penetrate the Catskills. The narrow valleys, rocky soils, and steep mountainsides did not favor tillage of the soil, and there were no minerals. Most men, at the time, had an overall aversion to entering "the deep unknown of woods."

Remarkably, Kingston, which was less than twenty miles away, was nearly 150 years old before settlers began to enter the mountainous region. There was little attempt to settle the Beaverkill valley until after the Revolutionary War. Permanent settlers did not arrive until shortly after the Declaration of Peace in 1783.

By 1785, a trail had been measured and cut from Lackawack (in the Rondout valley), through the forest, across the headwaters of the Beaverkill, to "Pawpacton" on the East Branch. It had marked and numbered "mile trees," 1 through 35, and was known as "the common road." It crossed the Beaverkill, Shin Creek, Willowemoc Creek, and the Neversink. The present-day Beech Hill Road, located above Lew Beach, is said to be a portion of this original route. Undoubtedly, hunters and trappers also traveled it and found their way into the Beaverkill and Willowe-moc valleys.

Settlers came mostly from Connecticut, and many were veterans of the Revolution. According to local legend, they were told of good flatlands located along the "Great Beaverkill" by scouts who had been in the Catskills, keeping an eye on the remaining Indians, who, it was feared, would aid the English.

These pioneers, at times, traveled Indian trails and, not surprisingly, settled in some of the very areas that had been sites of Indian settlements. In 1789, Jehial Stewart constructed a temporary shelter of bark and poles near the forks of the Great Beaverkill and the Whelenaughwemack.[1] Farther downstream, John Cook built a cabin at the mouth of Russell Brook, where the Indians formerly had a cornfield.[2] And in 1791, settlement also began at the mouth of the Whelenaughwemack (Beaverkill at East Branch).[3]

Originally, the river known today as the lower Beaverkill, below Junction Pool, was called the Whelenaughwemack; the upper Beaverkill was known as the Great Beaverkill. "Whelenaughwemack" is derived from the name used by the Lenni-Lenape, who lived at the mouth of the river, which was a noted rendezvous of the Indians before, during, and after the Revolutionary War. Since then, "Whelenaughwemack" evolved into "Welawemacks" and, eventually, "Willowemoc."

When the first settlers came to the region they learned the meaning of the name directly from the Indians: "It is 'the kettle that washes itself clean,' and the stream was so called because of the spring freshets, which carry off all the driftwood, etc., from its banks."[4]

On the heels of these pioneers came many more "Yankees." These men were knowledgeable woodsmen and expert with an ax; they quickly went to work clearing the land and constructing log cabins from the trees they had felled. Wildlife in the region was plentiful, and while hunting tales of wolves and panthers became a part of pioneer history, it was deer, bear, partridge, squirrels, and especially wild pigeons that found their way to the dinner table.

Shad, too, became an important food supply each spring. Just as the Indians before them had done, neighbors joined together when the fish arrived, made collective efforts to capture them, and shared the catch with one another.

Until fields could be cultivated for livestock, the wild grasses found in abandoned beaver meadows were cut and used as fodder. A few of the settlers living along the "big flats," upstream

---

[1]Quinlan, *History of Sullivan County,* p. 493.
[2]Wood, *Holt! T'Other Way,* p. 243–244.
[3]*History of Delaware County, N.Y., 1797–1880,* p. 212.
[4]George W. Van Siclen, *Forest and Stream,* May 6, 1880, p. 175.

of the Forks, traveled to the Susquehanna River and traded with the Indians for seed corn, for planting.[5] (Today, two hundred years later, these same fields that were used by the Indians are still planted with corn, which is sold to passing motorists from roadside stands in Rockland.)

Those living along the river flats were fortunate; their land was level and mostly cleared. Away from the floodplain, hillsides were steep and stony, with outcroppings of rocks, which made deep plowing impossible. The high mountains and narrow valleys caused morning and evening shadows to be long; frosts could occur late in the spring and early in the fall. Farming the land was not easy, and many looked to the forest for survival.

When the first white settlers followed the Indian trails into the mountains, they found the forest of the Beaverkill region to be a predominantly northern hardwood forest. Many of the first settlers took advantage of the immense forest and rapidly descending streams and became, by turns, lumbermen or raftsmen, farmers, and hunters.

"Rafting" became the first and principal industry of the pioneer settlers. Rafts were constructed from logs or rough-sawed planks and floated to Philadelphia, two hundred miles downstream, on the lower Delaware River. The Delaware and its headwater streams, like the Beaverkill, provided cheap, uninterrupted transportation for lumber from the remote forests of the Catskills.

Rafting on the Beaverkill began in 1798; the first men to really know the river were those who risked their lives floating and steering rafts of lumber down its waters. Each spring, after ice-out, they braved the chilling flows of a swollen river and steered their crudely made rafts through rapids, around fast and dangerous twists and turns, and past perilous boulders. For men who had spent their youth as soldiers of the Revolution, witnessing the dangers and excitement of war, rafting held a special appeal.

Most settlers were directly involved in rafting, either piloting rafts, working as oarsmen, or hauling logs to the stream; others simply sold the lumber, but it touched the lives of all who lived in the valley.

When the rafting industry began, sawmills, eager to supply the lumber, sprang up on almost every stream. In time, there were more than thirty mills located above the Forks of the Beaverkill and Willowemoc. These early mills were all powered by waterwheels and were generally quite small; the number of men employed at sawing logs was usually less than ten. In the beginning, they used only soft woods, such as hemlock, pine, spruce, and basswood.

---

[5]Willis, *The Pioneer,* p. 18.

While the steersman keeps his eyes on the river, raft passengers pose for the camera.

© Delilah Babcock

In 1860, the steam engine and circular saw began replacing the small waterwheel mills. Steam mills were larger and could handle more board feet of timber; this, in turn, increased the number of rafts that were floated each spring.

Four types of timber made up the rafts: toggle timber, square timber, sawed timber, and ordinary logs. Nearly 80 percent of all rafts were made of hemlock, the bulk of which was used for wharves and pilings along the Philadelphia riverfront. The sale of timber gave settlers a cash crop, while at the same time it helped in clearing the land for cultivation. The economic impact on the community was extensive—so much so that often notes were given and taken that read: "Thirty days after a general rafting freshet I promise to pay _____ or bearer."

Farmers and their oxen spent the winter in the woods, cutting and hauling logs to the river. After the ice went out in the spring, the stream bank, or docking bank, swarmed with activity. Everyone hastily constructed "colts," which measured, on the average, 22 feet by 80 feet. These were tied up in every sizable pool or eddy along the Beaverkill while the men waited for a "fresh," or rising river. When rains raised the flow, hundreds of rafts were started, almost simultaneously. Colts were floated downstream, by one to three men, to the confluence of the East Branch of the Delaware. Here they were lashed together to form a raft, which was generally 40 to 50 feet wide and 150 to 200 feet long. If the raft was not broken up by the river, the trip to Philadelphia, in clear weather and with a good fresh, took four to four and a half days.

Raftsmen were a hardy lot; they were generally fearless, rough, tough, daring men. More than a few lost their lives in their attempts to challenge the river when it was at its wildest; some "kept their courage up by putting their liquor down."[6] Through perseverance and bravery, the ever-exciting adventure down the river culminated with a sense of victory, when tidewater and Philadelphia were reached safely.

After receiving payment for their timber, the men started their long and sometimes adventurous journey home. With their coils of rope, augers, and assorted tools, the raftsmen became famous figures on the stagecoaches between Philadelphia and New York City. From New York City they took a night boat to Newburgh and then a stagecoach to Monticello. Some, wishing to save the stage fare, walked the sixty or seventy miles from Newburgh or Kingston, and others walked the entire distance, all the way back from Philadelphia to the Beaverkill!

To make the Beaverkill safer for raftsmen, the falls at Butternut Grove (Cooks Falls), which were considered a navigational hazard, were dynamited. Two years later, in 1875, over three thousand rafts passed down the Delaware River. A record keeper at Lackawaxen counted 3,140 by the 4th of May. The number of rafts floated each year increased steadily, peaking in the late 1870s or early 1880s, when hundreds of thousands of feet of hemlock logs found their way downriver.

Railroads, and more importantly, the lack of salable hemlock, caused the decline of the rafting industry. In 1888, the last raft went down the Willowemoc; and in 1904, veteran raftsman L. D. Francisco ran a pair of rafts to Easton, Pennsylvania. Later that year, the last raft of any kind went down the Beaverkill from Spooner's Eddy to Callicoon.

Though gone, the rafting industry will never be forgotten. The spirit of the men who challenged the river with their courage is remembered in the names of pools along the Beaverkill. These rivermen were the first to identify the pools and rapids that formed their experiences. A dangerous and dreaded area was at the mouth of the Beaverkill, where it was joined by the East Branch of the Delaware; the swirling currents made it one of the most difficult places to keep a raft from smashing against rocks, and so this hazardous junction, with its crooked channel, was known as the Jaws of Death.[7]

Others with self-descriptive names include Whirling Eddy, Hell Hole, Brown's Race, and Pull Hair. Pools such as Ferdon's Eddy, Cairns, and Ben Gray's pay tribute to Beaverkill landowners, who were also raftsmen. Even today, when local residents speak of the bygone days when tim-

---

[6]*Walton Reporter,* November 20, 1926, p. 2.
[7]*Bloomville Mirror,* May 25, 1858, p. 2.

ber was floated downriver to market, they do so with admiration. If their family lineage includes one who actually participated in these early river adventures, there is more than a hint of boastful pride.

The bend in the river and dangerous rocks were the reason raftsmen named this
Hell Hole or Whirling Eddy.

4

Steamboats, Stagecoaches,
Trout-Fishing Tourists

When settlement in the region began, men either walked or rode on horseback; most trails were too narrow to allow travel with a team. As more people found their way into the area, Indian trails and bridle paths became wagon roads, yet remained difficult to travel. They were rough-cut, nothing more than a swath with the trees cut down; stumps, boulders, and other obstructions were left in the roadway. Since wagons had no springs, people traveled only by necessity.

By the early 1800s roads began to improve, and more comfortable stagecoach travel came into existence, at least on nearby turnpikes. Turnpikes opened up the Beaverkill to tourists, who traveled up the Hudson by steamboat to Newburgh and Kingston and then came overland by stagecoach. While some were attracted by the scenery and wildness of the uncultivated mountains, many more came seeking trout—which, it was said, the region had in abundance.

The Ulster & Delaware Turnpike was constructed north of the Beaverkill; in 1802, it ran from Kingston into neighboring Delaware County. To the south, the Newburgh & Cochecton Turnpike opened in 1808, allowing travel from Newburgh across Sullivan County to the Delaware River. It was over this route that many raftsmen traveled on their way back to the Beaverkill.

These same raftsmen carried the word out to the civilized world that the Beaverkill offered trout fishing of the first order. And soon, on their return trips, they were sharing steamboats to

Newburgh and stagecoaches to Monticello with fishing tourists, who had learned of the Beaverkill and Willowemoc in the tackle shops of Philadelphia and New York.

Many of the first anglers headed for the Darbee House, which was located on a knoll overlooking the famous junction of the Beaverkill River and Willowemoc Creek. Samuel and Hannah Darbee constructed the first hotel in Westfield Flats (now Roscoe) between 1805 and 1810. Upon the accidental death of Samuel, this "publick house," known to sportsmen for many years, became simply "Mrs. Darbee's."

Meals, for which Mrs. Darbee's was celebrated, cost "a shilling, or one and eight pence, if toddy was ordered." Inside the hotel were seven immense stone fireplaces, a ballroom, and many fine paintings by artists who had boarded there while trouting. Outside, drawn and cut in outline on the side of the building, were large trout, taken from the Beaverkill:

Eminent doctors, artists and men of letters came for the excellent nearby trout fishing, relaxation, and charms of the wild countryside.

© Jack Niflot

The junction of the Beaverkill and Willowemoc.

Mrs. Darbee told of a party of men stopping there, who expressed a wish before retiring for the night, that they might see wolves. Arising in the night, which was bright with moonlight, Mrs. Darbee looked down on the flat toward the Beaverkill bridge, and saw wolves playing like lambs. The guests were awakened, and their wish had materialized.[1]

Prior to 1820 or 1825, there is very little written history of the Catskill region, especially as it relates to trout fishing. This is primarily due to the fact that the Catskills, including the Beaverkill, had barely been settled, and those few newspapers available rarely reported on activities other than politics. In addition, historical data regarding trout fishing in America before 1830 is rare.

The *American Turf Register and Sporting Magazine,* the first of its kind in the United States, made its debut in 1829; by this date the Beaverkill was already well known to trout fishermen. Though the magazine featured fishing articles of predominantly English origin, the reputations of the Beaverkill and Mrs. Darbee's found their way onto its pages:

> Make your headquarters at Mrs. Darbys [sic] and you will be sure to find excel-
> lent accommodations, and capital fishing. The Williewemauk, Calikoon, and Beaver-
> Kill, are three of the finest trout streams in this country; the trout are large, very nu-
> merous, and of the most delicious flavor.[2]

In 1831, the *Spirit of the Times* began publication in New York and was the first weekly all-around sporting journal. With the emergence of publications that featured articles and advertisements on trout fishing, the sport began to have a greater following.

During the 1830s, trout fishing was becoming a popular pastime; to exemplify this fact, one need only look at the many tackle stores in New York, dealing in rods, reels, flies, and other fishing paraphernalia. Fishing enthusiasts frequented Abraham Brower's on Water Street, Charles Taylor's on Maiden Lane and Broadway, and Lewis' at New and Wall Streets. On Fulton Street alone were the shops of T. W. Harsfield, J. B. Crook's, Thomas Conroy's, John Brown's Anglers Depot, and the famous Pritchard Brothers.

While Mrs. Darbee's attracted many of the earliest anglers who found their way to the Beaverkill, farther upstream Murdock's, another pioneer fishing resort, was building an equally

---

[1]*Liberty Register,* April 6, 1923, p. 2.
[2]*American Turf Register and Sporting Magazine,* August 1838, p. 369.

impressive reputation. James and Hannah Murdock owned a section of the stream above Shin Creek (Lew Beach), and there were few veteran anglers in New York who did not visit their delightful fishing retreat. The Murdocks had provided lodging to the very first trout fishermen who found their way up the valley to explore the primitive, unbroken wilderness of the upper Beaverkill.

Early angler fishing lower Shin Creek Falls.

© Jack Niflot

James Murdock had come to the Beaverkill valley in 1835, when it truly was a wilderness. That same year a wealthy New York gentleman had constructed a beautiful Gothic cottage near the banks of the Beaverkill for an invalid relative. It was Murdock's duty to care for the man, and as part of the exchange he was given the privilege of entertaining a limited number of anglers.

After the owner died, Murdock purchased the property and operated what early trout fishermen viewed as "the" place to stay when fishing the upper Beaverkill. Guests at the pioneer resort enjoyed walks, picnics to Beaverkill Falls, trout fishing, moonlight rides, and Hannah Murdock's cooking.

In the years that followed, the notoriety of Murdock's and Mrs. Darbee's grew, along with the fame of the Beaverkill. Amid a mountainous landscape, the stream, with its pure, icy waters that abounded in trout, attracted increasing numbers of fishing tourists.

But travel in and out of the region remained difficult, particularly in spring and early summer, when rains turned the roadways into a mass of soft mud and fording streams became impossible. One angler who experienced these early adventures, Robert Barnwell Roosevelt, wrote: "I am proud to say I have travelled that country when it took the stagecoach twelve hours to go twenty-four miles, and if we were in a hurry, we walked, and sent our baggage by the coach."[3]

---

[3]Roosevelt, *Game Fish of the Northern States of America and British Provinces,* p. 37.

5

The Troutist

At first, at least in the Catskills, the native brook trout were referred to simply as "trout"; and an angler who pursued them among the mountain streams was, at times, known as a "troutist."

One of the first to fish the Beaverkill was a Catskill native by the name of Fitz-James Fitch, who was born in Delhi, Delaware County, in 1817. Being a pioneer troutist, he sampled the Beaverkill when it was special: when its trout were naive and inexperienced and possibly as numerous and unsuspecting as they would ever be again.

Early in his professional career, he became the county judge of Greene County; he held that position for several years, before leaving the mountains and opening a law office in New York. "Judge" Fitch, as he was known throughout his life, was very popular in the fly-fishing circles of his day. A highly regarded fisherman and distance caster, he was recognized by his peers as being "courtly, precise, considerate, and observant of all the little amenities of social life; he was withal a loyal friend and charming companion."[1]

Judge Fitch first came to the Beaverkill in 1838, accompanied by William Adams of New York and John Smedburgh of Prattsville. They made the journey with a team of three-year-old

---

[1]*Forest and Stream,* December 12, 1896, p. 471.

horses that belonged to Smedburgh. The trio repeated the trip every year, with the same pair of horses, for twenty-one years! They always started out on or near the 24th of May and would stay ten days, always at Murdock's. They were gentlemen of the old school. ". . . none of them was ever known to utter a profane or coarse word, to fish on Sunday, to travel in or out on Sunday, and although abundantly supplied they were never known to offer a single drop of liquor to any one, even a guest."[2]

After spending but ten years in New York, the Judge's health began to fail, and his physician advised him to return to the mountains. He spent the following summer fishing along the Neversink, living in a little streamside shanty. The Judge was so rejuvenated by the experience that he decided to spend the greater part of every summer along the Catskill streams, fishing Rondout Creek, Dry Brook, Mill Brook, the Neversink, and the Beaverkill with regularity.

Judge Fitch was an excellent trout fisherman, and he kept accurate accounts of his fishing experiences for fifty consecutive years. He recorded every trout he caught, even those he returned to the stream. He began keeping records in 1845, the year he caught the least— 91; his best year was 1863, when he caught 1,089. After the first five years, all of the trout were caught on a fly. Two years before his death in Prattsville, in 1896, it was reported that the Judge had caught a remarkable 28,478 trout! This feat probably has not been duplicated, and it places Fitz-James Fitch right up there with the best of Catskill anglers.

While it may appear that the Judge was a victim of "fishing for count," he knew there was more to fishing than catching fish, and said so: "There are many things besides catching fish that give pleasure to the

Catskill Rivers, Austin M. Francis, Nick Lyons Books, New York, 1983.

Judge Fitz-James Fitch, a pioneer troutist of the Beaverkill.

fisher; vigorous, healthful exercise in the open air and usually in the midst of beautiful scenery. He should keep his eyes open and see everything worthy of admiration—the waterfall, the landscape, the towering mountain and the pretty, tiny flower at his feet."[3]

---

[2]J. S. Van Cleef, *Forest and Stream,* March 16, 1901, p. 209.
[3]*The American Angler,* July 24, 1886, p. 1.

The Judge took his amazing numbers of trout on wet flies, a fact that should not be lost to those fly fishermen today who bypass their use in favor of dry flies and nymphs. Like most early Catskill anglers, he generally used a cast of three flies, of which his favorites were the Gray Hackle, Coachman, and Beaverkill.

The Beaverkill, one of the first popular trout flies tied in America, was named by Judge Fitch to honor his favorite stream. The pattern stems from an unknown fly of English origin that the Judge found in his fly book and used with great success. He took the fly to Harry Pritchard, a well-known New York fly tier, and requested three dozen more like it. The fly was first tied by Pritchard in 1846[4] or 1850.[5]

Fitz-James Fitch made other notable contributions to American fly fishing. From 1864 on, he was a very capable rod maker and invented a rod grip known as the Fitch grip. Under the pen name of Fitz, he frequently contributed articles on fly fishing and rod making to fishing journals such as *The American Angler*. His invention of the creel, with the familiar shoulder strap and waistband, was much welcomed by anglers of his day. Previously, they had struggled with cumbersome baskets, which were carried laboriously by a single strap over the shoulder and rocked back and forth with the casting motion. Fitch came up with the idea in the summer of 1859, while staying at Murdock's and fishing the Beaverkill.

Though he invented the means with which to carry one's catch away from the stream, Judge Fitch, nevertheless, was an early proponent of catch and release. He wrote about releasing trout in the 1880s, a time when the idea was not practiced by many: "I look with great pleasure and pride upon my trout scores . . . but I look with more pleasure and pride upon the figures which tell me of the number of those trout that were put back in the stream."[6]

One of the most interesting gifts Judge Fitch gave to fly fishing was the record keeping of his early experiences. From him we are able to glean an idea of the population and size of the trout he and other pioneer anglers found in the Beaverkill.

Those anglers who first cast their lines into the flowing waters of the Beaverkill encountered only one species of trout: the brook trout, *Salvelinus fontinalis*. While they prefer cold, clean, well-oxygenated waters and thrive in streams, their natural habitat includes lakes and ponds. *Salvelinus* means "char"; *fontinalis,* "living in cold springs"; and as their name implies, brook trout prefer to live where water temperatures are coolest.

---

[4]Sturgis, *Fly Tying,* p. 104.
[5]Smedley, *Fly Patterns and Their Origins,* p. 5.
[6]*Shooting and Fishing,* August 22, 1889, p. 326.

Early fishermen found brook trout to be plentiful, from the headwaters all the way downstream to the junction of Willowemoc Creek. Below this point, because of warming water temperatures, the stream offered limited trout fishing. The farther upstream one traveled, the more abundant trout became; brook trout were most numerous upstream of the hamlet of Beaverkill.

Though their population was great, the brook trout of our forefathers' day was a predominantly small fish. And it was many years before fishermen spoke of, or wrote about, lengths of trout; in these pioneer days of trout fishing they measured their success by the pound—not of individual fish, but of the total catch! Anglers who first waded the waters of the Beaverkill carried baskets that, when filled, contained an approximate weight of the accumulated fish. The most popular sizes held fifteen, eighteen, and twenty-four pounds.

The lack of size was of small concern to those who delighted in stream fishing; they found attributes in the brook trout that were unequaled by other fish:

> The lines of grace and beauty, so gratifying to the poet and the artist, culminate in absolute perfection in the trout. The perfect symmetry, the harmonious blending of colors, the graceful motions of this exquisite of the brook, give it a value of great price, to all who look at it with appreciative eyes. Look at its large round eyes, orbs of light nev-set; its snow white body; look at its sides clad in mail of rainbow hue dotted with pink stars in sky blue tints.[7]

Native brook trout.

---

[7]*The People's Press,* (Kingston) August 29, 1861, p. 1.

At least one angler, as reported in an area newspaper, found a way to use the brook trout's scientific name to improve his casting stroke:

> An eccentric fisherman once thought the last portion of the name sounded so pleasantly, and had such a musical rhythm, that he used to steady himself when throwing the fly, by gently murmuring in a slightly ascending and descending scale, fon-ti-na-lis.[8]

As noted previously, one who fished the stream when it yet contained its "original" strain of brook trout was Fitz-James Fitch, who kept a diary of his angling experiences. Writing about the Beaverkill in the 1840s and '50s, Fitch recalled "when one hundred 'saving' trout per day, weighing from fifteen to twenty pounds, was considered but the average sport."

In order to obtain some idea of how large these trout were on the average we can use the maximum weight of twenty pounds, or 320 ounces, and realize that the average weight of the fish is 3.2 ounces. The conversion length of a trout weighing 3.2 ounces is approximately 8½ inches.

More accurately, perhaps, Fitch writes of a day when the sport was "exceptionally good" toward the end of May in 1859. He recorded: "I had scored, as memoranda made at the time shows, 121 trout, having thrown back perhaps half that number of 'small fry.' The weight of those saved was twenty-five and a half pounds."[9]

On this exceptional day, the total weight in ounces is 408, with the average weight of the 121 fish being 3.4 ounces, or a brook trout again measuring approximately 8½ inches. An 8½-inch brook trout is not a large fish, but it is respectable; it should be remembered that this was the average of 121 trout.

Large native brook trout taken from the Beaverkill.

Then, as now, habitat often dictates how large a fish will grow, and brook trout between 12 inches and 15 inches were taken in the

---

[8]*Kingston Weekly Freeman & Journal,* May 2, 1879, p. 1.
[9]*The American Angler,* April 22, 1882, p. 259.

deeper pools. In-stream dams, constructed by sawmills or tanneries, often created some of the largest and best pools, from which would come the biggest trout in the Beaverkill—brook trout that measured 15 to 20 inches, with weights of from 1 to 3 pounds. These were rare; generally any trout caught that weighed a pound or more made the newspapers, and not just locally but in other parts of the Catskills as well.

How rare a trout this size was can be seen from an article on the weights of native trout by James S. Van Cleef, a protégé of Judge Fitch's. Van Cleef also provides insight into the existing population of brook trout in the Beaverkill, prior to the introduction of stocked trout:

> I took in one year, about 1859, three trout, two of which weighed 1 lb. each, and one 1 lb. 5 oz.
>
> About that time I commenced fishing with a fly exclusively, and have taken quite a large number of trout weighing 15 oz., but none tipped the scales at 1 lb.
>
> Judge Fitch, after fishing the Beaverkill with a fly for about forty years, told me that he had never taken a trout in that stream with a fly that would tip the scales at 1 lb.[10]

Native brook trout larger than 3 pounds were unusual, and those taken were almost always caught in ponds and lakes. So rare were they, in fact, that for many years P. T. Barnum offered a cash prize of one hundred dollars for any brook trout weighing 4 pounds, delivered alive and un-injured to the aquarium department of his New York museum, "the trout to be warranted to live one week in a stream of fresh water."

One such trout was delivered to Barnum in the 1850s. Fishing-resort owner James Murdock received a "great price" for a 5-pound, 2-ounce brook trout he captured in the pond known today as Big Pond, located near Turnwood.

Another even larger fish, and the largest brook trout ever reported from the Beaverkill valley, also came out of Big Pond. In June 1860, Charles Woodward of Andes caught a magnificent 24-inch trout weighing 6¼ pounds.[11] Appropriately enough, when the region was first surveyed in 1809, the pond was known as Trout Pond; it later became Big Trout Pond and, finally, Big Pond.

In time, fishing writers and newspaper editors referred to the native trout as "speckled trout" or, more fondly and more often, "speckled beauties." Whichever name was used, the fact remained that the fish was greatly admired and always held in high esteem:

---

[10]J. S. Van Cleef, "Trout Waters and Trout Weights," *Forest and Stream,* May 21, 1898, p. 413.
[11]*Ulster Republican,* June 6, 1860, p. 3.

Big Pond produced the two largest brook trout to come out of the Beaverkill Valley.

The speckled trout, that prince of the pure, cold, spring water brook or pond, like the sportsman who follows him, is in a class by himself. He is the aristocrat of fishes. Brainy and valiant, he is a delight from his capture to his place on the table.[12]

In the years ahead, Catskill fishermen would be introduced to other species of trout, which they would accept and value as game fish; but it is doubtful that any generation of anglers ever held the same affection and warm attachment as did those who knew and loved the "speckled beauties."

---

[12]C. M. McDougall, *Forest and Stream,* February 21, 1914, p. 245.

6

James Spencer Van Cleef— A Beaverkill (and Sand Pond) Reminiscence

Countless men have fished the Beaverkill—novice and expert, from near and far, for recreation and sport. Some made infrequent trips, while others became regulars. A few who fished in the era of the speckled beauties left behind a record of their experiences; this is fortunate, since it is from these men that we are able to learn about the Beaverkill in its earliest years.

One man who contributed significantly to the history and preservation of the Beaverkill watershed was James Spencer Van Cleef (1831–1901).

Van Cleef was a prominent attorney who lived and practiced law in the not-too-distant city of Poughkeepsie. For more than twenty-five years he contributed articles and letters to *Forest and Stream*, writing "out of his rich experience and abundant knowledge of angling and anglers." His readers looked forward to his articles, which he usually closed with his familiar "J.S.V.C." Van Cleef wrote fondly of the bygone days of the Beaverkill, its trout, and its people.

He first visited the stream in 1857, when he was twenty-six years old. The following year he joined the trio of Judge Fitch, William Adams, and John Smedburgh and stayed at Murdock's, where the veteran anglers took the young man under their wing and taught him the "gentle art."

James Spencer Van Cleef, early Beaverkill angler/conservationist and founder of several Catskill trout-fishing clubs.

An enthusiastic angler, he enjoyed the friendship of, and shared the stream with, many of the more prominent trout fishermen of his generation, including Thaddeus Norris, Fred Mather, John Burroughs, and Harry Pritchard.

He wrote of being at Murdock's on one occasion when most of the guests apparently did not recognize Harry Pritchard. In addition to being a longtime, well-known professional fly tier, Pritchard had a reputation as an excellent tournament fly caster and was an "ex-champion fly-caster of the world." The roll cast as we know it today was, for many years, known as the Pritchard cast. Harry and his brother Thomas operated a fly shop and tackle store on Fulton Street in New York that was a popular rendezvous for anglers. Wrote Van Cleef:

There was a large number of anglers at Murdock's when Pritchard put in an appearance, none of whom seemed to know him, and all of whom were disposed to enjoy a little fun at his expense on account of his hesitancy in speech, but when Harry Pritchard proposed to fish upstream instead of down, there was a huge guffaw.

At that time, the Beaverkill had suffered from one or two severe freshets, and the ordinary angler was rarely able to take more than 6 or 8 lbs. of trout. Pritchard, in his early life, had been employed to catch fish on an estate in Ireland, and had there learned the merits of fishing upstream. Pritchard carried, on this occasion, a creel which would contain 15 or 18 lbs. of trout, and every night when he came in, his creel was full of large trout.[1]

In another reminiscence, Van Cleef recalled the religious attitude of the early settlers of the Beaverkill valley and how their customs were shared by the trout fishermen of his era. Natives never fished on the Sabbath, and if a visiting angler defied this rule he was ordered to leave the stream and never return. The gentleman angler who visited the Beaverkill recognized the inhabitants' welcome invitation to fish on their private property and, in return, respected the Sabbath as a day of rest and quiet.

---

[1] J. S. Van Cleef, *Forest and Stream,* September 11, 1897, p. 210.

The harmony that existed between visiting anglers and local people culminated each Sunday as they came together for religious services, as depicted in the following story:

Two miles below Murdock's, there was a little hamlet [Lew Beach] consisting principally of a church, an old graveyard, a grocery, blacksmith shop and cobbler's shop. At this point a small stream joined the Beaverkill from the east, with the charming name of Shin Creek, and those who fished this stream with its ragged edges and narrow gorges and came in with sore ankles, have always recognized this name, which was adopted by the Post Office Department as exceedingly appropriate.

The church at this place was built in the forties or early fifties by the joint contribution of several denominations, and when some minister did not happen to be on the stream to take charge of the service, it was usually conducted by a Methodist minister, who preached some six or eight miles elsewhere in the morning, and then afterward walked to Shin Creek to conduct the service there in the afternoon. . . .

The anglers in those days esteemed it a privilege as well as a pleasure to contribute from year to year, something for the purpose of keeping this church in proper paint and repair, and also to quietly add to the collection taken on every Sabbath day for the benefit of the minister. . . .

On the Sabbath day every one attended the services in this little church, rain or shine, often riding ten miles or more from up the stream, for this was the only church between the head of the Beaverkill and a place ten miles below it. It was always full.

There was a person then living in the neighborhood by the name of Hotchkiss, long since gone to his rest, and by common consent he led the music. He always came in his shirt sleeves when the day was warm, and when the hymns were given out he usually stood at the front seat, threw his foot over the back, and after listening to his music fork started the tune, which on almost every Sabbath was either "China" or "Mear" and sometimes both.

I have heard the best church music in the country, but I have never heard anything which seemed to bring every person who joined in these services nearer to the Heavenly Throne of God than these simple services in this little church in which every one joined, many of them with tears in their eyes . . . And these services and teachings bore rich fruit. The Sabbath was always observed as a day of holiness and rest, and what is more, these services made their visible impress upon the daily lives of all who lived upon this stream.[2]

One can see that James Spencer Van Cleef enjoyed a special relationship with the Beaverkill and its people, and he wrote warmly and intimately of his personal experiences.

S A N D   P O N D

Van Cleef also wrote often about the preservation of streams, trout habitat, and conserving natural resources. In 1868, he purchased Sand Pond and the 143 acres surrounding it. The pond, located deep in the forest at the headwaters of Willowemoc Creek, was noted for its exceptionally large brook trout, and was thus the frequent target of illegal netters. Following his purchase, Van Cleef took out an advertisement in the local newspapers, announcing his purchase of "the pond generally known as Sand or East Pond" and forbidding trespassing and fishing in the pond under the penalty of the law.

Newspapers at the time reported on the event, stating that a "company of sportsmen from the City of Poughkeepsie" planned to create a trout preserve at Sand Pond for their own private use during the summer.[3]

Van Cleef and his friends constructed a lodge overlooking the 14½-acre lake, and it was here that the first organized trout-fishing club in the Catskills was founded. Having obtained leases on four miles of Willowemoc Creek, they decided to call their group the Willowemoc Club. In 1870, the club purchased Sand Pond from Van Cleef and renamed it Lake Willowemoc. Membership was limited to twenty, and the first president was Cornelius Van Brunt, who, like Van Cleef, was an attorney from Poughkeepsie.

Sand Pond was eminent among Catskill trout ponds because of its sizable brook trout; brookies weighing between 2 and 3 pounds were not uncommon. It was reported that a party of anglers from Ellenville once caught a number of trout and graded them according to size—the first thirty averaged 2½ pounds! Brook trout measuring between 12 inches and 16 inches were common, and in 1872, club records revealed that the average size taken weighed 1 pound; the largest, 2¼ pounds.

Though of good size, the trout of Sand Pond were never very plentiful, mostly because of limited spawning opportunity. Writing about Sand Pond a couple of years after the club took owner-

---

[2]J. S. Van Cleef, "The Sabbath Day on the Beaverkill," *Forest and Stream,* May 18, 1901, p. 387.
[3]*Rondout Courier,* February 26, 1869, p. 2.

ship, Cornelius Van Brunt described the lake as having an even depth of only five feet, with a heavy growth of aquatic vegetation. He also wrote that the only stream entering the lake was almost inaccessible, and that the trout were accustomed to spawning along the shoreline "without much regard to the character of the bottom, and a very few by great effort went upstream. The result in the past has been that the greater part of the eggs were destroyed, and the young when hatched had no refuge."[4]

Club members immediately set about to "help the fish." They constructed a "spawning race" (artificial spawning bed) and then raised the lake level to cover it. They also cleaned the stream of siltation, debris, and barriers and made it easier for trout to enter to spawn. This example of habitat improvement and the club's foresight is remarkable, considering the work was accomplished in the 1870s!

Members also recognized that the brook trout of Sand Pond were special and took great care to preserve the quality of the fishery. They not only limited their sport to fly fishing but put into practice a unique form of catch and release. A guest of Van Cleef's who fished the lake describes the custom:

> The hook was carefully extracted and they were consigned to a wired creel, which was fastened to the stern of the boat. Taken ashore, the fish were transferred to a spring near the landing, where they were closely watched, and if one showed symptoms of any mortal hurt, he was forth with dispatched for table use. The rest were put back into the pond, except such as might be needed on the "festal board." And thus the fish are caught over and over again affording abundant sport with no destructive waste.[5]

These were indeed knowledgeable anglers who understood their fisheries resources and acted wisely in their preservation. Incredibly, the Willowemoc Club membership employed most of the primary techniques of modern fisheries management. They restricted the method of angling, reduced creel limits, practiced catch and release, and increased spawning and productivity through habitat improvement.

James S. Van Cleef continued purchasing vast tracts of wild forest lands surrounding the headwaters of the Willowemoc and Beaverkill. He and other members of the Willowemoc Club acquired thousands of acres, including Balsam Lake, Thomas Lake, and a portion of the upper

---

[4]*Forest and Stream,* April 23, 1874, p. 173.
[5]*Ellenville Journal,* July 20, 1877, p. 1.

Beaverkill. In 1883, they founded the Balsam Lake Club, and after they constructed a lodge, or club-house, their trips to and from Sand Pond became less frequent. Finally, in 1889, the Willowemoc Club members abandoned their interests at Sand Pond and settled permanently at Balsam Lake.

As a lasting tribute, founding member George W. Van Siclen dedicated the reprinting of an English classic to the Willowemoc Club. Van Siclen was considered a scholarly angler, and in 1875 he brought out *An American Edition of the Treatyse of Fysshynge wyth an Angle,* by Dame Juliana Berner.

In his dedication, he reminisced wistfully of the little lake deep in the forest and of the companionship he enjoyed along the Willowemoc:

> The present Willowemoc Club is not composed of Indians; nor is its club-house
> an Abbey, but a house of hemlock boards, with comfortable rooms; floors uncarpeted,
> except by the bedside; and a broad piazza, furnished with easy chairs, and overlooking
> a beautiful lake, full of trout; with an appanage of acres of woodland, and four miles of
> a fine trout stream.
>
> There I shall go when the apple trees are in blossom. And to please the congenial
> spirits of the modern monks who form that club, and the brethren of the angle through
> our land, is this little book reprinted.

George Van Siclen had fond memories of Sand Pond, and one day he most assuredly cherished occurred in 1877, when he caught three trout on one cast. Using a Black Gnat, Cowdung, and Coachman, Van Siclen hooked and successfully landed three brook trout, measuring 10 inches, 12¼ inches, and 16 inches respectively—38¼ inches of trout!

For more than forty years, James Spencer Van Cleef fished the Beaverkill and Willowemoc, and during that span he was important in the preservation of both the trout resources and the history of these two famous streams. In time, Van Cleef came to believe that the only way to preserve trout waters, or to restore streams to their former productivity, was through the control of private clubs or associations. He was a dedicated conservationist at a time when there were but a few. He deplored the practice of destroying the forest lands, which he strongly believed were crucial to the protection of watersheds. On occasion, he even delivered his message to the Fisheries Society and read papers before the society on the decadence of trout streams. During these years he was a member of the State Association for the Protection of Fish and Game, and was retained as counsel for the Senate Committee on Fish and Game. Van Cleef was recognized across the state as a conservation leader, and in 1895 he wrote the general fish and game laws for New York State.

7

"Scarcely Less Famous than the Beaverkill"

Not everyone who came to the Beaverkill fished the stream. Early anglers also found their way to the extreme headwaters and discovered Balsam Lake—a fairly shallow, cold-water lake of approximately twenty acres that teemed with brook trout. In the early days of Catskill trout-fishing history, Balsam Lake was "scarcely less famous than the Beaverkill."[1] What the lake's brook trout lacked in size, they made up in numbers; catches by fishing parties numbered in the hundreds, and sometimes even the thousands.

During this period, the public roamed freely over the land, hunting, trapping, and fishing the many lakes, ponds, and streams, very much as the Indians had done. Even though the almost two million acres of the Hardenbergh Patent had been divided into fifty-two "Great Lots" and then subdivided, the Catskills remained sparsely settled. Most of the land was still owned by a relatively few absentee landlords, the majority of whom had never even seen their holdings. These tracts were vast areas of wild, mountainous, unbroken forest, and as such, it was difficult, if not impossible, to prohibit their use by the public.

---

[1] *Kingston Weekly Leader,* June 7, 1889, p. 7.

From the time Balsam Lake was discovered, it had been a favorite haunt of outdoorsmen. Not only did the lake have a bountiful supply of trout, but the area surrounding it was populated by a large number of deer, many of which found their way to markets. Sleds of venison went weekly from the backwoods to the settlement of Kingston.

By the 1840s, reports on the fishing at Balsam Lake appeared frequently in the weekly newspapers in and about the Catskills. They generally described the rugged countryside, the difficulty of travel, and the phenomenal number of trout caught and kept by fishing parties.

The first visitors to these waters far from any roads experienced great hardship. They traveled the last several miles on foot, through a wilderness, over steep mountains, with no trails to guide them.

One story illustrating the perils and primitive nature of such a trip appeared in the February 1853 *Rondout Courier.* After abandoning their sleigh at the last clearing, five Rondout sportsmen, lured by the traditional stories of Balsam Lake,

> started afoot for the fishing ground at 10 A.M. The route was over three dreaded mountain ridges, trackless, precipitous, clothed in dense forest, and with snow some three feet deep on the heights, and a trifle less in the gorges, ravines and valleys. To add to their toil, a crust had formed on the snow some two feet deep and on this was a dry powdered snow of a foot, and the wayfarers broke through the crust at every step. Four hours of wearisome effort brought them to Balsam Lake, an inconsiderable pond lying hemmed in by the feet of three or four mountains. Here a fire was built, and holes cut in the ice. The trout were abundant, biting at anything, a bit of white rag answering as well as the best bait, and, so eager were the fish, when one was drawn out others jumped out of the water in unsuccessful pursuit of the line.[2]

The majority of those who made raids on Balsam Lake came from within the Catskills or from the larger communities just outside its borders, such as Kingston, Rondout, and Ellenville. Quite often their goal was not merely to have a good time and catch fish but to collect and take home a supply of trout that would serve as food in the months ahead.

An article in the *Prattsville Advocate* in 1847 reported on the typical success of a party of five: "On returning to the house and summing up the sport of the two days, we found we had taken thirteen hundred and six fine trout, most of which we pickled for home consumption."[3]

---

[2] *Rondout Courier,* February 11, 1853, p. 2.
[3] *The Spirit of the Times,* September 18, 1847, p. 352.

Hunters and fishermen made camp for days, even weeks, along the lake's shoreline. Upon arriving, they made rafts to fish from or fashioned canoes by hollowing out large trees. They slept on beds of hemlock boughs, in crude shanties, or under open skies. Bonfires, ostensibly made to provide light and warmth, also illuminated the woods, keeping away panthers and other wild animals:

> Soon after we started our watch fires, we retired for the night; but our rest was soon broken by a shriek from the midst of the forest, which greatly alarmed us; for we soon became aware of the near approach to our camp of some of the wild beasts that infect these woods.[4]

Men from towns and cities hired guides, who were acquainted with forest life. They came to Balsam Lake to live in the style of backwoodsmen and once there, they were often joined by men who *were* backwoodsmen. Gentlemen-sportsmen met and mingled with tough characters—dead-shot, mountaineer market hunters. The lake was a rendezvous for men of vastly different backgrounds and social standings; yet, in the confines of the forest, they joined company and shared campfires. Their love for the outdoors brought them together; they sang songs and feasted on a hindquarter of venison and delicious trout. As the fires burned low, the men exchanged woods lore and told tales of bears, wolves, and panthers.

---

[4]*Bloomville Mirror,* July 27, 1858, p. 2.

8

"Wagon Fishermen"

During the 1840s and '50s, the reputation of the Beaverkill continued to grow, attracting trout fishermen and the attention of America's earliest angling writers. John J. Brown, a New York tackle dealer, is often credited with the authorship of the first useful American angling book.

His pocket-sized manual, titled *The American Angler's Guide*, was published in 1845. The book was very popular with the angling public and went through several editions. Brown included chapters on fish, tackle, bait, and angling. And he attempted to persuade his readers to try their hand at fly fishing. He claimed that the sport was not difficult, and to prove his point, he wrote of his personal experiences with the rugged raftsmen of the Delaware:

> The scientific and graceful art of throwing the artificial fly is a beautiful accomplishment but not so difficult as is generally imagined. In the months of May and June, the raft and lumberman from the Delaware and rivers of Pennsylvania are seen in the fishing tackle stores of New York, selecting with the eye of professors and connoisseurs the red, black and grey hackle flies, which they use with astonishing dexterity on the wooded streams in their mountain homes.[1]

---

[1] Wetzel, *American Fishing Books,* p. 38.

Brown also advised his readers to "fish the Beaver Kill, the Mongaup, the Willewemack, and other kindred streams."[2]

In 1848, the Erie Railroad skirted the western Catskills and followed the upper Delaware River through the borders of Sullivan and Delaware Counties. The railroad not only provided swifter transportation to and from New York but made the Beaverkill accessible to those outlying areas with rail connections to the city. The number of trout fishermen increased, and inn ledgers began recording guests from as far away as Kentucky, Maryland, and Pennsylvania.

Most Erie travelers, however, disembarked at Callicoon, where they were met by the buckboards of Murdock's, Flint's, Tripp's, or one of the newer boardinghouses, as more farmers were opening their doors to the additional fishing tourists. The road from Callicoon was long and rough, and travel was uncomfortable and tiring; once they reached their destination, anxious fishing parties often stayed for days or weeks before returning.

One who fished the Beaverkill often during these early years was Thaddeus Norris. An expert fisherman, rod maker, and writer, Norris was known as the dean of American anglers. In 1864, he wrote *The American Angler's Book,* which contained lists of fish, flies, and tackle, and recounted personal angling experiences. The volume became extremely popular; even today, many consider it the best of the old-time fishing books.

Though he lived in Philadelphia, Norris spent many days in the 1850s fishing the waters of the Willowemoc and Beaverkill, experimenting with flies and fly-fishing techniques. When visiting the area, he usually stayed at the Boscobel, which was what Chester Darbee called the resort previously owned by his mother, and which earlier fishermen had referred to as Mrs. Darbee's.

Thad Norris and some friends who also "enjoyed the gentle art" formed themselves into an association under the unassuming name of Houseless Anglers. Included in the group were Chester Darbee and Peter Stewart, a well-known local hunter and woodsman. Norris dedicated the popular *American Angler's Book* to these com-

© *Forest and Stream, Oct. 9, 1897*

Thaddeus Norris, "Dean" of
American anglers.

---

[2]Brown, *The American Angler's Guide,* 1849 ed., p. 413.

panions, writing fondly of his experiences on the Beaverkill and of how much he enjoyed a tradition that he and his friends called the Noonday Roast, during which "many pleasant hours have been passed under the dark sugar-maple or birch cooking, eating, smoking, chatting, sleeping, many a long story has been told, and perhaps occasionally a *long bow* drawn."[3]

Because of its inaccessibility, for nearly half a century the Beaverkill furnished twenty-five to thirty miles of as fine fishing as any stream in the state. With the coming of the railroad and an increase in fishing tourists, a greater burden was placed on its trout resources. New roads were built, and though they remained crude and primitive, they often paralleled the stream, allowing further exploitation by anglers who visited the fishing grounds by wagon and camped at streamside.

"Wagon fishermen" carried their comforts and luxuries with them, bringing bedding, a good supply of food, a stove, and lanterns. They found a comfortable place for their horses and made themselves at home. These men were not bound to any one place and lived right on the stream at all of the best fishing spots. When one area was fished out, they moved to another and worked the stream relentlessly.

© *The Speckled Brook Trout*, Edited & Illustrated by Louis Rhead. R. H. Russell, New York, 1902.

"A Cool Spot in Leafy June," a somewhat dated illustration by Louis Rhead.

---

[3]Norris, *The American Angler's Book,* p. 497.

During the 1850s, reports circulated that the Beaverkill was being "fished to death," and its speckled beauties were decreasing in size, as well as in number. Veteran anglers saw wagon fishermen as an unethical lot who exploited the trout population of the Beaverkill. Local newspapers seem to bear this out, as reports of incredible catches surfaced: "A party of gentlemen returned to this village last week from a fishing excursion to our mountain streams, having caught about 1,400 trout during their absence."[4] And two weeks later: "A party of four gentlemen, from Kingston, returned last week, having caught between 1,700 and 1,800 brook trout."[5]

Reports such as these were becoming all too common, as fishermen seemed "intent upon exterminating as many trout as possible." Writing on the subject years later, Robert Barnwell Roosevelt stated:

> When the railroad was first opened, the country was literally overrun, and Bashe's Kill, Pine Kill, the Sandberg, the Mon Gaup and Callicoon, and even the Beaver Kill, which we thought were inexhaustible, were fished out. For many years trout had almost ceased from out of these waters, but the horrible public, having their attention drawn to the Adirondacks, gave it a little rest. . . .[6]

---

[4]*Kingston Journal,* June 20, 1855, p. 2.
[5]*Kingston Journal,* July 4, 1855, p. 2.
[6]Roosevelt, *Game Fish of the Northern States of America and British Provinces,* p. 37.

9

Tanneries

It was not angling alone that began taking a toll on the trout populations of the region. The pristine waters of the Beaverkill and Willowemoc would soon also be choked with the odorous, noxious substances of the tanning industry.

During the 1850s, an increasing number of tanneries began to appear, up and down the watershed. Wastes discharged from this stream-related industry caused fish kills and loss of trout habitat, not only on the Beaverkill but all over the Catskills, and wherever hemlock trees grew in abundance.

Commenting on the problem in his *American Angler's Book,* Thad Norris wrote:

> The tannery, with its leached bark, and the discharge of lime mixed with impure
> animal matter extracted from the hides, flowing in and poisoning the trout, have done
> more to depopulate our waters in a few years, than whole generations of anglers.

In the Catskills, the process of making leather with tannin, extracted from the bark of the hemlock, started as early as 1817. The first tannery appeared in Greene County, and the industry developed so rapidly that by 1825 tanneries in that region were producing more leather than in the

43

rest of New York State combined. Tanners depended on hemlock, which flourished in the Catskills, especially on the northern and eastern slopes, where dense groves grew in moist, sheltered ravines and lower valleys. Hemlock was a limited resource, and when the trees were exhausted in Greene County, the competition for the bark forced the tanneries to move south, following the supply of mature trees into the heart of the Catskill range and into Sullivan and Ulster Counties.

Catskill hemlocks were said to be the richest in tannin; pioneer tanner Zadock Pratt once avowed that "the farther you go from the Catskill mountains, the less tannin you find in the hemlock."[1]

Another need of the tanner was a good supply of water. Streams provided inexpensive waterpower, as well as the large amounts of fresh water necessary to the various stages of the tanning process. As was often the case, they were also considered convenient for ridding the tannery of its unwanted wastes, which were simply discharged into the nearby waterway.

Early on, it was deemed more practical to construct tanneries in the forest, and cart the hides in and out of the mountains, than to haul the bulky bark out. Hides were brought up the Hudson River by sloop, and then overland by oxen or horses to the tanneries. Many of the hides that were sent to the Beaverkill region originated from places as far away as Odessa, Russia, and Rio de Janeiro, Brazil. Some arrived by railroad at Callicoon and then were brought by wagon, over roads so rough that only two trips per week could be made; the wagons forded the Willowemoc at the present site of the Hazel bridge.

The hides were first limed or sweated. After the hair and excess flesh were scraped off, they were placed in a series of curing vats containing "ooze" made from ground hemlock bark and water. As the hides progressed through the vats, they were subjected to solutions of increasing strength. Since large quantities of clean water were needed to control the tannic acid, the vats were sunk in the ground near the stream. Eventually, the hides were removed and dried, then treated with fish oil, then dried again and treated with tanner's oil. To tan a hide by the hemlock method took from six to eight months; the leather produced was mainly used for shoe soles and it had a distinctive red-brown color.

During the peeling season, an army of men stayed in the forest, near the hemlocks, living in temporary log houses and crude shanties. One, who became a bark peeler at the age of thirteen, described his first experience in such a shelter:

---

[1] *Ulster Republican,* March 16, 1859, p. 1.

One of them, about 16 by 20 feet, I was in. There were two beds, a fireplace, a small stove, some benches and a table in the one room downstairs. Above there was a loft where the men slept on the floor. There was a ladder alongside the chimney leading up stairs, and right under that ladder there was a big black bear chained. I tell you, my eyes stuck right out when I seen that bear, for I had come down from Prattsville, where there was a village. There was an old woman cooking and smoking a pipe over the kettles. In that house lived the owner and his wife, six children, four workmen, the bear and a couple of dogs.[2]

There were loggers, who felled the trees; peelers, who stripped off the bark; and teamsters, who hauled the bark back to the tannery. The work was difficult and dangerous; the men were not paid well, and the hours were long and tiring. Accidents were frequent, and when bark peelers were trapped and crushed under the heavy weight of a giant falling hemlock, they paid with their lives.

Life as a bark peeler, working for the tanners and living in the forest, was difficult and trying:

We had pretty hard sort of grub in them times and durned few of the barkpeelers saw fresh meat mor'n once or twice a year, less of a Sunday or a holiday some of the men dug out a woodchuck or caught a coon. There was plenty of deer around sure enough, but firearms wuz scarce, and cost a heap, so thet most of the time we ate salt pork and trout.[3]

The flow of sap in the spring made it easier to remove the bark, so it was peeled in late April, May, and June and hauled to the tannery in winter, on sleds and drays. The bark peelers referred to the sap as "slime" because of its stickiness; their predicament in dealing with this problem is best described by H. A. Haring, author of *Our Catskill Mountains:*

With the "slime" came much personal inconvenience. For, in their task of peeling the bark, the men would inevitably lean against the sticky sap. They would get stuck against the tree, against the fresh bark, against the leaves of underbrush, even against

---

[2]DeLisser, *Picturesque Ulster,* p. 191.
[3]DeLisser, *Picturesque Ulster,* p. 155–156.

each other! Then again, the sap dried on their clothes, which—it has been said—were never taken off during the two or three months of the peeling season.

It was commonly said in the Catskills, at the time, that "you could smell a barkpeeler coming—even before he left the woods."

The tanneries, too, were a smelly business. The sap or slime on the bark would ferment and sour; and fish oil, animal hair, and the decaying flesh taken from the hides fouled the air. Curing vats, with their concoctions of tanbark and lime, were emptied into the waterways, killing fish and polluting the waters downstream.

In 1832, the first of the tanneries had appeared in the Beaverkill valley when Linus Babcock constructed a dam across the river and built a tannery at the hamlet of Beaverkill. By the 1860s, the demand for leather had increased to such an extent that there were eight tanneries operating in the area. One was located on the Little Beaverkill at Morrston; four were on the Beaverkill at Shin Creek, Beaverkill, Westfield Flats (Roscoe), and Butternut Grove; and three were along the Willowemoc, at Willowemoc, DeBruce, and Westfield Flats. The tannery at DeBruce was constructed in 1856, just downstream of Mongaup Creek, and was the largest, employing about one hundred men.

Competition for the hemlocks was great, as each tannery depended on the bark for survival; trees were cut down wherever they could be reached. Those found along stream banks were felled across the water, peeled, and left, bank to bank, obstructing the stream. While many of the hemlocks along the Beaverkill and Willowemoc were hauled to the river and rafted to market, it is estimated that 95 percent of the trees were left where they fell.

Many deplored this wasteful practice of cutting down hemlocks, taking the bark, and leaving the greater part of the tree to rot. Trout fishermen were united in their dislike of the tanners and complained bitterly about how they despoiled the countryside and polluted the streams.

It did not take the tanners long to devastate the hemlocks in the Beaverkill and Willowemoc watershed. The industry peaked about twenty years after it had begun and then slowly declined, closing shortly after 1885. The tanners were so complete in their destruction of the hemlocks that many believed the giant evergreens would never return. Today, a little more than a hundred years after the industry left and moved west into Pennsylvania, hemlock groves of mature trees are again found in abundance.

Because of the extensive abuses and wasteful practices of the tanning industry, there has been a common misconception that prior to this period the Catskills were dominated by hemlocks. The Catskill forest before the ravages of the tanners was similar to the forest that is present today, as depicted by surveyors' maps and field notes, collected prior to 1812, before there was any considerable human disturbance or forest exploitation.

Records of early surveys are a useful means of determining what the forest was like; trees marked as witness, or bearing, trees and recorded on maps were an unbiased sample. Robert P. McIntosh, who studied surveyors' field records, found, "In 21 of 22 surveys of the Catskill forest, beech was the most common tree; and in most of these, hemlock was the second most common tree. Beech comprised 50% of the total density, hemlock 20%, sugar maple 13%, and birch 7%."[4]

One of the earliest survey records of the Beaverkill valley, on file in the Ulster County Clerk's Office in Kingston, is a map made by Jacob Trumpbour, dated 1809. The survey covers an area of 8,250 acres of the upper Beaverkill, in the present-day area of Turnwood, Alder Lake, and Shin Creek. As with the findings of McIntosh, this map depicts 56.4% beech, as the most common trees used as survey markers, followed by 17.6% maple, 10.3% birch, and 5.1% hemlock.

---

[4]McIntosh, *The Forests of the Catskill Mountains,* p. 9.

10

Pigeon Fever

Because of its abundance of beech trees and vast forest wilderness, the Beaverkill region was also famous as a gathering place for the phenomenon known as the wild pigeon. To the early settlers, they were a wonder of nature, coming north each March, filling the sky with numbers impossible to comprehend or describe.

The story of the wild pigeon, or passenger pigeon, as it is now called, is one of greed, wastefulness, and senseless slaughter. To exploit a species so abundant and reduce it to extinction is unconscionable. The passenger pigeon was a beautiful, slender bird, fifteen to seventeen inches in length, with delicately pinkish tinted gray feathers and a long tail of eight to nine inches. Passenger pigeons had a wingspan of twenty-three to twenty-five inches and resembled mourning doves, though much larger.

Passenger pigeon

© The Audubon Society Encyclopedia of North American Birds, John K. Terres, Alfred A. Knopf, N.Y., 1980

A bird of the wilderness, the pigeon chose to nest in the forests north of central Ohio, from the Mississippi River to New Hampshire. Sullivan County was well known for its vast nestings, as were the mountainous sections bordering Sullivan, Ulster, and Delaware Counties. A favorite nesting area was the headwaters of the Beaverkill, Willowemoc, Neversink, and Esopus, stretching from Turnwood to DeBruce and Willowemoc, all the way over to Frost Valley and Denning. Passenger pigeons nested in immense numbers, covering thousands of acres; they chose areas of dense forest, with plenty of water and mast. While they ate a wide variety of seeds and berries, they preferred mast crops, especially the nutritious beechnut.

Their incredible flights were a wonderment to all, and attempts to adequately describe their numbers taxed the powers of even experienced writers. One of the earliest to try was John J. Audubon, who encountered passenger pigeons along the Ohio River in 1813 and gave this account:

> The air was literally filled with pigeons; the light of noon day became dim, as during an eclipse; the pigeons' dung fell in spots not unlike melting flakes of snow; and the continued buzz of their wings over me had a tendency to incline my sense of repose.[1]

Bringing darkness to daylight did indeed cause anxiety and apprehensiveness among those who witnessed these great flights of pigeons. Some early colonists of New England looked upon them with reverent wonder; they saw flights as "ominous passages of approaching disasters" and believed that pigeons were always more numerous in the springs of sickly years. Pigeons flying through the sky, wave after wave, in countless numbers, presented an image of "fearful power" and frightened beast as well as man: "Our horse, Missouri, at such times has been so cowed by them that he would stand still and tremble in his harness, whilst we ourselves were glad when their flight was directed from us."[2]

When pigeons arrived at the nesting grounds, they selected mates, and for the next two days went about the business of constructing a nest, entirely from sticks and twigs. They then took turns tending the nest, which usually contained but one or, at most, two eggs. Early in the day the males would leave to drink and feed, returning about midmorning; then the hens would leave, staying away until three o'clock in the afternoon. This pattern occurred daily, rain or shine, for twenty-eight days. After fourteen days the egg hatched, and the young, known as squabs, were

---

[1] *The Ulster Sentinel,* September 26, 1827, p. 4.
[2] *Forest and Stream,* September 12, 1914, p. 336.

cared for by both parents. For the next two weeks, squabs were fed a substance known as pigeon milk, which the parent birds produced in their crop or throat lining.

Trees were filled with nests, often fifty or more in a single treetop. The nests were nearly flat, flimsy, and not very secure; any disturbance to the nesting bird usually resulted in the egg or squab being tossed to the ground. So many pigeons would collect in the trees that their accumulated weight would break the branches, leaving a nesting site desolate, as if a great hurricane or tornado had swept through the forest.

Noise and chaos were companions of a nesting ground, and the screaming and squealing pigeons made when roosting could be heard for miles: "From an hour before sunset until nine or ten o'clock at night there is one continued roar, resembling that of a distant waterfall."[3]

Even when feeding on the forest floor, pigeons were a sight long remembered. They were so numerous and close to one another that the ground could scarcely be seen, and those who witnessed these events marveled at how they left not a leaf unturned in their search for beech-nuts.

While pigeons were hunted and killed by hawks, owls, and every other predatory form of wildlife, their greatest enemy was man. When a nesting site was discovered, the news spread over the countryside, and all of the male inhabitants became afflicted with "pigeon fever." "Farmers, mill men, bark peelers, raftsmen, and tavern loafers"[4] would leave their customary occupations, intent on sport or plunder, to slay without limit. Shortly, they would be joined by professionals, netters and gunners, who descended on the roost with every variety of weapon and method known, to destroy or capture passenger pigeons while they tried to nest. The birds were shot, netted, poked out of nests with long poles, clubbed, and choked by men using pots of sulphur, "making the birds drop in showers."[5]

When they were in season, nothing was talked of, or eaten, but passenger pigeon. To those settlers trying to survive the rugged existence of Catskill mountain life, they were a welcome source of food. There was pigeon stew, broiled pigeon, pigeon potpie, and pigeon served in every style imaginable. They were salted down in barrels for winter use and shared with less fortunate neighbors whose food supply was not as plentiful.

While some were killed for home use, the greatest number found their way to markets in major cities. Commercially minded men were attracted to this great natural food resource and killed

---

[3]*Forest and Stream,* September 12, 1914, p. 337.
[4]*Forest and Stream,* June 2, 1906, p. 868.
[5]*Forest and Stream,* September 12, 1914, p. 336.

or captured pigeons primarily for sale to restaurants and hotels. Before the advent of clay pigeons, gun clubs also purchased many of the birds for use as live targets.

Once a roost was located, rough roads were cut into the mountainsides to enable wagons to haul pigeons to market. Buyers would erect coops or cages for holding live birds and haul in barrels and ice for shipping dead birds. Day after day, two-horse wagons loaded with pigeons wound their way out of the forest, passing over the Newburgh & Cochecton Turnpike to the Hudson, to be taken by sloop or steamboat to New York. If a rafting freshet coincided with nesting pigeons, most every raft leaving the upper Delaware carried a load of the birds, which were sold all along the river to Philadelphia.

The carnage that occurred when men invaded a nesting area is difficult for those living today to imagine. A mountain resident writes of a trip to a nesting at the headwaters of the Beaverkill and Neversink:

> The flock is said to be spread over a space of ground some ten miles long and two miles wide. The trees there are filled with nests in every direction, and the ground is almost covered with eggs and dead pigeons. The hunters shoot into crowds, and when the birds do not fall within a few steps, they make no effort to find them, but try again. There was an immense number of hunters on the ground and when the party from this place came out, they met some 150 or 200 persons armed and equipped—for the work of slaughter—who were just "going in."[6]

As long as passenger pigeons existed in great numbers, they were easy quarry for hunters. They were not shy or wary as most game, and they allowed men with firearms to approach them at astonishingly close quarters. This resulted in a most destructive fire, and the slaughter of pigeons was assured: "Many a time I have fired until the old gun became so hot I could scarce bear my hand on the barrels and was forced to cease for awhile to allow them to cool before I dared reload again. The flocks were so dense I literally made it rain pigeons."[7]

While some professional pigeon men resorted to the use of firearms, many more who made their living exploiting the birds used nets. One man who pursued pigeons for many years among the beechwood forests of the headwaters describes the method in graphic detail. After constructing a "bough house," a bed was made by leveling the ground nearby:

---

[6]*Kingston Democratic Journal,* May 9, 1860, p. 2.
[7]*Forest and Stream,* February 16, 1895, p. 126.

Upon this we sprinkled wheat with anise seed to tempt the pigeons. A net was placed on one side of the bed fastened with saplings which sprung back so that when a rope was pulled at the bough house the net would be thrown over the bed. We had flyers and stool pigeons. Their eyes were sewed shut so they could not see; a flyer had a string attached to its legs. When thrown in the air it would fly up a short distance and drop down in a natural way as though it had found an inviting spot. This would attract the attention of pigeons which might be flying in the vicinity, sometimes drawing them from a considerable distance. Then the stool pigeon tied at the end of a lever that could be worked up and down with a string, would be made to fly. By and by down would come the flock of pigeons with a roar to the bed. While eating the grain the net would be sprung. Then a rush for the bed to hold down the net and kill the pigeons by biting them in the neck. The dead birds would be thrown in a basket, the feathers carefully picked off the bed, the net again set, when everything would be in readiness for the next flock.

It's down right mean to kill them, but it's business—business, not sentiment. I remember the first time I bit a pigeon and killed it. Ugh! I thought I tasted it for a week. Die easy? O, yes, just a little bite on the back of the neck, and the pigeon is dead before you can wink.

It was always the rule to let one or two escape so as to bring back another flock to the same feeding ground. How many did we usually catch? Why, at one haul we could cover 150 perhaps, but the usual number was from 75 to 100. I knew of a man near Kingston who netted 3,000 pigeons in half a day. It was an ordinary thing to catch 1,000 in a day. Those were great days my boy.[8]

While all must share responsibility for the extinction of the passenger pigeon, it was many people's conclusion that the netting of birds for market deserved most of the blame. The number of birds sold commercially was incalculable, and could only be reckoned in the billions. When railroads penetrated all parts of the country, they brought the prey closer to markets. In addition, the telegraph was used to apprise the netters as to the whereabouts of the pigeons. Express companies were anxious for the netters to know where the pigeons were, since they charged between six and

---

[8]*Kingston Weekly Freeman & Journal,* March 7, 1889, p. 3.

twelve dollars per barrel and anywhere from four thousand to five thousand barrels were generally shipped from each nesting.

By the 1890s, one hundred to two hundred men were engaged in netting pigeons all the time. With increased communications, netters, gunners, and buyers seemed to arrive at a roost at the same time as the pigeons, and they were joined by a multitude of hunters, amateurs, and greenhorns, who surrounded and destroyed nesting grounds.

Reports by sportsmen repeatedly indicated that the passenger pigeon was in trouble. The size of the flocks kept diminishing, while the destructive forces exploiting them multiplied.

The cry for their protection was a long time coming, and once the birds began their downward spiral, it was too late. An article calling for a closed season appeared in *Forest and Stream* as early as the fall of 1876, when there were still abundant numbers:

> If we wish much longer to hear over our heads on bright March mornings the rush of his breezy wings speeding in swift flight above the waking woods, battalion after battalion sweeping on from horizon to horizon almost in a breath; if we wish our October lunch of his broiled tender flesh, or care for "squabs on toast;" even if we wish to pack them in a box, and liberate him only to cut short his sudden joy with our shot "at 21 yards rise," the pigeon, which is not only useful and beautiful, but a delight, must soon be protected by law from wanton capture in what should be for him as well as other birds, a "close season."[9]

By 1890, pigeons were scarce everywhere in the East. Traditional nesting grounds were now being abandoned, and the birds were being driven westward into the forests of Michigan, Wisconsin, and Canada. Even though everyone was aware of the wholesale slaughter of pigeons for commercial purposes, there were those who refused to believe the birds were in danger of becoming extinct. They believed that, owing to the birds' persecution, the pigeons simply disappeared to a distant and unexplored part of the country and hid themselves.

The last large flocks nested along the upper Beaverkill in 1877. In the final days, reports of passenger pigeon sightings grew very scarce. The few that reached the public came out of the Catskills and, not surprisingly, from their old nesting grounds, in the vast hardwood forest of the Beaverkill. When the birds were seen, the numbers were a pittance, compared to their former abundance; but because of their scarcity, a flock of any size caused a sensation.

---

[9]*Forest and Stream,* September 21, 1876, p. 104.

A few years after their disappearance, naturalist John Burroughs caused a stir when he gave accounts of passenger pigeon sightings to the readers of *Forest and Stream*. Pigeons were spotted at DeBruce in the fall of 1904 and, two years later, at Willowemoc. In 1907, Burroughs made a trip to Sullivan County to verify a report of about a thousand pigeons seen in May: "The locality was a few miles north of Livingston Manor, near the Beaverkill. I am fully convinced that the pigeons were seen,"[10] wrote Burroughs. Quite possibly, the last sightings were of a small flock preparing to nest along the Beaverkill in 1909, and a flight of about three hundred, seen over Willowemoc in 1910.

In 1914, the Cincinnati Zoological Gardens announced that its lone female, the last remaining passenger pigeon, had died in her twenty-ninth year. In 1878, the zoo had received eight passenger pigeons, and while a number of birds were hatched, all had died except Martha. Desperate to find a mate for the bird, the zoo made an offer of one thousand dollars, but in all the years before Martha's death, no one came forward to claim the reward.

The prevailing view of the people toward the extinction of a species so beautiful and so numerous was one of profound regret. Not everyone, however, took a sentimental view of their passing. Some found "its manner of life and vast numbers incompatible with agricultural interests." They determined that "when the wilderness ceased to exist, the earth had no place for the wild pigeon."[11]

---

[10]*Forest and Stream,* July 13, 1907, p. 53.
[11]*Forest and Stream,* May 26, 1906, p. 827.

11

"The Trout Are Playing Out"

During the 1860s, the Beaverkill's trout population received a small reprieve when the Civil War (1861–65) consumed men's passions.

Those anglers who traveled to the stream during these years again found brook trout in abundance. Two men who journeyed over from Delhi and stayed at Murdock's wrote of their experiences to the editor of the *Bloomville Mirror* in June 1864: "We kept a record of each day's work, and the number caught by each, which gives the following result . . . a grand total for the three and a half days, 776 trout."[1]

One other interesting report of this period was found by Kenneth Sprague of Roscoe, while he was glancing through a diary his grandfather kept for many years. The entry was dated April 14, 1865: "Went fishing at Baxter's with Harry Mott; not much luck. Went to Buck Eddy [Willowemoc Creek, just upstream of Roscoe] and caught 109 trout. This night President Lincoln was assassinated."[2]

[1] *Bloomville Mirror,* June 28, 1864, p. 1.
[2] *Liberty Register,* May 16, 1940, p. 6.

Several significant events were pivotal in the history of the Beaverkill; the first occurred when railroads penetrated into the remote areas of the Catskills. Following the Civil War, an epidemic known as "railroad fever" spread across America. Visions of great commercial activity and national expansion were on the minds of everyone; bankers, manufacturers, farmers, and resort owners dreamed of prosperity and profits. Railroad construction became widespread, and new lines found their way from population centers even into the tiny, secluded hamlets bordering trout streams.

Construction started on the Rondout & Oswego Railroad in 1869. This line began in Kingston and wound its way up the Esopus valley, over Pine Hill, and into Arkville. A mere fifteen miles from Arkville, the upper Beaverkill was now accessible to anglers, who traveled up the Dry Brook valley, over a wagon road, and around Balsam Lake Mountain to the headwaters.

Even before it was completed, fishermen began using the line; and additional exploitation of the mountain streams was not only swift but dramatic. The *Kingston Journal* reported on the first trout shipped, via the new railway, in the summer of 1870:

> Several thousand speckled trout from the brooks of Shandaken, Olive and other sections of Ulster, have been brought to town of late. The Rondout & Oswego railroad cars transverse the trout districts of the county, and not only afford cheap travel for those who indulge in piscatorial sports, but also bring fish to market in so short a space of time after being caught, that they are nearly as hard and fresh as when first taken from the water.[3]

A second railroad, and one that had an even greater impact on the Beaverkill and Willowemoc, began laying its tracks in 1868. The New York & Oswego Midland Railroad ran from New York to the very doorstep of the Beaverkill. The line traveled through Sullivan County to Morrston (Livingston Manor), along the banks of lower Willowemoc Creek to Westfield Flats (Roscoe), and then followed the Beaverkill downstream, all the way to East Branch and on to Lake Ontario. At this time, Westfield Flats contained "3 hotels, 4 stores, 3 blacksmith shops, 2 wagon shops, 1 cabinet shop, 1 harness shop, 2 shoe shops, 5 saw mills, and 2 tanneries."[4]

Known simply as the Midland, the railroad officially opened July 9, 1873. The last spike was driven on the banks of the Beaverkill at Whirling Eddy, a pool the raftsmen called Hell Hole.

---

[3]*Kingston Journal,* July 13, 1870, p. 3.
[4]*Delaware Gazette,* June 18, 1873, p. 2.

The "Mountain Express" enabled city anglers to commute regularly, on weekends, to the Beaverkill.

With the coming of the railroad, the Beaverkill was easy to reach. In fact, the Midland opened the door to a flood of anglers who could now get to the stream in a matter of hours and could commute regularly on weekends. Coincidentally, trout fishing in the 1870s became increasingly popular, being fueled by the publication in New York of *Forest and Stream,* a weekly journal devoted to fishing, hunting, and outdoor life in general.

Forest and Stream made its debut on August 14, 1873, and in a short time began informing its readers on the pleasures of trout fishing and how to use the new railroad to reach the Beaverkill:

> One of the best trout regions within striking distance of New York lies on the
> borders of Sullivan and Ulster counties, and includes the famous Beaverkill and Wil-
> lowemoc rivers. By taking the 6 o'clock morning train of the Oswego Midland Rail-
> road the angler can reach Morrston at noon, distance one hundred and seventeen miles,
> enjoy the afternoon fishing, and fish all the next day until 3½ o'clock, when the train
> will bear him back to this city and land him at Cortland or Desbrosses street at 10½
> o'clock, with his fish fresh and ready for the morning breakfast.[5]

---

[5]*Forest and Stream,* July 9, 1874, p. 346.

Railroads brought the beautiful mountainous scenery of the Catskills, with its fresh air and pure waters, to the threshold of the metropolis. With low travel rates, good railway accommodations, and inexpensive board, it was not long before the entire region became one vast summer resort. Now city dwellers could escape the heat and toil of their fast-paced lives and spend time in the country, vacationing, much to the satisfaction of hillside farmers, boardinghouse owners, and hotel keepers.

Recognizing that trout fishing held a strong attraction for summer visitors, railroad officials began promoting the Beaverkill through advertisements in sporting magazines and journals. For many years the Ontario & Western, which replaced the Midland, ran "hunters' and fishers' specials," with Pullman drawing-room cars that carried the names of the famous streams, such as the Neversink, Willowemoc, and Beaverkill.

On the heels of the railroad came more hotels and boardinghouses, which catered to the new fishing tourists. In 1878, the Midland published the first of many annual guides to "healthful summer resorts among the mountains." This first edition informs anglers who arrive at Morrston:

> Here Emmet Sturdevant will meet you and take you to his house, or to Cooper's or Matt Decker's on the Willowemoc, or good old Murdock or Jones Brothers will seat you in a springy buckboard for the Beaverkill. Who has not heard of "Murdock's on the Beaverkill"? Many a clergyman and lawyer and business man has eaten motherly Mrs. Murdock's cakes and maple syrup during the last twenty-five years, and has gathered new strength and health from absorbing the perfect air as he struggled along the stream, and then came home, with a full basket, wet and hungry, to absorb his own trout as they came crisp and hot from her skillful hand.[6]

The enthusiasm for trout fishing continued to grow, and it received an added boost from the publication of a number of books on angling, most notably *I Go A-Fishing,* by W. C. Prime (1873); *The Fishing Tourist,* by Charles Hallock (1873); *Pleasures of Angling,* by George Dawson (1876); and another by Hallock, titled *The Sportsman's Gazetteer* (1877), which included a directory to fishing resorts in the United States.

This growing popularity was illustrated locally in an article that appeared in the *Ellenville Journal:*

---

[6]*Summer Homes on the Midland,* p. 25.

The number of both City and Country who affect to be "trout fishers" is largely increased. It is said to be a rule in New York business circles that all applicants for positions of any kind, from that of bar-tender up through all grades of clerkships to a silent partnership, must be provided with a trout-pole, fly book and fish basket. No man or boy can "come the gorilla" in the stock exchange who doesn't own or can't borrow a German silver mounted fly pole. No law student can be admitted to the bar until he knows the difference between a "Limerick" and an "Aberdeen," and owns a pair of hob-nailed "stogas." And the last time I was on the Beaverkill I encountered, rod in hand and creel on his back, a tailor's apprentice, fresh from Gotham, in a brand new suit of silver-grey corduroys! And in the country, the highway from boyhood to manliness leads through a trout-stream as certainly as through a cigar box. Hence the poor trout have next to no chance at all.[7]

Fishing the Willowemoc at DeBruce.

© Jean Boyd

The multitude of new anglers placed greater stress on the dwindling trout supply. Many believed that the railroads would be the end of trout fishing and that the streams would never recover from this new onslaught of fishermen, who fished so persistently. At this time, the trout population of the Beaverkill was still dependent upon the natural reproduction in the stream. No stocking or planting of domestic trout had occurred, and the native brook trout were still of the original strain.

---

[7] The Rev. Dr. E. W. Bently, *Ellenville Journal,* July 20, 1877, p. 1.

With more and more fishermen vying for fewer trout, competition developed the practice known as "fishing for count." Eager to best one another, anglers no longer kept only the larger "saving" trout but began keeping every fish, right down to the smallest fingerlings, and then boasted of the numbers they had taken. Year by year, overfishing reduced the average size of the trout.

Because of their relatively small size, trout were hauled from the stream by a "jerk of the wrist," which served to make quick work of the fish while at the same time did not disturb the water. Without laws to regulate anglers' success, the number of trout one angler could remove in a single day was extraordinary: "A party of five brought home 800 trout"[8]; "a party of twenty captured 1,500 in a single day." . . . "There have been by actual count over 2,000 fish in the cellar [at Murdock's] at one time."[9]

The trout were disappearing, and it was a matter of time until the free fishing enjoyed by everyone was doomed. Until then, the public roamed the countryside, camping and fishing freely wherever they chose. Most farmers whose lands adjoined the Beaverkill took in fishermen and, like the inns and boardinghouses, allowed their guests to fish over their neighbors' water. But now the demand was greater than the stream could produce, and hordes of new anglers were tramping the stream, anxious to fill their baskets.

George W. Sears, the popular outdoor writer who used the pseudonym Nessmuk, bluntly told his readers:

> Salmo Fontinalis is becoming small by degrees, and deplorably scarce. . . . It is the constant, indefatigable working of the streams by skilled anglers, who turn out in brigades, supplemented by the granger, who takes his boys along in a lumber wagon, camps on the stream until he has "salted down" several butter tubs full of trout, and saves everything large enough to bite. . . . Anglers increase as trout diminish; and such streams are infested by anglers from April to August, to an almost incredible extent, nearly all of whom basket anything more than four inches long. . . . The trout are playing out.[10]

---

[8] *Kingston Journal,* May 29, 1872, p. 3.
[9] *Ellenville Journal,* August 3, 1872, p. 1.
[10] *The American Angler,* November 19, 1881, p. 19.

12

Unlimited Trout

The idea of replenishing streams or ponds by stocking developed early in the history of sport-fishing in America. Locally, stocking began long before there were fish hatcheries, before Americans even knew how to artificially propagate trout.

The first reported Beaverkill watershed stocking occurred as early as 1833, when Benjamin and Jacob Misener transported brook trout they had captured from Pease Brook, Hankins Creek, and other nearby streams and placed them in Long Pond [Tennanah Lake].[1] Afterward, and for many years, Long Pond was known for its large brook trout. During the 1860s and 1880s, it was still furnishing anglers with an occasional brook trout that exceeded 4 pounds!

The first attempt at managing the state's fisheries resources began with the formation of the Board of Commissioners of Fisheries in 1868. There was a Fish Commission even before there was a Forest or Game Commission; Chapter 285 of the Laws of 1868 authorized "an Act to appoint Commissioners of Fisheries for the State of New York." Its first members were former governor Horatio Seymour, Robert Barnwell Roosevelt, and Seth Green.

---

[1]"History of the Town of Fremont, Sullivan County," *Republican Watchman,* August 30, 1940, p. 1.

From the outset, the commission focused its efforts and finances on fish propagation. Its plan was to replenish streams throughout the state by stocking them with domestic, or hatchery-raised, trout. A pioneer fish culturist, Seth Green had established the first hatchery in America at Caledonia, New York, in 1864.[2] While Dr. Theodatus Garlick of Cleveland, Ohio, had fertilized the eggs of trout and hatched them successfully as early as 1854, it was Seth Green who made hatchery fish profitable, a "recognized art of practical significance in this country."

In the summer of 1870, the Fish Commission constructed a "hatching house" at Caledonia and named Seth Green as the superintendent. The site was leased from A. S. Collins, who had acquired it from Green years earlier. At first, the hatching house was used only for the propagation of whitefish and salmon trout (lake trout).

In 1875, the site was purchased outright by the Fish Commission and a larger, more complete hatchery was created on the very land where Seth Green had started his hatchery years before. Until this time, brook trout had not been hatched at public expense. Now, with these improvements and the ever-growing rail transportation, the commission was ready to meet the "urgent demands" of the public and replenish the state's trout waters. Caledonia was an excellent location for the distribution of hatchery fish. Major railroad lines ran within a mile of the facility and connected with others that traveled to all sections of the state.

In its year-ending report to the legislature, the commission announced it expected to have a supply of one million brook trout fry, for distribution to all persons desiring them, to stock public streams and ponds in the state.

The ease with which trout eggs could be taken and fertilized, producing thousands of fry from a single pair of fish, was seen as an extremely exhilarating idea. The Fish Commission was making a major effort to replenish its waters by offering an unlimited number of free trout to all the people of the state of New York!

"Securing the trout spawn," the ease with which trout eggs could be taken and fertilized, was seen as an extremely exhilarating idea.

© *Harper's New Monthly Magazine,* November 1868

---

[2]Heacox, *The Compleat Brown Trout,* p. 83.

The first stocking of trout taken from a hatchery and placed directly into the Beaverkill appears to have occurred in 1876.[3] On February 16 of that year, Charles Mead, a founding member of the Beaverkill Association, received from the state hatchery at Caledonia 20,000 brook trout fry. These fish were placed in the waters of the association (now the Beaverkill Trout Club) and were one of the first shipments of brook trout ever made from the state hatchery.

It became the commission's policy to issue an annual news release advising the public that trout or other fish could be had for free, by ordering them directly from Seth Green, Rochester, New York. Every winter, newspapers throughout New York informed the public when it was time to order trout fry. All that was required was that the recipient give a general description of the waters to be stocked, how many fish were desired, and an affidavit that the fish were placed in public waters. Unless picked up at Caledonia, the fry were shipped in tins, delivered by a messenger. In such cases, the person ordering the fish was to include directions specifying which rail route to come by and who to call for settlement, since it was expected that the messenger's expenses would be paid.

Railroads became eager participants in the Fish Commission's plan to restore the state's trout streams. They ordered their baggagemen to carry cans of young fish and crates of fish eggs and to assist anyone loading and unloading the same. "Conductors have also instructions to stop express trains at any streams, to leave fish, providing they can do so without missing connections."[4]

In addition to carrying cans free of charge, the Ontario & Western began stocking trout along its line. Trout fishing was an important asset to the railroad's passenger service, and officials determined early that stocking was necessary to ensure satisfied travelers. Their records show that in 1878 only 20,000 trout were acquired. In just a few years the number of fish put into streams by the O. & W. grew dramatically: In 1884 they placed 310,000 fish; in 1885, 460,000; and in 1886, 900,000![5]

Stocking was deemed so vital to the railroad that in 1890 the O. & W. constructed a special car, designed strictly for transporting and distributing trout and other fish along the many miles of streams and lakes bordering their rail line.

About the same time that the Caledonia hatchery was being readied for the production of brook trout, Seth Green received eggs of two new species of trout he believed would be instrumental in restocking the state's exhausted waters.

---

[3]New York State Fisheries Commission, annual report, 1877, p. 10.
[4]*Hancock Herald,* April 15, 1880, p. 2.
[5]*Walton Chronicle,* April 7, 1887, p. 2.

One shipment, from the German fish hatchery at Huningen, contained 2,500 fertilized eggs of the "European brook trout" (brown trout). Unfortunately, it arrived in a "horrible state of putrefaction," with not one good egg in the lot. It was the second time that brown trout eggs had failed to survive the trip across the Atlantic.[6]

The other shipment arrived on March 31, 1875, and contained eggs of the "California mountain trout" (rainbow trout). These were sent by a Mr. Newell of San Francisco, and while a great many of the 1,800 eggs perished because of high temperature, the hatchery did manage to hatch 260 trout.

In the rainbow Seth Green thought he had found a further way to rejuvenate the trout waters of New York. He believed that rainbow trout could withstand warmer water temperatures and endure greater hardships and, therefore, live in waters vacated by the native trout.

Poor forestry practices and the discharges of deleterious wastes by streamside industries were fouling the homes of brook trout, which were too delicate to reside in anything but the purest and coolest waters. Other streams throughout New York were naturally too warm to have ever supported many native trout.

In the spring of 1878, those survivors of the San Francisco shipment reached three years of age and were ready to spawn. Their eggs were hatched, and the fry were distributed throughout the state, becoming the first rainbow trout introduced into eastern waters. Only one of these shipments reached the Catskills: A. S. Hopkins of Catskill, New York, received 1,006 "California mountain trout" and placed them in the waters of Greene County.[7]

Rainbows were first placed in the Beaverkill on June 30, 1880, when Ed Sprague and James Murdock received a shipment of 30,000 fry and stocked them in the upper Beaverkill and Shin Creek. A few days later, Montgomery Dodge placed rainbows in the waters of the lower river. On July 6, 1882, H. E. Street stocked 25,000 in Mongaup Creek, a tributary of the Willowemoc.

By the end of 1881, more than a million rainbow fry were being stocked per annum. Speaking before the New York Association for the Protection of Game, Commissioner Robert Barnwell Roosevelt stated, "They are the coming trout! They are perfection."[8]

Unforeseen doubts, however, began to surface rather quickly. Reports to the Fish Commission claimed that rainbows were not readily found the year after they were introduced into a stream. It was feared that many were preyed upon when they were first planted. Rainbows

---

[6]*Forest and Stream,* April 22, 1875, p. 166.
[7]New York State Fisheries Commission, annual report, 1880, p. 44.
[8]*Forest and Stream,* December 21, 1881, p. 411.

spawned in the spring; therefore, the fry were stocked later in the season, at a time when other fish were feeding greedily. In addition, it was rumored that the fish were migratory and that when they reached a certain size, they worked their way downstream.

During these years, rainbows were not stocked in the Beaverkill with regularity or, for that matter, in large numbers. Because of this, there is very little information available as to how successful these early rainbow stockings were. Those fish that did survive apparently did very well; some grew to exceptional size. Two of the largest were caught in the same pool, under the bridge at Craig-e-clare. This long, deep-ledge rock pool was the home of a 6-pound, 3-ounce rainbow, caught in 1892 by the Reverend Robert Joscelyn of Minnesota. In 1894, another monster was taken by Joseph Kelley of Lew Beach that measured 23¾ inches and weighed an even 6 pounds!

13

Beecher, Burroughs, and Buntline

Three of the most notable and colorful anglers to fish the Beaverkill in the 1870s were James Beecher, John Burroughs, and Ned Buntline. Each, in his own way, enriched the lore of the Beaverkill.

The Reverend James C. Beecher was the brother of Harriet Beecher Stowe and Henry Ward Beecher. His sister, an ardent abolitionist, wrote *Uncle Tom's Cabin,* which became a sensation, "the first powerful blow dealt to American slavery."[1] The book evolved into one of the most popular plays produced on the American stage. Henry Ward Beecher, too, was an antislavery leader, as well as a clergyman, and was one of the most conspicuous figures in the public life of his time.

During the war over slavery, James Beecher commanded an all-black regiment. Harriet, to show her pride in him, devised a banner that portrayed "a rising sun with the word LIBERTY above it in immense crimson and black letters, and below it the inscription 'The Lord Is Our Sun and Shield.'" James carried the flag into battle at Charleston.[2]

---

[1]Knox, *Life and Work of Henry Ward Beecher,* p. 34.
[2]Hedrick, *Harriet Beecher Stowe,* p. 305.

During the trouting season of 1874, the Willowemoc Club invited the Reverend Mr. Beecher, then pastor of the Poughkeepsie Congregational Church, to spend his vacation at their lodge. The Reverend loved nature and the outdoors; he usually spent his vacations fishing and camping in the most secluded parts of the country. On his visit to Sand Pond, he decided to explore the surrounding wilds of that primitive region and took off from the lodge with only his knapsack. After a lengthy journey through the forest, he discovered a lovely lake, encircled by high mountains and densely wooded peaks.

He was so delighted with the natural beauty of the place and its pristine surroundings that he camped along the lake's shore for six weeks, subsisting by hunting and fishing. Being a skillful angler, he did not have to venture far, since the lake had an abundance of brook trout. Believing he was the first person to discover the lake, he decided he had the right to name it Beecher Lake. This is understandable; maps of the region were rare, and even the most popular at the time, J. H. French's survey map, printed in 1858, failed to show any lake where Beecher found his, between Balsam Lake and Alder Lake.

The lake, its serenity, and the beautiful valley of the Beaverkill affected the forty-two-year-old preacher so deeply that he decided to abandon the comforts of city life. At the end of his vacation he resigned from his flourishing pastorate, giving up the very lucrative salary of three thousand dollars to live in the peacefulness of his newly found wilderness retreat.

Unbeknownst to Beecher, the lake that he found was called Thomas Lake and was owned by James Spencer Van Cleef. Van Cleef was willing to part with the lake, but with certain conditions. In September 1874, he sold it to Beecher, along with 150 acres, reserving the right to fish the lake for himself and members of the Willowemoc Club.

After purchasing the property, James Beecher decided to spend the first winter at the lake. He braved the punishing wind, cold, and deep snows alone, living in a tent. His only companions were "winter storms and the night cries of the mountain wild beasts."[3] There were no nearby neighbors, and the nearest road of any kind was seven miles away; yet he found the experience, with its solitude and peacefulness, uplifting:

> A sailor by nature and a minister by grace, I love to sit here by the hour and look
> out upon these surroundings. They are a source of never-ending enjoyment. During
> the winter months I am still more fond of this retreat, for as the beautiful snow lies so

---

[3]*New York Times,* August 27, 1886, p. 2.

still and quietly all about us, there is nothing to disturb or discolor it. Here is true re-
pose and communion with nature.[4]

All that winter, he walked through the woods and deep snow; it was nine miles to the nearest post office, where the mail arrived once a week.

James Beecher was educated at Dartmouth and Andover Seminary, and while he was a clergyman by profession, he was also a skilled and able carpenter, blacksmith, and glazier. He cleared
land along the lake and cut a trail several miles through the forest, so lumber could be hauled in
for a permanent dwelling. Along the lake he constructed, with his own hands, a beautiful one-
and-a-half-story house. After he and his family moved into the home, he avowed he would never
go back to village life, even though he received many offers to return to the pulpit. "I can obtain
more real enjoyment and comfort here with $300 a year, than with $3,000 in New York," he stated.

The Beechers were kind and caring people; Mrs. Beecher began teaching school and introduced books, for the first time, to the families of the backwoodsmen. They provided clothing to
needy children who wore simple homespun. Their many acts of charity and good work endeared
them to their neighbors; it was said that they gave to the poor of the valley so generously that they,
too, were often "poor of purse."

Almost immediately, James Beecher began preaching locally at the two regional school-
houses, and though he had to travel a great distance on horseback, he never missed a Sunday service. The scattered settlers journeyed by horse and wagon over the roughest of roads to Shin Creek
(Lew Beach) to hear this Beecher, who had chosen to live among them.

Those living along the Beaverkill came to love the "hermit" preacher, and they joined together and constructed a wagon road for him, from the post office to his home at Beecher Lake.
To repay this kindness, he used his carpentry skills to place doors and windows in their crude log
cabins or make other repairs and improvements. After the road was finished, he purchased a horse
and wagon for Mrs. Beecher, but he continued to make his own journeys by saddle horse.

During the years he lived in the valley, James Beecher was at times visited by his famous sister and brother. Henry Ward Beecher, too, was a "lover of the trout-rod" and undoubtedly fished
the Beaverkill when he came to Beecher Lake. On occasion, he even served as guest preacher and
delivered Sunday services. He was a preacher of national fame, known for his originality of
thought and his highly emotional and florid sermons. For nearly half a century he was pastor of
Plymouth Church, where he "fearlessly preached freedom for the slave, and [his] words have elec-

---

[4]*American Agriculturist,* September 1881, p. 354.

trified a continent and sent a thrill to the heart of the whole English speaking race."[5] When President Lincoln visited New York and was asked what he would like to see, he chose Plymouth Church in Brooklyn, where Henry Ward Beecher delivered his antislavery sermons.

Henry Ward Beecher was an extremely popular figure. Though he had a great many admirers and was known across the land as a fiery orator, however, in the backwoods of the Beaverkill even someone of his stature and reputation could go unnoticed. One legend that has been preserved in the valley tells about a time when he was delivering a sermon and in the audience was an equally famous man by the name of Joe Jefferson. Jefferson was a veteran fisherman who had visited the stream for many years, frequently staying at Murdock's. He relaxed by sketching the natural beauty of the Beaverkill, but it was the stream's trout that he was after; and while he was a great success as an angler, Joe Jefferson was best known as an actor, especially for his role in *Rip Van Winkle*.

From 1866 on, he played annual tours, and children across the country were taken to see "Rip." Jefferson became one of the best-known and best-loved figures in America, and his performance was recognized as "one of those rare and precious things which come only in a generation."[6]

On this particular Sunday, the service was held at the little one-room schoolhouse above Shin Creek;[7] since it was a warm summer day, the minister preached from the doorway. During the service he saw and recognized Joe Jefferson, who, he noticed, was not paying very close attention.

"They would not know me, but maybe my dog Schneider would," he said, louder than necessary. "Jefferson looked up (for that was Rip's dog's name) and said, 'who am I listening to?' and they told him it was Henry Ward Beecher."[8]

James Beecher died in August 1886. Upon his death, the Poughkeepsie *Evening Enterprise* commented on the "hermit" preacher's life among the settlers of the Beaverkill:

> He had endeared himself to the dwellers of that mountainous region by his simple mode of life and his continuous acts of kindness and benevolence. During his entire residence among them he was always ready to help the poor and suffering with hands and money; foremost in every good work, and with all his eccentricity, he was looked upon by those people as a good man, worthy of their highest respect.[9]

---

[5] Knox, *Life and Work of Henry Ward Beecher,* p. III.
[6] Malone, *Dictionary of American Biography,* p. 16.
[7] Today, located at the end of the meadow on Joan Wulff's property.
[8] Tiffany, *Pioneers of the Beaverkill Valley,* p. 23.
[9] *Evening Enterprise,* August 27, 1886, p. 2.

Another who enriched the lore of the Beaverkill through his writings was John Burroughs. Famous throughout America as a naturalist, poet, philosopher, and writer, this Catskill native was an early saunterer and trout fisherman of the Beaverkill.

Born in Roxbury, Delaware County, in 1837, Burroughs had fished mountain streams since boyhood, acquiring his love for the sport from his grandfather Edmund Kelly.

John Burroughs, like many who grew up on farms in Delaware County, learned to fish the small brook trout streams that seemingly flow through every farmer's field. Even today, these little streams are important to country youngsters, who find in them not only the delightfully pretty "native" trout but also small adventures. They provide a challenge; a boy or girl can bring home a treat for the table, gaining praise and respect as an angler, or fail to deliver, and experience humility. Such trout streams build character.

In July 1860, when he was a grown man of twenty-three, Burroughs set out with a friend to find the source of the Beaverkill and to fish in famous Balsam Lake. Off in the wilderness, far from settlements, they camped and lived on the fish and game they captured.

Perhaps they heard the howl of wolves, or the screech of a bobcat or panther; whatever the cause, their first night in the wilds of the Beaverkill was a memorable one. They took turns keeping up the fire; Burroughs had the first watch and "fired shots in several directions lest the creatures which seemed to be lurking out there in the darkness should close in on them."[10]

They survived the night and the following day camped on the shores of Balsam Lake, where they tried to fish for trout; but they couldn't manage the flies until some men came along and showed them how.

In the years that followed, Burroughs made other trips to the area, to the Willowemoc and Mongaup as well as the Beaverkill.

In 1868, he and some friends set out to fish Thomas Lake (Beecher Lake), the small trout pond hidden in the forest between Alder Lake and Balsam Lake. They hiked in from Mill Brook valley, and while the distance was not great, the terrain was steep, and the going was rough and difficult. The men got lost and were about to give up and return home, but Burroughs convinced them to stay. He went ahead and eventually found the lake; then he returned and got everyone lost again:

> I would have sold my interest in Thomas's Lake at a very low figure. I heartily
> wished myself well out of the woods. Thomas might keep his lake, and the enchanters

---

[10]Barrus, *John Burroughs: Boy and Man,* p. 319.

guard his possession! I doubted if he ever found it the second time, or if any one else ever had.[11]

At last they found the lake, and along its shore a crude raft, which they used to cast their flies for the trout they were assured were there. They did not catch very many during their stay and had to be satisfied with catching sunfish, which took the hook more readily.

But it was Balsam Lake that really charmed him—which is not surprising, since it is beautiful and secluded and its infinite population of trout were always eager to take the hook. In his ever-popular work *In the Catskills,* he described a trip made in 1869:

> Balsam Lake was oval-shaped, scarcely more than half a mile long and a quarter of a mile wide, but presented a charming picture, with a group of dark gray hemlocks filling the valley about its head, and the mountains rising above and beyond. We found a bough house in good repair, also a dug-out and paddle and several floats of logs. In the dug-out I was soon creeping along the shady side of the lake, where the trout were incessantly jumping for a species of black fly that, sheltered from the slight breeze, were dancing in swarms just above the surface of the water. The gnats were there in swarms also, and did their best toward balancing the accounts by preying upon me, while I preyed upon the trout, which preyed upon the flies.[12]

Writing to a friend about this particular trip, Burroughs declared:

> I wish you could have had some of the trout we caught. At Balsam Lake, during a thunder shower that drenched Johns and me to the skin, I caught from a dug-out 75 as beautiful trout, in about two hours, as ever swam. It was such fun! Sometimes I would haul in two at a time, as I had two flies on my line.[13]

John Burroughs was a great observer, an angler who took the time to look closely at his catch and appreciate the great natural beauty of the native brook trout:

---

[11]Burroughs, *Wake-Robin,* p. 191–192.
[12]Burroughs, *In the Catskills,* p. 215.
[13]Barrus, *The Life and Letters of John Burroughs,* p. 140.

It pleased my eye so, that I would fain linger over them, arranging them in rows and studying the various hues and tints. They were nearly uniform size, rarely one over ten or under eight inches in length, and it seemed as if the hues of all the precious metals and stones were reflected from the sides.[14]

Burroughs was inspired by his beloved Catskills, their farmlands and mountain streams. He wrote with a unique style and shared with the world his observations of rural life and nature. Trout fishing often found its way into his writings. His trips to the Beaverkill valley first appeared in *Wake-Robin* in 1871; in *Locusts and Wild Honey* (1879), he included the wonderful essay "Speckled Trout." Burroughs's writings endeared him to the American public, and by the turn of the century he was considered the foremost among American nature writers. He camped with Theodore Roosevelt and enjoyed the friendship of such noted men as Oliver Wendell Holmes, Ralph Waldo Emerson, Henry Ford, Thomas Edison, Walt Whitman, and John Muir.

John Burroughs loved fishing for the native brook trout of Catskill streams. He had the heart of a fisherman and possessed the special gift of being able to write with simplicity and beauty of his experiences:

The fisherman has a harmless, preoccupied look; he is a vagrant, that nothing fears. He blends himself with the trees and the shadows. All his approaches are gentle and indirect. He times himself to the meandering soliloquizing stream; he addresses himself to it till he knows its hidden secrets. Where it deepens, his purpose deepens; where it is shallow he is in-different. He knows how to interpret its every glance and dimple; its beauty haunts him for days.[15]

No one who fished the Beaverkill was as widely known as Colonel Edward Zane Carroll Judson. Judson, who went by the pen name of Ned Buntline, was one of the most famous and colorful literary figures in America. He, too, was a native of the Catskills, being born in Stamford, Delaware County, on March 20, 1823; and like John Burrroughs, he developed a childhood love of trout fishing, the outdoors, and writing. However, that is where any similarity between the two men ends.

---

[14]Burroughs, *In the Catskills,* p. 217.
[15]Orvis and Cheney, *Fishing with the Fly.*

John Burroughs, fly rod in hand, explaining the nature of the pussy willow.

As a child, Ned Buntline learned to fish from his father, who made his own rods, tied his own flies, and was an expert on a trout stream. From him, Buntline developed a lifetime love of fishing, and when not off to a war or similar adventure, he could be found fishing in the Adirondacks, Catskills, and Poconos.

He had a burning desire to be an American hero, and he spent the greater part of his life trying to reach that goal. Ned became an adventurer at an early age, running off to sea as a cabin boy and serving as an apprentice in the navy. When he was but thirteen years old, he rescued the crew of a vessel that collided with a ferry boat and received from President Van Buren a commission as midshipman for his bravery.

Ned Buntline's wild and romantic life almost ended in 1846. In Tennessee, he killed a man whose wife he was having an affair with. At the trial, the man's brother opened fire, and Ned escaped by leaping out a courthouse window. He was recaptured and hanged by a mob in the square; however, friends cut the rope and saved his life. Another version of the story is that the hangman's noose broke when the trapdoor was opened, and Ned, with his neck intact, was, by law, freed!

That year he began writing cheap, sensational fiction. He was the first of the dime novelists, and is credited with pioneering the technique. In time, Ned Buntline became known as the "King of the Dime Novels." This "fertile writer of fiction" wrote more than four hundred of the adventure books, and in many of his earliest stories, he was his own hero; later he exploited "various more or less authentic Westerners."[16]

His confrontations with the law continued, however, when a few years later he was convicted of leading the famous Astor Place Riot in New York and spent a year in prison. In 1852, he was indicted for causing an election riot in St. Louis, in which several persons were killed and houses and property destroyed.

---

[16]Malone, *Dictionary of American Biography,* p. 237.

Constantly seeking adventure, and guided by intense patriotism, Ned took part in every war he could. He was a veteran of the Mexican War, the Seminole War, and the Civil War. When there were no wars, he found other ways to pursue danger and excitement. He was once a bounty hunter, and he roamed the Yellowstone region as a fur trader; he saw much of the old West when it truly was "wild."

After years of controversy, his public image soared shortly after he met William Frederick Cody at Fort McPherson, Nebraska, in 1869. At the time, Ned Buntline was reputed to be the best-paid writer in America, and Cody was the regimental butcher and buffalo scout. Ned conferred on him the name Buffalo Bill and proceeded to write a series of dime novels that featured Buffalo

Ned Buntline.

© Sarony, From *My Angling Friends* by Fred Mather, Forest and Stream Publishing Co., 1901

Bill as the hero. *Scouts of the Prairies,* a very successful play, followed; it starred Cody and introduced him to eastern audiences, who were eager to see the famous plainsman. Through his writings, Ned also immortalized the legends of Wild Bill Hickok and Texas Jack.

Always fond of firearms, Ned once had the Colt factory make him an order of guns. The Buntline Special was a unique, .45-caliber six-shooter with a twelve-inch barrel and an overall length of eighteen inches. The weapon also had a detachable walnut stock, which allowed the owner to convert it into a small repeating rifle. Engraved on the walnut butt of each gun was the name NED. Buntline presented one of these guns to famed lawman Wyatt Earp, and it is reported that twenty years later the Dodge City marshall was still wearing his Buntline Special.

Age began to slow Ned down; age, and the many wounds he had received in campaigns and gun scrapes. His face and hands were scarred, and he had begun to feel the pain of a few unextracted bullets, which had made him somewhat lame. He was aging rapidly, and looking older than his years. In 1871, at the age of forty-eight, a wealthy but weary Ned Buntline retired permanently to his Catskill roots at Stamford.

He was now content to challenge the trout and find excitement along the waters of the Beaverkill. And the stream must have filled his need for adventure, as he made numerous trips and annual pilgrimages from his elegant residence, called Eagle's Nest—so many, in fact, that he had a special wagon constructed to travel the rough and narrow roads leading in and out of the Beaverkill region. The wagon was extra long, with back-to-back seats, and was pulled by a pair of fancy bay horses.

Ned and his wife, Anna, spent a good part of each summer visiting Catskill trout streams. She, too, was an accomplished angler, and Ned, proud of her skill with a fly rod, let everyone know she had "deftly drawn her share of the speckled beauties from their native element to the shore."[17]

Ned Buntline regularly opened the season along the banks of the Beaverkill, a tradition he looked forward to every year. He loved the Beaverkill, and in the last years of his life the stream gave him tremendous pleasure. In his special wagon, among the fishing gear, Ned packed a large American flag. Whenever he stopped at an inn or boardinghouse in trout country, the flag was hoisted. On the Beaverkill, he stayed at Tripp's Brookside Paradise, just upstream of the Turnwood covered bridge, and they always flew the Stars and Stripes in tribute to his intense patriotism. City sportsmen learned to look for this emblem as a sign that Ned Buntline was on the stream.

Even in the backcountry, Ned Buntline could draw a crowd. In the summer of 1871, while camping in the meadow near Beaverkill Falls, he described in his diary a talk he gave in Sunday school, where he found a large crowd "who had been informed that I would talk to them. Did so, with temperance for my theme, and the beauties of nature and the wilderness for my text."[18]

Ned Buntline also contributed to sporting literature, writing fishing articles for such publications as *The American Angler, The Rod and Gun and American Sportsman, Forest and Stream,* and *Turf, Field and Farm*. He wrote about the Beaverkill, and since his wife fished alongside him, he became enthusiastic about female anglers. In the fall of 1881, he wrote an article for *The American Angler,* recommending that more women enter the sport and write of their experiences. He ended the piece with an appeal: "What I want most to see now in *The American Angler,* is some live, spirited, true—sketches from some of our Female Anglers. There are plenty of them—so come on ladies and blest be he, who first cries—hold enough!"[19]

"Fishermen are born such—not made!" he wrote in an essay for Orvis and Cheney's *Fishing with the Fly,* published in 1883. And while he did not consider himself a great caster, or as skilled as some of his talented companions, he understood trout. Ned also possessed the practical experience and cleverness of one who had grown up along trout streams, and he believed the statement applied to himself.

And he was a good fisherman, holding his own with the best of them; he once took a beauty of a native brook trout out of Alder Creek, which flows into the Beaverkill at Turnwood. The

---

[17]*The American Angler,* November 19, 1881, p. 22.
[18]*Bloomville Mirror,* July 4, 1871, p. 2.
[19]*The American Angler,* November 19, 1881, p. 23.

trout weighed 2¼ pounds, and like many of the largest fish taken from the Beaverkill, it was captured in a large, deep pool created by a milldam.

Ned Buntline died in July 1886. His funeral was one of the largest ever held in the Catskills; special trains were run on the Ulster & Delaware Railroad to bring more than eight hundred people to Stamford. Mourners and citizens watched in admiration as two hundred veterans of the Grand Army of the Republic marched over to Eagle's Nest, to accompany his remains to the cemetery.

Throughout his life, Ned Buntline was a controversial figure. He was "both hymn writer and inveterate duelist, he could lecture on temperance while being accused of drunkenness."[20] Ned possessed a flamboyant and vain nature, which caused some people to despise him, others to admire him. He was a bona fide rabble rouser, and tremendously popular. The rugged old sportsman was friends with the best anglers of his day, and fished with many of them, including the legendary Seth Green.

Fred Mather, a noted fish culturist and one of the earliest writers for *Forest and Stream,* wrote a series of articles titled "Men I Have Fished With," which evolved into a book with the same name, featuring many of America's best-known anglers. Writing about Ned Buntline, Mather states:

> When I fished with Ned in the Catskills, the drift of his talk would give an uninformed person the impression that his services to the country were equal to those of Grant, Sherman or Sheridan. His vanity was not balanced by modesty or humor, yet he was always clean of speech, as I knew him.
>
> Only last week, Col. Kerrigan wrote me: "When you write up Ned Buntline, don't put wings on him. He was a grand, good man all the same, and there is no use in trying to hide his faults, for he had plenty of them; other people have worked up Ned's faults, and you know that he was a man in whom the good predominated."[21]

---

[20]Kovalik, *Ned Buntline: King of the Dime Novels,* p. 3.
[21]*Forest and Stream,* July 24, 1897, p. 69.

14

Clubmen

During the 1870s, overfishing had become a major problem; and one solution that was gaining in popularity among landowners and anglers was the establishment of private, or posted, water. In this era trout-fishing clubs were founded on the Beaverkill, and for the first time notices began to appear along the stream, advising anglers that they were no longer welcome.

Trout populations must have been in a deplorable state, as evidenced by the fact that legislation was introduced in Albany to halt trout fishing. This desperate attempt occurred in the spring of 1874, when "an Act for the preservation of fish, commonly called speckled trout" was introduced to the legislature. The bill prohibited anyone from catching or fishing for trout, in any stream, in Ulster and Delaware Counties, for a period of two years. While the bill passed in the assembly, it failed in the senate.[1]

Stream posting actually began in the Catskills on Willowemoc Creek, in 1868, when the Willowemoc Club was established at Sand Pond. The club leased four miles of the Willowemoc upstream from the tannery at DeBruce. In a letter to *Forest and Stream,* dated March 19, 1874,

---

[1]*Walton Weekly Chronicle,* April 2, 1874, p. 1.

Cornelius Van Brunt, club president, advised readers that he and several others had formed the Willowemoc Club, not only to have a pleasant place to fish but, more important, to put a halt to the destructive practice of keeping every fish, no matter how small. Immediately they met with opposition; however, attitudes changed as landowners witnessed an increase in the stream's trout population. The founders of the Willowemoc Club set in motion a policy of stream preservation, through private ownership, that exists on the Beaverkill and Willowemoc to this day.

In 1872, Junius Gridley, Edward B. Mead, Daniel B. Halstead of Brooklyn, and Robert Hunter of Englewood, New Jersey, spent the entire summer boarding on the upper Beaverkill. They slept in tents the first year and constructed a small clubhouse, approximately a mile and a half upstream of Beaverkill Falls, in 1873. These men were the parent group of the Salmo Fontinalis Club; whether they operated their club in the traditional manner or leased and posted the stream is not known.

Posting on the Beaverkill began in earnest downstream of Shin Creek, on the farm of Royal Voorhess. Like other farmers whose lands adjoined the stream, Voorhess received a substantial portion of his income from boarding fishermen. And like others, he was concerned, because his guests were bringing in fewer fish and were traveling farther upstream, where trout were more plentiful.

Most farmers were reluctant to post their lands and prohibit fishing. They were afraid they might incur the wrath of anglers, who had always fished over their waters, and they held a "fear of some secret attempt at retaliation."[2] Something, however, had to be done, and Royal Voorhess believed he had found the answer.

On July 1, 1875, Voorhess obtained leases along the stream from several adjoining landowners, for the "exclusive rights of fishing, and preserving of the trout and other fish." The leases included a ten-foot strip along either side of the stream and were for a period of five years, with an option for five more. After obtaining the leases, Voorhess and several of his regular boarders filed a certificate of association and founded a society known as the Beaverkill Association: "The business of said society shall be fishing and other lawful sporting purposes."[3]

The leases and the certificate of association were filed and recorded in the Sullivan County Clerk's Office on September 9, 1875. The original trustees of the organization were Royal Voorhess, Whitman Phillips (Franklin, N.J.), Edward A. Hastings (Brooklyn, N.Y.), Henry Bacon, and Charles Mead (Goshen, N.Y.). This filing was the first of its kind in either Sullivan or Ul-

---

[2] *Forest and Stream,* April 2, 1885, p. 188.
[3] Misc. Book No. 2, Sullivan County Clerk's Office, p. 603.

Beaverkill Trout Club, formerly the Royal Voorhess property, and home of the Beaverkill Association.

ster County, making the Beaverkill Association the first fishing club of record on the Beaverkill. In the years ahead, the Beaverkill Association would evolve into the Beaverkill Trout Club, which yet today maintains the Voorhess homestead as its clubhouse.

The practice of posting had begun, and soon others would follow. On July 5, 1877, the *Walton Weekly Chronicle* reported that the Mead brothers, from Brooklyn, would build a boardinghouse on the one thousand acres they owned at Quaker Clearing, and that no one would be allowed to fish on their property except their guests.

The Meads built their resort at the headwaters, far beyond where others had settled. The land had been partially cleared long before by a Quaker who had abandoned the idea of farming in such a rugged area. This was the most remote section of the Beaverkill, and the last to be inhabited. Visiting anglers were surprised to find not only a homestead but notices prohibiting fishing as well. One angler who visited the Meads during their opening season felt a touch of pity for these city people, who found themselves far off in the wilderness, and stated:

> It saddens one to see refinement buried alive in such a place. Over twenty miles to the nearest town, no church, no doctor, no neighbors, and no prospect for any advance in civilization for a lifetime. In the summer one vast forest, in the winter one expanse of snow, the only visitors are an occasional deer, or a starving bear; their lullaby, the screech of a wildcat, the howl of a hungry wolf, mingled with the roar of a biting wind which seeps through the valley with a restless fury.[4]

Those most concerned over the trout fishing in the Beaverkill were the veteran anglers who had fished the stream before its slide into mediocrity. One such angler was George W. Van Siclen,

---

[4]*Liberty Register,* February 7, 1879, p. 2.

© Holland Society Yearbook—1888

George West Van Siclen.

who fished its waters each season for many years. He, like Royal Voorhess, became convinced that measures had to be taken to halt the overfishing.

Van Siclen was a founding member of the Willowemoc Club; along with other club members, he would hike three miles through the forest from Sand Pond to fish the Beaverkill and Balsam Lake. Now, in 1878, after obtaining a lease and the cooperation of adjoining land owners, he and other club members formed a new fishing club, known, appropriately, as the Beaverkill Club.

Van Siclen was an authority on angling and an expert caster; he helped organize some of the first casting tournaments in Central Park. He also contributed articles and letters to *The American Angler* and *Forest and Stream* on a variety of angling subjects. One letter that appeared in *Forest and Stream* must certainly have upset many who fished the Beaverkill:

NO MORE TROUT FISHING IN THE UPPER BEAVERKILL

No more trout fishing in the upper Beaverkill. Please give notice through your columns. Last summer while I was at Weaver's there came down from "Quaker Clearing" three men on a buckboard, and they boasted "over four hundred trout"; I could not see nor imagine where they had so many stowed away, but after a while they opened a twelve-quart butter firkin and showed me the poor little things. They claimed four hundred, 'and I guess they told the truth.' I think that not one of the "fish" was six inches long. Now this sort of thing must be stopped, and I have made up my mind to stop it on that stream. How many of us have fished the Beaverkill! We used to put up at Murdock's or Flint's or Walmsley's or Leal's, or camp out, and catch our creels full; but now-a-days the smallest creel half full of seven inch trout is good luck.

After the sight of those poor little innocents my plans were soon laid. I obtained the next day, from Joseph Banks, a long lease of the stream across his two lots; I have since made arrangement with Mead Brothers, at the old Quaker Clearing. Van Cleef and Van Brunt, the owners of Balsam Lake, have joined me, and so has Ransom

Weaver. I have hired a patrol to guard that stream from Balsam Lake down to Weaver's west line and I have posted notices and the fishing of the upper Beaverkill in Sullivan and Ulster counties, New York, is going to be preserved. All gentlemen sportsmen will keep away from there after this notice, unless they have my permission to fish, and all others will wish they had stayed away if they disregard it. It is unpleasant for me to write in this positive manner—it sounds boastful and ungenerous—but somebody had to take hold or the fishing would be gone from there in another two years. . . .

This notice will undoubtedly cause great disappointment to many, especially to sportsmen of Ulster, Delaware and Sullivan counties, N.Y., but I do hope that it will be regarded, because we have the legal right and title and the means to enforce it, and we shall certainly do so. It is but fair to add that any one stopping at Weaver's or Mead's will be allowed to fish over their respective pieces of stream, but not on Balsam Lake nor the "Bank's lots." The increasing fondness for real sports sends more hunters and fishermen afield every year, and forests and streams near the great cities are almost stripped of fin and feather. Those who cannot take time to go far have but one resource—to preserve the game by restricting the privilege.

Yours Respectfully,

Geo. W. Van Siclen[5]

The stream section referred to was several miles in length and included practically all of the water upstream of Beaverkill Falls. To make sure that local anglers also were notified of the upper Beaverkill posting, Van Siclen followed up by writing to newspapers all over the Catskill region. He requested editors to give his letter space before the fishing season opened, since "this is a matter of such general interest" to the fishermen where their paper circulated.

Virtually every newspaper in the mountains published a letter similar to the one that appeared in *Forest and Stream*. Van Siclen again stated how he disliked the idea of preventing fishing that had been, for so long, free to all, and he emphasized that the fishing was gone, due to careless fishermen who killed every trout they caught.

---

[5]*Forest and Stream,* April 4, 1878, p. 162.

The trout population must have indeed been low on the Beaverkill, and the public must have sensed the urgency or recognized the need of Van Siclen's action. There was no outcry, at least not in print, nor were there any angry follow-up letters on the stream closing. For that matter, the only editorial comments looked favorably on the idea. The *Hancock Herald* told its readers that the trout once so numerous were now very scarce, and the cause was the careless and destructive fishing by the public. The paper urged landowners and lessees to protect their fishing interests and post their water.

More posting did follow, and on the Beaverkill there were few, if any, complaints by the angling public, which seemed to recognize the action as justified and necessary for the preservation of trout fishing.

Another area newspaper, the *Ellenville Journal,* chose to speak out against the exploitation of Balsam Lake. Even though the lake was remote and travel difficult, men continually raided the lake's trout population, in winter as well as summer:

> Every winter barrels of trout are scooped out with nets through holes cut in the ice on Balsam Lake and whose business is it? Parties of ten or a dozen "campout" for a week at a time on the shores of these secluded ponds; each one fired with the ambition to beat his fellows in the numbers of trout taken. Hence it is fish, fish, from dawn to dusk, and everything that bites from two inches to twenty, must be kept and counted.[6]

This type of outcry was not lost on the owners of Balsam Lake. In 1878, Cornelius Van Brunt and James S. Van Cleef broke up the boats at the lake, posted it, and hired a watchman. In response, the *Kingston Freeman* reported that as Balsam Lake was now "guarded by a mountaineer with a big dog and a springfield musket, it is not a popular place with the public generally."[7]

By this time, a rough road or trail ran over the mountains from Seager, in the Dry Brook valley. It traveled the west side of the foot of Graham Mountain to Samuels' Clearing on the Beaverkill. The road was steep, windy, unreliable, and fraught with hidden dangers. While it made the lake more accessible, it was a deplorable road, and was best described by Ned Buntline, who in 1881 was invited by the owners to fish Balsam Lake. Buntline made the trip with his special buckboard, which was followed by an ox sled loaded with two boats to fish from. They traveled "through swamps hub deep, over roots, fallen logs, rocks as large as a small house stuck up

---

[6]*Ellenville Journal,* July 20, 1877, p. 1.
[7]*Kingston Weekly Freeman & Journal,* May 2, 1879, p. 1.

edgeways, lengthways, crossways and every other way, making turns so short that we had to lift the latter end of the wagon around to pass and even unhook traces to get between huge trees."[8]

Buntline avowed that should he be elected to join the club, the only way he would ever visit Balsam Lake again would be as a passenger in a hot-air balloon!

In 1884, a clubhouse was constructed on a hillside overlooking the lake, and the Balsam Lake Club, which had been founded the year before, began operations. The parent group of anglers forming the organization was the same as the group that had formed the Willowemoc Club in 1868, and the Beaverkill Club in 1878. Just as he had been the first president of the Willowemoc Club, Cornelius Van Brunt also became the president of the new organization.

In 1886, the Balsam Lake Club began leasing portions of the Beaverkill and acquiring others. By 1887, they owned 4½ miles, including waters previously leased by the Beaverkill Club. Through continuing land purchases, the club amassed more than three thousand acres, including six miles of the upper Beaverkill, by 1894.

From the time settlers began salting down barrels of its trout, Balsam Lake has maintained a seemingly inexhaustible population of brook trout. The main reason for this bountiful supply is the small stream entering the lake at its north end. The stream has ideal spawning habitat, and each fall great numbers of trout enter its waters to reproduce. They do so very successfully, thereby replenishing the lake with an apparently infinite number of new trout.

The reputation of Balsam Lake was that its trout "always seem to be hungry and bite very freely."[9] Yet even during days of year-round slaughter, they remained abundant, and no matter how many were removed, the trout maintained a length generally between 6 and 8 inches.

One angler who fished the lake for almost forty years, beginning in 1845, remarked after his last visit that he "found to my surprise no appreciable diminution in number and size of the trout in it. They are uniform in size, from three to five ounces."[10]

Records of the Beaverkill Club in 1880 reveal that 1,364 brook trout were kept, with a total weight of 205¾ pounds. The average trout taken weighed .15 pound, which, according to conversion charts, would be a trout of approximately 7.5 to 7.9 inches.

When the Balsam Lake Club took over the lake, it, too, enjoyed incredible catches of brook trout. Early records reveal the following:

---

[8]*Forest and Stream,* October 27, 1881, p. 252.
[9]*Liberty Register,* February 7, 1879, p. 2.
[10]*Kingston Weekly Leader,* June 7, 1889, p. 7.

1885	—	2,135
1886	—	3,521
1887	—	3,163
1888	—	1,879
1889	—	2,350
1890	—	2,030
Total	—	15,078

While the lake's trout were small, they were generally of the same size as those found in the club's headwater section of the Beaverkill. Club members were not concerned with the size of trout, though; they enjoyed the outdoors and the quality of the fishing experience.

The same year the Balsam Lake Club was founded, Charles Orvis and A. Nelson Cheney published a collection of articles written by well-known anglers of the 1870s, titled *Fishing with the Fly*. One of the contributions was by club member George Van Siclen. It was a sentimental essay about a day on Balsam Lake titled "A Perfect Day."

Van Siclen was a lover of trout and nature, and he did an excellent job conveying to his readers the happiness he found in the tranquility and beauty of Balsam Lake. He thoroughly enjoyed his escape from business cares and the din of the city. On this day Van Siclen reflected on the pleasantness he found about him:

> Soon seated in my boat I paddle to the shade of a tall, dark hemlock and rest there, lulled by the intense quiet. Ever and anon as I dreamily cast my ethereal fly, a thrill of pleasure electrifies me, as it is seized by a vigorous trout.
>
> I have long classed trout with flowers and birds, and bright sunsets, and charming scenery, and beautiful women, as given for the rational enjoyment and delight of thoughtful men of aesthetic tastes.

15

No More Free Fishing

Fishing clubs were formed because of the scarcity of trout and a desire for social communion. They were important to the preservation of the trout resources of the Beaverkill. In the 1870s, fishing clubs protected the remaining population of brook trout by immediately reducing fishing pressure. Before there were laws and officials to enforce them, clubmen initiated their own strict regulations on members, by reducing daily creel limits and restricting angling to fly fishing only. In addition, by employing a watcher to patrol the stream on a regular basis, they further protected the trout from illegal fishing, such as netting, poisoning, and dynamiting.

Early on, posting was accepted by the public, at least on the Beaverkill. However, as it grew in popularity and spread to other streams, where more and more water was being leased and posted by newly formed clubs, it began to be resented. On Rondout Creek, most of the headwaters were acquired by the Peekamoose Fishing Club; on the Willowemoc, by the Willowemoc Club; and on the West Branch of the Neversink, by the newly formed Neversink Club. Through leases, clubmen were acquiring all of the best trout-fishing water in the Catskills. In the spring of 1885, a reporter for the *New York Times* wrote that the Beaverkill, Neversink, and Willowemoc were no longer open to public fishing; and that natives who had fished these waters all of their lives, as well as visiting anglers, would be considered poachers if they attempted to do so.

No more free fishing.

No stream posting angered the public as much as the closing of the West Branch of the Neversink. The stream had been very accessible to anglers, especially those from the Kingston area. When a Kingston newspaper carried the notice that the public could no longer fish in those waters, it triggered a war of words that raged for years.

The conflict began with letters and editorials in local newspapers, then spread to sporting journals. One area newspaper decried the idea of leasing streams as "preposterous" and declared, "Why, there are men enough in New York City with money to control every trout stream in Ulster and Sullivan County."[1]

An outdoor writer compared posting to monopolizing sunsets! He added, "And only those of sufficient wealth should see the recurring glories of the evening sky."[2]

One of the most persistent and outspoken critics of the clubmen was Robert E. Best, a Kingston fur dealer, who had fished the Neversink for many years and did not take kindly to the idea of the posting of his favorite stream. In a series of blistering letters, he questioned not only the legality of leasing trout streams but the very character of the men doing such an "un-American" deed:

> These migrating vagabonds hailing from New York, forming themselves into clubs, and leasing fishing streams for their selfish purposes, have been on the increase for some years. As a rule they spend but little or no money in the country where their nests exist, and where they have their drunken orgies, and sing their obscene songs. A few barrels of rum brought with them from New York, with what chickens they can steal from hen roosts, and the trout they can catch from the stream that has been stocked from the State hatcheries and placed there with Ulster County people's money, form their stock of summer substance.

[1]*Kingston Weekly Freeman & Journal,* April 30, 1885, p. 5.
[2]*The American Angler,* March 1892, p. 288.

It is but two years ago that an old and gray-haired man, born near the waters of the Beaverkill stream, wandered to its edge to catch a small mess of fish for a sick daughter. He was ordered off by two members of a club, who had leased that portion of the stream, upon which they told him he was a trespasser, and because the old man in his infirmity, could not move fast enough to suit them, they cruelly knocked him down, and kicked him when down in a most brutal manner. One of the assailants, a member of the New York City club, was the keeper of a house of prostitution, and the other, the keeper of a gambling den in New York City. Pretty specimens indeed of humanity to come to Ulster County to teach the natives to obey the laws of New York. . . .

In this free country, thanks to God, the rich and poor are equals. Let the man be a millionaire or a bark peeler, let his hands be soft and white, or horny and brown, give him free fishing and free fowling in free America. However humble may be the man's calling in his home the dainty and delicious trout is one of God's good gifts to earth to his children. He has vouchsafed it to all whether his smoke curls from a palace chimney or a bark peeler's shanty.[3]

Charles Hallock, past editor of *Forest and Stream,* laid much of the blame for stream posting on the Fish Commission, for allowing the streams to deteriorate. He took issue with the commission, which seemed to believe that stocking more fish was the solution to improving trout fishing. He pointed out that after years of stocking, the fishing was not any better and argued that the Fish Commission should abandon the idea that stocking alone was the solution to good fishing. Hallock stated that the commission followed a policy of spending the public's money on "making fish so abundant that they can be caught without restrictions and serve as cheap food for the people at large, rather than to expend a much larger sum in 'protecting' the fish, and in preventing the people from catching the few which still remain (or did remain) after a generation of improvidence."[4]

Forest and Stream also took issue with Best's assessment of the clubmen and came to their defense: "Knowing the high character of the gentlemen composing the Neversink Club, the Balsam Lake Club and the Willowemoc Club, most of whom are personal acquaintances, we regard the article written to the *"Freeman"* as a most vile slander."[5]

---

[3]*Kingston Weekly Freeman & Journal,* March 26, 1885, p. 3.
[4]*Kingston Weekly Freeman & Journal,* April 30, 1885, p. 1.
[5]*Forest and Stream,* April 9, 1885, p. 201.

Streams were being purchased and "preserved," and many felt that only men of wealth would be allowed to "enjoy a day's sport in fishing for trout."[6] Another noted angling authority who spoke out on the situation was William C. Harris, editor of *The American Angler:*

> Men have felt galled to see legal notices prohibiting them from taking fish from streams where their fathers freely fished before them and where they had as freely angled away the Saturday afternoons of their boyhood.
>
> This is a natural and by no means ignoble sentiment, but a little consideration will show any man that it is no more practically possible to leave all fishing waters free to all than it is to do away with farm fences and turn the crop fields of the country back into meadow-grazing lands free for all.
>
> We have nothing whatever to say for or against this system. We only point out a known fact and draw the plain conclusion that every angler who cares to provide for his enjoyment in years to come had better lose no time in securing some good angling privilege somewhere.[7]

Fishermen were not the only ones upset over the leasing of trout streams; hotels, inns, and boardinghouse owners also became alarmed at the amount of stream mileage lost to posting. Such businesses had increased steadily ever since the railroad came through the region, and they viewed free fishing as vital to their success in attracting tourists. Boardinghouse and resort owners prepared petitions that they hoped would influence legislators into preparing a bill preventing the leasing of trout streams.

One club member responded to their concerns by stating:

> If the fishing in these streams would always remain as good as it was when the hotels were built and railways introduced into this section, their argument would be better, but unfortunately the reverse is the case. Four years ago I ceased fishing the Beaver Kill and adjacent waters, the river almost devoid of fish; that parties from a distance were in the habit of visiting the streams with the apparent view of carrying away as many fish as possible, regardless of size, hiring small boys to increase the catch, and making

---

[6]*Ellenville Journal,* May 17, 1889, p. 1.
[7]*The American Angler,* November 5, 1887, p. 1.

use of other unsportsmen like ways of depleting the streams. I have heard parties boast that they had carried away 1,100 fish (some of which were scarcely two inches long), the result of three days fishing, besides all they ate.[8]

The most persistent argument put forth by those opposed to the leasing of streams was that if the stream was stocked with trout by the Fish Commission, it should remain open to the public. Stocking, it was stated, brought the streams back to their original value as trout waters, and was done at public expense. Therefore, it was reasoned, the trout in the streams were public property, and it should be illegal to post such waters.

Clubmen did not disagree that the state owned the fish, even in their wild state; but, they argued, they had the "right of property, and can exclude any person from trespassing upon their grounds for the purpose of fishing."[9] In effect, they granted that individuals had the legal right to catch state trout, as long as they did not trespass over private land to do so.

When streams first began to be stocked, they were, for the most part, free to everyone; and when trout were planted in those streams, the public benefited from the stocking. Although not public waters in the strictest sense (since they flowed over and through private lands), they were public waters for all intents and purposes, since the public had "unrestrained" access and use of them for fishing.

As the growth of angling increased, the fishing privileges grew in value, and these waters that had always been free were posted, and became in fact what they had always been legally: private waters.

All that the Fish Commission required of one ordering fish was an affidavit that the trout would be placed in public waters. Very frequently, those ordering and stocking the fish were not stream owners, nor did they have permission of the owners. Yet "free" fishing advocates insisted on fishing the entire stream, on the grounds that the stream had been stocked at public expense.

One stream owner remarked:

> The result has been that many of our finest streams have been practically destroyed by stocking through acts of trespass to which the State has really been a party, and it is a grave question whether a claim for these injuries to the rights of riparian owners could not be successfully made to the Court of Claims of this State.[10]

---

[8]*Forest and Stream,* April 9, 1885, p. 207.
[9]*Forest and Stream,* April 9, 1885, p. 207.
[10]J. S. Van Cleef, *Forest and Stream,* December 8, 1900, p. 453.

The argument over the public's right to fish in streams once stocked by the state continued for years, and led to more frequent confrontations between fishermen and the stream watchers hired by the clubs. These disputes were, at times, taken before a judge; however, trespassers hauled into court were usually released, as it was almost impossible to procure a verdict against a man guilty of trespassing on private club water. Most often these arguments were settled with fists, stones, and even drawn revolvers! Some fishermen refused to recognize the rights of clubs to prohibit fishing and when asked to leave hurled insults at the watchman. When this occurred, the watchman would fill his pockets with stones, follow the trespasser, and throw stones in the water ahead of him, spoiling his fishing. This occasionally escalated into a fistfight, where one side or the other was treated to uncomfortable bruises or a good ducking in the stream.

Not all watchmen were challenged in such a manner; one who was usually avoided was Sturgis Buckley, who patrolled the Beaverkill for the Balsam Lake Club. Buckley acquired a reputation as a determined, uncompromising stream watcher. It was said, rather sarcastically, that he wore a "winning smile," which "made would-be poachers fish, or cut bait."[11] Those daring enough to fish "his" water did not do so openly; they would hide along the stream, wait for Buckley to pass by, follow him until it was time for his return trip, and then follow him again. When they became familiar with his pattern, they would fish the area that he had just left.

The idea of posting also began to catch on with farmers. While some refused all attempts to "fish over them" and would threaten to shoot, others gave permission to fish for a fee of twenty-five cents a head. Farmers did not have time to patrol their water, nor could they afford to pay someone else to do so. One way to keep an eye on the water was to pasture an angry bull next to the stream. Another was the practice of having a large, aggressive, hungry-looking dog run freely. When someone was fishing, the dog let it be known, and a very uneasy angler was only too happy to toss a quarter to the farmer and be rid of the annoying beast.

After years of exploitation and overfishing, trout fishing on the Beaverkill seemed destined to improve. One *Forest and Stream* writer reported:

> We are glad to hear from some of the veterans who have for many years made it
> a point to fish these brooks, that last season's catch showed a very marked improvement
> over the previous years as that did over the one of 1888, both in size and number.
>
> This happy state of affairs has been partially brought about by the liberal stock-
> ing of these waters by the wise management of the Ontario & Western R.R., but there

---

[11]*Walton Reporter,* April 28, 1900, p. 8.

is another cause which has helped the brooks, and that is the headwaters of the two streams [Beaverkill and Neversink] are controlled by clubs and private parties who limit the fish caught both in size and numbers, and absolutely prohibit fishing in the little side streams where the fingerlings seek shelter from their larger brethren, thus assuring a constant source of supply. Reasonable people begin to see the advantages of having parts of streams controlled in this way, as it certainly improves the whole of the waters. They cannot lock up their fish, and they naturally will drop down stream, particularly as they grow large.[12]

Once posting began, it spread quickly. Undoubtedly it became a case of self-preservation; as water became posted it placed an even greater burden on that which remained open. Commenting on the increase in posting, the Livingston Manor correspondent to the *Walton Reporter* wrote:

> Fishing is very poor around here this season. The primary causes are undoubtedly excessive legislation and the profusion of notices posted on the banks of the stream in endless variety of form and nearly every language from Hebrew to Choctaw, which has so bewildered the trout that they know not what to do.[13]

---

[12]*Forest and Stream,* January 15, 1891, p. 517.
[13]*Walton Reporter,* May 14, 1892, p. 8.

16

"Who Would Not Be a Game Protector?"

Year after year, season after season, ever-increasing numbers of anglers were removing more and more trout from the Beaverkill and other area streams. They did so without restrictions, as there were virtually no laws. The only law was one of common decency, which was adhered to by those fishermen who considered themselves sportsmen: anglers who knew it was unwise to keep fingerlings and who killed only reasonable numbers of trout. Laws restricting the number of trout that could be taken or setting limits on the size of the fish did not appear until 1876, and many believed it was too little, too late.

In New York State, fish and game laws are based on the premise that ownership of all fish and wildlife is vested in the state. This principle has been handed down from the common law of England, and while a statewide law restricting the use of seines was adopted as early as 1813, most laws were enacted to meet the specific needs of a particular locality. These early fish and game laws were enacted by county government, through the Board of Supervisors. Enforcement was the duty of all sheriffs, constables, and other police officers.

One of the earliest laws pertaining to trout in the Beaverkill watershed was enacted by the Sullivan County Board of Supervisors on April 3, 1849, and was titled "An Act for the preservation of Deer, Birds and Fish, and for the destruction of certain wild beasts."[1]

---

[1] Misc. Book No. 1, Sullivan County Clerk's Office, p. 1.

Section No. 7 of the law prohibited the use of the berry *Coculus indicus* or any other poisonous substance for the purpose of fishing.

Section No. 10 set a season for trout, protecting the fish only during the spawning season between August 1 and November 1.

And Section No. 11 allowed that:

> All penalties imposed by this act may be sued for and recovered by any individual or by the overseers of the poor of the town where the offense is committed in a suit to be commenced in two months after the commission of the offense and when sued for by the overseers of the poor shall be for the use of the poor of such town.

The act also established bounties to be paid: for wolves, ten dollars; panthers, five dollars; wildcats or catamounts, two dollars; and foxes, fifty cents.

In 1857, the state legislature passed a law prohibiting the taking of trout with anything other than a hook and line; they could not be taken by "net, seine, weir, basket, spear, grapple or trap." A feature of this law, and of fish and game law in general, was that all penalties imposed by the act could be sued for and recovered, with one-half going to the complainant. Known as the moiety system, it allowed any person to bring suit and recover one-half of the fine, with the other half going to the poor. Though this system continued for many years, it was generally disliked by law enforcement officials.

In 1871, changes by the legislature gave more power to the county Board of Supervisors. A law provided for the election of game constables, with powers similar to civil constables, to be nominated at town meetings. Laws continued to be made at both state and county levels of government; one law passed by the Ulster County Legislature in 1876, dubbed Murdock's Trout Bill,[2] was proposed by Hardenbergh supervisor and longtime resort owner James Murdock. Murdock had witnessed decades of Beaverkill trout exploitation, and he believed a size limit was necessary to halt the keeping of undersized trout, especially fingerlings.

Concerns about overfishing became obvious when, just a few years later, the Sullivan County Board of Supervisors provided the ultimate protection to a nearby stream. In 1882, the board created, in a sense, an early no-kill regulation by passing "an Act for the preservation and protection of Brook trout in the Middle Mongaup Stream and its tributaries in the Town of Liberty, Sullivan County."

---

[2]*Kingston Weekly Freeman & Journal,* January 21, 1876, p. 1.

Section No. 1 of the law stated: "No person shall kill, or attempt to kill or catch any brook trout in the water of the Middle Mongaup River."[3]

The stream was protected for a period of three years, and a fine of twenty-five dollars was imposed for violating the law; one-half of the penalty went to the complainant, one-half to support the poor in the town of Liberty.

While increasing concern over diminishing trout populations brought about more restrictive laws pertaining to fishing, enforcement of these laws was, for the most part, nonexistent. Reports of trout being taken illegally with nets, spears, poisons, and dynamite were common and were the cause of public outrage. There were too few game constables appointed by the county to be effective. Sheriffs and other law enforcement officers were generally involved with what they considered more serious crime.

Finally, in 1880, the governor was authorized to appoint eight state game protectors, and while this was the beginning of fish and game protection, a more accountable and effective force was not established until 1888, when the Fish Commission appointed a chief protector, and fifteen game and fish protectors. These men were empowered to begin suits in the name of the people; one-half of the penalties recovered in civil actions would go to the state, and the other half would go to the game protector or the individual bringing the suit.

These pioneer game protectors had a most difficult time carrying out their duties; they had to bring suit, and in return they could be sued personally if they made a mistake, with no assurance that the state would back them up with an attorney. Laws pertaining to fish and wildlife were not always respected or readily accepted. Many people still adhered to the belief that in America the woods and streams were free, and laws limiting this freedom were looked upon with contempt.

Sometimes, game protectors were ridiculed for not enforcing the law, and then mocked when they did—often on the front pages of area newspapers. Some of the same editors who lamented the deplorable conditions of trout streams took issue when the lawbreakers were brought to justice, siding with the violators and claiming they were poor victims, ignorant of the law. There was also great animosity shown toward game protectors over the fact that they received one-half the fine, even though the money could go to anyone making the complaint.

An example of how difficult the job of game protector was can be seen in the experiences of Seth Walley, who enforced the laws in Delaware County, which included the lower Beaverkill. In the summer of 1893, Game Protector Walley received a complaint from a citizen about three men

---

[3]Misc. Book No. 2, Sullivan County Clerk's Office, p. 113.

spearing fish in the waters of Trout Creek. A Walton newspaper, with a touch of sarcasm, reported on the incident: "Here was an opportunity which [Walley] embraced at once of showing the people of Trout Creek that the suckers still had rights, and at the same time scooping in a nice little fee."[4]

Two of the men were immediately brought to justice and charged with illegally taking fish; the penalty for each offense was one hundred dollars, of which Walley received half. In an effort to extract some satisfaction by outwitting Walley, the third violator had his brother charge him with the crime before a justice in Walton. The defendant pleaded guilty and was fined one hundred dollars; but since the brother who brought the suit was entitled to one-half the fine, it was thus "kept in the family" and did not go to Game Protector Walley!

By doing his job and enforcing the law, Seth Walley became a very unpopular man, especially in the hamlet of Trout Creek. A year after the spearing incident, the *Hancock Herald* wrote openly of the desire to tar and feather Seth Walley. "But the self-constituted avengers were doomed to disappointment, for at sundown Mr. Game Protector quietly folded his tent and stole away. Whether he 'smelled a mice' or not, deponent sayeth not. Who would not be a game protector?"[5]

Two days later a Walton newspaper reported:

NOW THEY ARE AFTER SETH

Fish Protector Walley does not find his path strewn with roses in his pursuit of the infringers of the game laws. On the contrary the animosity of some has been aroused and their hands are "lifted up against" the officer of the law. Trout Creek has been a favorite field of operation for Mr. Walley and he has reaped a rich harvest from some of the farmer boys of that little hamlet and its environs. But this has been done at the cost of popularity, and 'tis whispered that before the dark shades of night surround that village Seth takes care that he is safe without its bounds. The lively young men of that vicinity have organized a "vengeance club" with the avowed purpose of "getting even" with Mr. Walley and are patiently biding their time when the unpopular official can be caught at some favorable opportunity, and then, woe be unto him.[6]

---

[4]*Walton Reporter,* June 17, 1893, p. 1.
[5]*Hancock Herald,* May 10, 1894, p. 1.
[6]*Walton Reporter,* May 12, 1894, p. 1.

Such obviously biased reporting could only have made it harder for Seth Walley, or any game protector, to enforce the law. And it delayed the acceptance of laws restricting or regulating fishing, as well as their receiving respect and recognition as being in everyone's interest.

Laws continued to be made by the county Board of Supervisors until 1895, when they became the duty of the state legislature. In general, trout season in the Catskills opened on May 1 and closed on August 31, to give the trout more protection throughout their spawning seasons, with no fishing allowed on Sunday.

This short season—only 106 days—continued for many years, from the early 1870s until the 1920s, and may have been responsible, as much as anything, for the fishing remaining as good as it did.

The Indian, too, had seen the importance of protecting trout during certain times of the year. This early wisdom is revealed in a tale by Dr. E. A. Bates:

> In the olden moons, at such a time, the boys of the village cut a long pole of sinewy willow, and at the end of a tough line made of the inner bark of the elm, they tied the sharp pointed fish hook made of bone. With a juicy piece of bear fat, they fooled the trout.
>
> Then one trout-fishing moon came when few trout were caught. The next spring, this happened again. Finally, a wise old fisherman opened one of the trout with his sharp stone knife and found it was full of eggs. So the council drew from the wisdom of old fishermen, and a careful watch was made, and then it was found that the trout always swam over their spawning beds just before the wild apple bloomed.
>
> From that moon on, and even today, the redman stays far from the home of the trout until the apple trees are in full bloom, for he dreams of a trout-fishing moon for his grandchildren.[7]

Size limits may have helped also, as they both increased and spanned an even greater time period. In 1876, with the passage of Murdock's Trout Bill, the size limit was 5 inches; by 1885, it had been increased to 6 inches, and by the late 1930s, climbed to 7 inches.

---

[7]Dr. E. A. Bates, *Sullivan County Democrat,* June 14, 1933, p. 8.

Part

II

17

Enter Salmo fario

Fred Mather, like Seth Green, was an early fish culturist who was interested in fly fishing for trout and writing about angling. However, he disagreed with Green and the Fish Commission about the rainbow being the salvation of New York's trout waters.

In a paper read before the American Fishcultural Association in 1884, Fred Mather, then fishery editor of *Forest and Stream,* registered doubts as to their worth:

> I have suspected the so-called rainbow trout to be identical with the steelhead salmon, *S. gairdneri,* which is a migratory fish.
>
> We have been waiting and watching the habits of this alleged trout with great interest in order to learn if its habits might not show it to be, in some respect, different from the steelhead. The evidence of the Commission tends to show that it is a migratory fish and, if so, it may escape to the sea and be lost.
>
> The promise of the rainbow trout was that in it we had a quick growing fish, which was not as sensitive to warm water as our own "fontinalis," a desideration which now promises to be filled by the brook trout of Europe, *Salmo fario*.[1]

---

[1] *Forest and Stream,* May 29, 1884, p. 350.

While fishing in Europe, Mather became familiar with brown trout, and he so admired the fish that he resolved he would introduce the species to America at the first opportunity. That occasion arose in 1883, when Mather took charge of a new hatchery located at Cold Spring Harbor on Long Island. The facility was a joint venture of the United States and New York Fish Commissions.

On December 28, 1882, he wrote to Professor Spencer F. Baird, of the U.S. Commission of Fish and Fisheries:

> My Dear Professor,
>
> We think it desirable to introduce both European brook trout *(Salmo fario)* and the grayling at the new hatchery at Cold Spring. Should you have an offer of any from your foreign correspondents we will be glad to receive and care for them.
>
> Very Truly Yours,
>
> F. Mather

The very next day, the commissioner replied that he had been offered plenty of trout eggs but had always turned them down. He would, however, ask Herr Von Behr, president of the Deutschen Fischerei Verein.

Professor Baird wrote to Herr Von Behr, announcing he was sending a shipment of eggs of lake trout, whitefish, and brook trout and concluded his letter: "Mr. Mather is about starting a new hatchery on Long Island, near New York, in which he will do a great deal of work for the United States. He thinks he would like to have some eggs of the European trout. Can you send him some?"[2]

Fred Mather began operations at the Cold Spring Harbor hatchery on January 1 and had barely had time to set up when he received, on the 28th of February, 80,000 brown trout eggs from Germany: 60,000 large eggs, and 20,000 from upper Rhine tributaries, which were smaller but were of the same species. Mather reported sending 10,000 large and 2,000 small brown trout eggs to the hatchery at Caledonia, and 2,000 large and 3,000 small eggs to the U.S. Fish Commission at Northville, Michigan.[3]

---

[2] *Forest and Stream,* March 24, 1894, p. 250.
[3] Fred Mather, New York State Fisheries Commission, annual report, 1886, p. 86.

As can be seen by the above correspondence, it appears that the introduction of brown trout into America was due to the suggestion of Fred Mather but was accomplished by Professor Spencer F. Baird.[4]

Hardly had the brown trout arrived in this country when anglers with European fishing experience began describing their merits in the pages of sporting journals. Some were convinced the brown trout would be welcomed by all, since they grew larger and were warier, gamier, and, therefore, superior to native brook trout. They stated that brook trout were easier to catch, took the fly more readily, and did not require the delicate approach that was practiced in England. One angler noted, "On many English streams the fish can only be taken with a dry fly, a practice unknown, so far as I know, in America."[5]

These comparisons annoyed more than a few anglers who loved their native brook trout and in no way thought it inferior to any fish. When English authorities declared their trout was "only a charr," American anglers took offense. One writer asked indignantly, "In what respect is a trout superior to a charr? Certainly the American charr is handsomer than the brook trout of Europe."[6]

In time, the brook trout of Europe would be judged on more than looks alone, and while discussion varied on the values of the fish, almost everyone agreed that the new trout should be placed in American waters.

Meanwhile, at Cold Spring Harbor, Fred Mather was having trouble hatching and raising the trout he received from Herr Von Behr. Those of the large type all died shortly after hatching. The smaller eggs taken from upper Rhine tributaries did better, with some 4,000 being placed in rearing ponds. These too, however, proved difficult for Mather and his staff:

> We were so proud of these fish that we often caught them to show visitors, and
> as often as we disturbed them we would find dead ones on the ground the next day.
>
> Those specimens jumped out of the wooden rearing ponds, and it was only when
> their numbers had been severely thinned by it that we learned that they seemed
> prompted to it every time they were disturbed either by putting a net to catch speci-

---

[4]There is evidence, however, to suggest that brown trout were first brought into this country one year earlier, by W. L. Gilbert of Plymouth, Massachusetts. Gilbert operated the "Old Colony ponds at Plymouth" and received 4,000 eggs from a gentleman from Guildford, Surry, England, in February 1882. Writing in *Forest and Stream* on January 7, 1886, Gilbert also reported that only about 25 good fry were hatched; however, in 1885, he succeeded in taking 3,000 eggs from them when they matured.

[5]*Forest and Stream,* January 3, 1884, p. 457.

[6]*Forest and Stream,* December 6, 1883, p. 367.

mens to show to visitors or at night by some animal swimming in the pond. In November, 1884, when they were a year and a half old, we removed them to a large breeding pond, and the next morning the ground was covered with them, although this pond had banks a foot higher than those of the rearing ponds. At present not over fifty are left, and learning their habits has been expensive.[7]

Fortunately for Mather, Herr Von Behr made another shipment of eggs, which were received on February 15, 1884, and on the 25th, the hatchery received 5,000 brown trout eggs from England. These were a gift of R. B. Marston of the London *Fishing Gazette* and were eggs taken from two of England's most famous trout streams; 3,000 came from the Itchen and 2,000 from the Wye.[8]

Secure in the knowledge that he now had backup stocks of the European trout, in May 1884 Fred Mather began placing 40,000 brown trout fry directly into New York public waters in and around Long Island. The following spring, in 1885, the Cold Spring Harbor hatchery expanded its range when it distributed 28,900 brown trout into the waters of Queens, Suffolk, Westchester, and Rockland Counties.

In November of that year, both Cold Spring Harbor and Caledonia reported taking eggs from brown trout hatched from the original shipment, received in 1883.[9]

In the spring of 1886, the Caledonia hatchery stocked its first brown trout, sending 116,000 fry throughout the state, with one shipment reaching the Catskills. On March 20, 4,000 brown trout were sent to E. D. Mayhew, for placement into Spring Creek, near Walton.

In December 1886, the New York Fish Commission announced that it would have a limited number of "German trout" available next season for stocking the public waters of the state.

In the spring of 1887, Montgomery Dodge purchased a round-trip ticket and traveled to Caledonia to pick up the first brown trout to be placed in the Beaverkill. "Gum," as he was known, owned and operated a hotel located just upstream of the Forks, on the Rockland flats. He was a genial host, well known to fishermen and, for that matter, the traveling public. It was said that men would ride half the night just to spend the other half at his popular Excelsior Hotel.

The records show that Dodge received 10,000 "German trout" at the hatchery on the 25th of March.[10] The trout fry were so tiny that had he peered into the large tins that accompanied him on

---

[7]Fred Mather, New York State Fisheries Commission, annual report, 1886, p. 72.
[8]Fred Mather, New York State Fisheries Commission, annual report, 1886, p. 73.
[9]*Forest and Stream,* November 26, 1885, p. 348.
[10]New York State Fisheries Commission, annual report, 1887, p. 58.

the train, it is doubtful whether he could have distinguished them from the native trout he was so familiar with. He had ordered the fish from Seth Green during the winter and was no doubt encouraged by the reports on the European import. Perhaps on the return trip he pondered how this new trout would do in the lower Beaverkill. It was said that they did well in larger, warmer waters, and that they would not wander off, as did the rainbow. He may have even envisioned a trout season lasting through the summer, and ultimately increasing his hotel business. It is unlikely he could have realized the tremendous impact the stocking of brown trout would have on the Beaverkill.

"Gum" Dodge did not make the trip to Caledonia alone. Jefferson Campbell of Roscoe also picked up an order of 10,000 German trout; these fish were for Warner Sprague, who placed them in the nearby Willowemoc.[11]

A little more than a week later, E. R. Sprague, who owned the Mountain View Villa at Lew Beach, picked up an order of 14,000 German trout and placed those fish into the waters of the upper Beaverkill and Shin Creek. On the 4th of April, J. G. Stevens of Livingston Manor received 7,000 fry and stocked them in the upper Willowemoc and its tributaries. Now this trout of Europe whose noble lineage descended from the Itchen, the Wye, and the Rhine was well distributed throughout the Beaverkill and Willowemoc.

In the lower river, brown trout found an environment that was extremely beneficial to their growth and survival. It was the most productive section of the Beaverkill, and the habitat was excellent: Pools were very large and deep, riffles rich in aquatic insects. Mayflies were abundant, and, coupled with a large and varied minnow population, formed a wonderful food supply. Perhaps most important, the water was generally too warm to support brook trout and so was virtually free of competitive game fish. These circumstances not only ensured their success but allowed brown trout to have a swift and dramatic impact on the fisheries of the Beaverkill.

Brown trout grew rapidly, and while some from the original stocking of 1887 may have been caught previously, the first reported catch did not appear in local newspapers until May 1890. Irving W. Finch, a veteran Roscoe angler, came into town with a German trout that measured 15⅝ inches in length, and weighed 1 pound and 9 ounces.[12] This trout, a little over three years of age, was one of the fry that had traveled the train with "Gum" Dodge on his trip from Caledonia.

Later that summer an even larger trout was seen living in Palen's millpond, which was located on a split channel of the Beaverkill, along the flats upstream of the Forks. Every man in

[11]New York State Fisheries Commission, annual report, 1887, p. 58.
[12]*Walton Reporter,* May 24, 1890, p. 1.

A large brown trout in excellent condition taken from the Beaverkill.

Rockland was said to be after the trout, but only "Gum" Dodge succeeded in hooking, and then losing, the big fish.

Over the next couple of years, reports of trout weighing 2 and 3 pounds became common. Before long, even larger fish were caught, as brown trout began to inhabit and dominate most of the best water on the Beaverkill, especially the large pools formed by mill-dams.

After their introduction, the U.S. Fish Commission attempted to have the new trout from Europe become known as the Von Behr trout. In 1889, Commissioner Marshall McDonald proposed "to give to this trout a name which is intended to perpetuate in America the memory of the man to whom we are much indebted for this valuable addition to our list of noble fishes."[13]

The commission believed it would not be difficult to introduce the new name, as all of the eggs and fry shipped from government establishments would be shipped as Von Behr trout (*Salmo fario*). But the name was never accepted by sportsmen, who, like Seth Green, referred to the fish as the German trout or German brown trout.

In the years ahead, brown trout thrived. They grew more rapidly and lived longer than brook trout, and thus reached lengths and weights never attained by the native species. Just a few years after their introduction, articles praising the fishing in the lower river began to appear. One of the first, and perhaps most descriptive, was written by S. K. Putnam, and titled "How to Fish the Lower Beaverkill"; it appeared in *The American Angler* in August 1893.

The author acknowledged that nearly everyone who visited the stream selected the upper Beaverkill for their sport but wrote that he wished to put in a good word for the lower portion of the stream. He stated that trout of the lower Beaverkill would average much larger than those upstream and that "many of more than two pounds" were being taken from the "beautiful pools and grand rifts" from the junction of the Willowemoc downriver to East Branch.

---

[13]*Forest and Stream,* December 5, 1889, p. 391.

Though written more than one hundred years ago, his physical descriptions of the pools and riffles sound very much like what Beaverkill anglers find today, and his advice on how to fish them is as useful now as it was then.

One year later, in 1894, an article in the *New York Times* titled "Midsummer Beaverkill Fishing" reported on the progress brown trout had made in Beaverkill waters and also on the difficulty in catching them, since ordinary trout tackle proved less than adequate:

> Just now an unsolved problem of the Beaverkill, and, in fact, of the Willowemoc, is how to capture the large brown trout, Salmo fario, which, planted at Rockland, are now by migration and propagation up the river as far as Sprague's [Lew Beach], and vary in weight from ten to the ounce to ten pounds.
>
> The European variety is piscivorous, and it preys on the American trout. A two pound brown trout caught the other day had dined on a quarter pound Salvelinus, and one of six pounds caught last year was digesting an eleven inch trout.
>
> An angler last month at Voorhess' hooked a brown trout of between four and five pounds, and at first the trout did not appear disposed to battle for liberty, but when it became convinced that the angler really meant it, it displayed its strength, and left with a leader and several yards of line, after breaking the angling wand in two places.[14]

THE OLD BRIDGE
Beaverkill,
Sullivan County

© Ed Van Put

A favorite pool of large brown trout on the upper Beaverkill, the Covered Bridge Pool at Beaverkill.

---

[14]*New York Times,* July 15, 1894, p. 12.

While the fish thrived and grew especially well, anglers were slow to praise or condemn them. Perhaps their uncertainty was simply due to a lack of knowledge of brown trout. This silence prompted the English editor R. B. Marston, who had gifted the Cold Spring Harbor hatchery with 5,000 brown trout eggs, to state:

> I confess that I have now and then wondered that so little is said in the American sportsmen's papers about the fish, after ten years trial. The last report I heard was not quite so favorable as it might have been and I sincerely hope that our trout is not going to prove such a disappointment in America.[15]

---

[15]New York State Fisheries, Game and Forest Commission, annual report, 1895.

18

"Beware the Brown Trout"

It was not long before Americans did indeed speak out about brown trout, and as Mr. Marston suspected, anglers began finding fault with the European trout. Disturbing reports began to surface, claiming that the browns grew to such large proportions because they were eating the brook trout, and driving the natives from the streams! Some trout fishermen believed there was no necessity to stock the fish and viewed their importation as a mistake. These sentiments began to spread, as the traditional large catches of native brook trout grew scarcer, and anglers attributed their empty creels "to the voracious appetites of the German trout."[1]

It soon became apparent that brown trout were competing with native brook trout for food, spawning areas, and habitat. Adjustments between the two species were often decided by water temperatures. Brook trout remained the dominant species in icy-cold feeders and at the extreme headwaters, where the colder temperatures were not favored by browns. In streams or stream sections where the two species could coexist, browns, by their more aggressive manner, replaced the native trout entirely. This was especially true on large portions of the Beaverkill and Willowemoc.

---

[1]*Walton Reporter,* July 6, 1895, p. 1.

The wisdom of stocking a fish that preyed upon their beloved speckled beauties was questioned by many, and enthusiasm for brown trout began to wane. In addition, browns were denounced as "logy and lazy" and for having a decidedly inferior flavor when served on the table. Comparisons between the species became more frequent, and it is not surprising that American anglers rallied to the defense of their own:

> In appearance the brown is scaly, flat, greenish-yellow, irregular in form, bad eye, homely overall. In the native the scales are invisible; he is gold and silver, round and symmetrical, and as beautiful an object as lavish nature produces. . . . As food, the flavor of the brown becomes "weedy" after the middle of May and is decidedly unpleasant to the taste, though early in the season he is not so bad. The native is sweet and delicious as long as the stream is up.[2]

By 1900, stocking applications for browns became so few that the state was forced to adopt a new policy regarding the fish. Brown trout production was cut back, and the number of breeding fish kept at hatcheries was reduced. The vast majority of applications received were for brook trout, as sportsmen no longer desired to place browns in their favorite streams.

On the Beaverkill, members of the Balsam Lake Club were proud of the fact that the German trout had never penetrated their headwater section of the stream—that is, until in 1906 one member came marching back to the clubhouse carrying an 11¼-inch German brown in his creel.

In 1907 the federal government not only cut back but totally halted raising and distributing brown trout in the United States. In answer to the change in policy, George M. Bower, commissioner of the U.S. Bureau of Fisheries, replied that in streams where brown trout had been introduced successfully, the brook trout either disappeared or became very scarce. He went on to state that brown trout were more cannibalistic and grew larger than native trout but that in no instance did brown trout prove superior to the native trout of this country.[3]

Charles Hallock, the editor of *Forest and Stream,* disagreed, and stated so in an editorial:

> The increase in size and numbers of the brook trout in eastern streams, through restocking is too slow. The presence of a few brown trout is welcomed by all who cast the fly, for in the waters where they are increasing there is fair sport now where there

---

[2]Benjamin Kent, "An Angler's Notes on the Beaverkill," *The Speckled Brook Trout,* ed. Louis Rhead, p. 110.
[3]*Forest and Stream,* May 25, 1907, p. 821.

was little or none a few years ago, and there are few men who would not rather take one of the big fellows than a score of native trout that barely exceed the legal minimum length.[4]

The debate over brown trout continued; and while they had many detractors, one who strongly defended the fish was the angling journalist Theodore Gordon:

> Since the introduction of the brown trout, two to three pounds is not uncommon, and many much larger fish have been taken. . . . The lower portions of the Beaverkill and Neversink are noble and beautiful rivers, and should afford more sport than they do now.[5]

Gordon was a close observer of the habits of brown, brook, and rainbow trout. He had an intimate knowledge of Catskill streams, both before and after the introduction of browns and rainbows. For years he wrote on the merits of stocking brown trout, and he believed they greatly improved the fishing:

> A few thousand "farios" placed in some of our rivers will produce greater results in the way of sport than thrice the number of native brook trout. I honor the sentiment which inspires the lover of the native fish, but I remember what the fishing was in the old days before brown trout were introduced, and what it is at the present time. The trout were numerous, but the average size was very small. . . . The first time I fished the Willowemoc, thirty years ago, one could take many trout, but a large pro-portion were smaller than I would now care to basket. It was the same on the Beaverkill and Neversink. We did not have nearly as many battles with sizeable trout as we do nowadays. We never killed any two or three pound fish or had occasional sight or touch of monsters that thrilled our nerves with wild excitement.
>
> It is natural and patriotic to exaggerate the fine qualities of our own trout and to remember with delight our early fly fishing experiences, but for the man who prefers a reasonable number of fairly large trout to many little ones the sport is better, upon the whole, in this part of New York than it was in the days of "fontinalis" only.[6]

---

[4]*Forest and Stream,* June 15, 1907, p. 1.
[5]*Forest and Stream,* March 19, 1904, p. 232.
[6]*Forest and Stream,* June 29, 1907, p. 1019.

Patriotism did indeed surface, along with strong prejudices against brown trout, during the days of World War I. One Catskill correspondent likened the German brown to its country of origin:

> A German brown caught in the Ouleout had his stomach full of brook trout, his finer and gentler brothers. That is just the way the German nation is doing or trying to do. It swallows all its smaller kindred among the nations, and it never stops until it has assimilated them all into its own carnivorous bulk. Call him German, therefore, and wage a war of extermination.[7]

Such dramatic talk fueled dislike for the fish and stigmatized brown trout as cannibals, a reputation that exists to this day. It was evident that the Conservation Commission was still having doubts about brown trout, even in 1923, when it issued a news release warning anglers that "the greatest care should be taken to see that the brown trout and the brook trout are not mixed in the waters of a lake or stream."

A news article titled "Beware the Brown Trout" informed its readers that the commission was taking a more cautious approach in the stocking of browns. Many applications for the species were being held, pending an investigation by a commission expert to determine if there was still hope of preserving brook trout fishing. Before a final determination was made to stock browns, the commission required that "a petition signed by 25 leading citizens or game clubs of the vicinity shall testify that it is futile and a waste of stock to continue the planting of native brook trout in the water in question."[8]

The argument over which species to stock continued for many years, and while there were those who favored brown trout from the beginning, the majority of American anglers did not. They were slow in their acceptance of the foreign game fish, and a sign of their contempt was the continued practice of calling them German trout.

William Schaldach, an outdoor writer and artist, summed things up rather nicely:

> Those few streams that still hold only native trout, let us treasure them and guard them carefully, but in the great majority of rivers where changed conditions are not favorable to fontinalis, let us plant the brown trout in numbers and let us cease calling him the "German" trout or "European" trout, for he is now an American citizen, and a most desireable one.[9]

---

[7]*Catskill Mountain News,* August 9, 1918, p. 2.
[8]*Walton Reporter,* March 23, 1923, p. 1.
[9]*Forest and Stream,* May 1926, p. 274.

19

The "Big River"

The trout-fishing history of the lower Beaverkill coincides with the stocking of brown trout. Their introduction created many more miles of trout water, as browns began inhabiting the water previously avoided by native brook trout—virtually all of the lower river below Roscoe and the junction of the Willowemoc. While there may have been controversy in the stocking of these foreign trout, their introduction to the Beaverkill was one of the most significant events in the stream's storied past.

Previously, Morsston (Livingston Manor) was where anglers disembarked from the train. From there, they traveled the DeBruce road to the fishing grounds at Willowemoc and DeBruce or the Beaverkill road to Beaverkill, Lew Beach, and Turnwood. In 1886, Roscoe listed only one resort in the O. & W. Railroad's *Summer Homes* guide.

Now, with brown trout well established in the lower Beaverkill, anglers no longer concentrated their efforts upstream. More and more fishing tourists were making Roscoe their headquarters and plying their skills on the lower river. As its popularity grew, trout-fishing regulars, especially local anglers, referred to the water below Roscoe as the "Big Beaverkill" and, more often, the "Big River." An increased demand for accommodations saw major new hotel construction up and down the stream: Central House (1890), Beaverkill House (1893), Beaverkill Mountain House (1894), Bonnie View (1895), and Campbell Inn (1901).

111

Beaverkill House, one of several fishing resorts constructed in the 1890s.

During these years, additional rail travel spurred the O. & W. to construct a new railroad station at Roscoe in 1895. Upon its completion, J. S. Underhill, a wealthy Brooklyn sportsman, presented the railroad with a handsome weathervane topped by a stately trout. The trout was a fitting symbol for the village, as the stocking of brown trout brought new prosperity to the Beaverkill in the 1890s.

Jeronimus Underhill fished the Beaverkill for more than fifty years, making his first trip to the stream in the 1840s. While he was known to be a skilled angler, he is best remembered for the wonderful gift he bestowed on the railroad station and the village of Roscoe.

In the years ahead, the trout weathervane greeted thousands of anglers who traveled the O. & W. seeking their favorite sport in the waters of the Beaverkill. Stepping off the train, passengers eagerly cast their eyes on the great copper trout to get the wind direction, which in some cases determined not only where to fish but whether to fish the dry fly upstream or the wet fly down.

The big trout remained on the Roscoe station for many years, serving as a landmark to several generations of Beaverkill anglers. It remained there until the 1950s, when a bankrupt railroad gave way to improved highways, increasing auto, truck, and bus travel. The railroad ceased operations in 1957; and shortly thereafter, before the old railroad station was razed, someone climbed

After the introduction of brown trout in the Beaverkill, more and more tourists made Roscoe their headquarters.

© Jack Niflot

onto the roof and removed the weathervane. Frank Trinkner, an outdoor columnist for the *Liberty Register,* wrote an interesting story on its demise:

© Ed Van Put

J. S. Underhill's famous gift, a weathervane to the Roscoe station.

Back when Roscoe was the trout fishing capital of the country and anglers came from just about every state in the union to fish the far-famed waters of the Big Beaverkill, the Little Beaverkill, the Willowemoc and dozens of smaller streams in the area, one of the first sights that greeted their eyes as they disembarked from the old O. & W. R.R. was the weathervane on top of the depot, topped by a fine figure of a trout that seemed to represent the very essence and spirit of the village which catered to fishermen from every walk of life. While many eyes that glanced upward to it at the beginning of a day's fishing to see if the wind was in the right quarter are now closed in a long sleep, there are still many anglers who will always remember Roscoe's trout weathervane as a golden symbol of the good times and good fishing of another age, for it maintained its proud position atop the station for 62 years.[1]

---

[1]*Liberty Register,* July 24, 1958, p. 6.

Trinkner notes that he telephoned the Roscoe state police and was told that no one had lodged an official complaint about the theft of the old landmark. He then contacted Doug Bury, the proprietor of the Antrim Lodge, who told him that he knew the "old trout" was missing and admitted cheerfully that he had had his eye on it himself. One longtime customer of the Antrim had suggested that Doug steal it for him—and he was thinking of doing the deed when the weathervane disappeared "right out from under his nose." Doug told Trinkner that he had a good idea where it went, and that it was not very far away. "In fact, he thought that a fellow with a sharp eye might see the hot trout appear in the environs of Roscoe, after it had cooled off a bit."

Trinkner concluded his column by stating that he hoped that Doug was right, since "we think that a lot of old time anglers would prefer to see their famous landmark stay in Roscoe, trout-famous for years."[2]

While the railroad station is long gone, the weathervane is not; today, a "fellow with a sharp eye" can still see the trout that was such a familiar sight to those anglers who traveled the rails to fish the "Big River" and meet the challenge of the brown trout.

If there ever was a golden era for trout fishing in the Beaverkill, it was, without a doubt, those introductory years, especially after brown trout began reproducing naturally in the stream. In the decade from 1894 until 1904, brown trout enjoyed a superiority in numbers and sizes that would never be equaled or surpassed.

In August 1894 three of the largest trout ever to be taken from the Beaverkill were captured within days of one another. Jasper Barnhart caught a 26-inch, 6-pound trout at the covered bridge, at the hamlet of Beaverkill, and Joseph Kelley took another 6-pounder under Wagner's bridge (Craig-e-clare). The biggest, however, was not caught but found floating in the Beaverkill, severely wounded though not quite dead. The giant brown had been speared; it measured 32 inches and weighed 8¾ pounds.

Anglers were, in fact, unaccustomed to catching such big fish, and more often than not these huge browns smashed tackle and got away. The following year, in the summer of 1895, even more very large trout found their way from the river into the spotlight of the local inns, taverns, and newspapers. Alex Voorhess of Lew Beach caught a 5-pound, 2-ounce German brown; Lee Davis caught another weighing 5 pounds. Joseph Kelley again caught a monster trout under the bridge at Wagner's, this one weighing 6 pounds and 15 ounces. Upriver, under Charles Sliter's dam, John Tompkins captured two beauties weighing 3½ pounds and 4½ pounds; and one week later, also under Sliter's dam, Egbert Tripp of Turnwood caught a 4-pound, 5-ounce trout and another mon-

---

[2]*Liberty Register,* July 24, 1958, p. 6.

ster German trout measuring 31 inches and weighing 10 pounds—by far the largest ever caught in the Beaverkill!

One other brown trout would make headlines in 1895; that June, a huge fish was again seen in Palen's millpond, which was located just downstream of the new state hatchery in Rockland. The magnetism of the trout was apparent when more than two hundred people turned out to witness its capture. The millpond was drawn down, and personnel from the Beaverkill Hatchery placed a net across the outlet. Somehow, in the excitement, the big trout managed to jump the net and escape into the raceway. George Cochran, who had been watching from the bank, leaped into the millrace and succeeded in capturing the fish with his hands. It was immediately placed in a nail keg, transferred to a tank of water, and taken to the hatchery.

The giant trout, which measured 31 inches and weighed 9 pounds, may have been from the original stocking of 1887. At the hatchery, it was placed in a display tank; in just a few days, several hundred visitors, from all over the state, came to view the huge fish. In time, the trout succumbed to injuries it had received when captured, and died. It was such a grand specimen that the supervisor sent the trout away to Rochester to be mounted, and upon its return it was placed on exhibition at the Beaverkill Hatchery.[3]

Palen's Millpond and Raceway, home of the giant brown trout, which was exhibited at the Beaverkill Hatchery in 1895.

© Ed Van Put

---

[3]Apparently, when the hatchery at Rockland closed in 1904, the large mounted trout was presented to the Palen family, whose heirs still maintain a home alongside the historic gristmill. The magnificent brown trout is still there, on a dining-room wall, under a handsome glass dome, immortalized forever—just a stone's throw from the site where it captured the attention of an entire community. The tag reads:

Brown or German Trout: Length—30½ inches, Weight—9¼ pounds
Caught June 20, 1895.

While Beaverkill brown trout were finding their way onto the pages of newspapers and sporting journals, they were not the only fish to do so. During this period, another species appeared in the lower river.

In 1895, *The American Angler* reported that five Atlantic salmon were captured in the Beaverkill; and on October 1, 1896, the *Roscoe-Rockland Review* reported, "Another salmon has been taken from the Beaverkill. This one on Saturday last—from an eel rack or weir—about a mile above Trout Brook. The salmon was 37 in. long and weighed 14 lbs."[4]

These salmon were believed to be some of those planted in 1892 in the East Branch of the Delaware River, at City Brook and Read Creek, and in the West Branch of the Delaware, at Deposit, by the Pennsylvania Fish Commission. They were of Penobscot origin. In 1895, more than one hundred of these salmon, averaging 12 to 15 pounds, were caught in the New Jersey portion of the Delaware River and in Delaware River tributaries in Pennsylvania and New York.

One year later, in 1896, Cooks Falls residents' attentions were drawn to the river when two enormous fish were spotted in the deep covered-bridge pool:

> Quite an excitement now prevails here watching the two large trout in the Beaverkill just above Cook's Falls bridge. By the looks of them as near as can be estimated they are about thirty inches long. They are beauties and can be seen at any time of the day. No charge for looking at them.[5]

Over the next several years, many more record-setting browns were taken from the waters of the Beaverkill. Each year, area newspapers reported on trout in excess of 5 and 6 pounds. For example: Alex Voorhess of Lew Beach caught a 5-pound, 4-ounce brown in 1898; in 1899, William Miller of Roscoe took one measuring 25 inches and weighing 5 pounds; in 1900, William Keener captured another 25-incher, which weighed 5 pounds; and in 1901, Irving Finch caught a brown trout that was 26 inches in length and tipped the scales at 6 pounds. The last two veteran anglers also hailed from Roscoe, and caught their trout in Ferdon's Eddy, downstream of the Forks.

---

[4]Quoted in the *Roscoe-Rockland Review,* October 1, 1896, p. 8.
[5]*Walton Reporter,* August 16, 1896, p. 1.

20

William Keener and Louis Rhead

The first angler to establish a reputation for catching extraordinary brown trout on the "Big River" was William Keener. Born in Andes, Delaware County, in 1848, he came to Roscoe with his parents as a child, and throughout his life he lived within sight of the Beaverkill. His knowledge of the river was unequaled; he knew the pools, the riffles, and the favorite haunts of trout. Viewing the river on a daily basis made him familiar with its great fly hatches and how the trout adapted to the seasonal variations of flows and water temperatures. Keener had a thorough understanding of the river and knew when and where to fish.

He caught big fish, and newspapers regularly made mention of them; their reports often attached the tag of "champion" or "expert fisherman" to his name. He caught many at the Forks (Junction Pool), a pool he popularized as much as anyone. Keener was a familiar figure there, fishing a pair of big wet flies or a favorite bucktail. The pool was but a short walk from the Roscoe House, which he owned and operated.

For years, the Roscoe House was a popular sportsman's rendezvous; and anglers, amateur and veteran alike, sought the wisdom of its proprietor. William Keener knew the ways of trout and was the most knowledgeable Beaverkill fisherman of his generation.

Roscoe House, a favorite gathering place of old-time Beaverkill anglers.

Trout fishermen of every era are only too eager to exchange ideas, debate techniques and theories, discuss flies, and exaggerate their success on the stream. In these early days of brown trout, talk turned from how many to how big. "Fishing for count" was on the way out, and this next generation of anglers would measure their success in inches and pounds.

A few, however, finding brown trout more difficult to catch than native brook trout, hired local anglers to fish for them, while they sat indoors:

> Some men sit in a barroom all day, after engaging a couple of local anglers to fish
> for them. Their ideas of what constitutes sport are peculiar, but they usually return to
> the city with a large number of trout. Doubtless they enjoy a fine reputation at home.[1]

But it was not just the trout that were taken:

> Up in the Catskills a city fisherman occasionally is taken in by the countrymen.
> One day a man fresh from the city desiring to make folks believe he was a great fish-

---

[1]*Forest and Stream,* June 27, 1908, p. 1020.

erman purchased what looked like a basket of beautiful trout offered by a mountaineer. He examined several of the speckled beauties lying on the top and paid a good round price for the basket full. When he arrived home he found only a few trout on the top the rest being suckers. When the mountaineers heard of it they merely remarked that suckers were easily caught![2]

One can only imagine the conversations that took place at the bar of the Roscoe House. Keener was known as a quiet man, and as one who did not give advice unless asked, preferring to listen to others; "but when asked for an opinion he would voice it in a pointed manner with but few words, often to the discomfort of wiseacres and always to the pleasure to those who knew him."[3]

One who knew him well was Louis Rhead, the noted artist and angling author. "He swears awful at times," wrote Rhead. "You see at a glance his [Irish] ancestry, and though born in the Catskills as his father before him, he was the fiercest Home Ruler for the Old Sod I ever met or heard of."[4]

William Keener.

Keener caught many memorable fish, but perhaps his greatest catch was a "double," taken at the Forks. He hooked and landed a 3-pound, 9-ounce brown trout and a 4-pound smallmouth bass; the bass took the end fly, and the trout the dropper. He was fishing with Louis Rhead, who mentioned their longtime friendship and Keener's notoriety as a fly fisherman in his *American Trout Stream Insects* (1916). Rhead wrote of the piscatorial feat in *Fisherman's Lures and Game-Fish Food* (1920) and again in *Forest and Stream* in August 1923, where he devoted an entire article to describing Keener's unusual catch. Though the two fish often inhabit the same waters, hooking a trout and a smallmouth at the same time is a rare occurrence, even for those who regularly fish with two flies. In all probability, Keener's landing of those two large fish will never be equaled.

[2]*Kingston Weekly Leader,* May 18, 1901, p. 1.
[3]*Livingston Manor Times,* July 23, 1924, p. 1.
[4]*Forest and Stream,* August 1923, p. 722.

William Keener was so well known and respected by sportsmen everywhere that when he died in 1924 *Forest and Stream* printed his obituary on its editorial page, which was edged in black. Commenting on his character, and contributions to trout fishing, it stated:

> By nature he was unusually mild and gentle-hearted, with a fund of native Irish wit and humor, well known to that race. It was as good as a play, to hear his quips and sallies on those boasters and braggarts one so often meets out fishing. His own nature was the very opposite, modest in the extreme, generous, charitable, and possessed of a very winning manner to his intimate friends, of whom he had many. The thousands of anglers who now enjoy the fine fishing of the Beaverkill and Willowemoc are much indebted to Mr. Keener, who has for many years upheld the best traditions of the craft, and used uncommon sense in properly stocking the streams, by placing the young fish in situations where they had ample food and quick growth. No angler in the entire state of New York was better known, and none more esteemed.[5]

Appropriately, William Keener's final resting place is not much more than a long cast to the waters of the Beaverkill. This friend to so many anglers lies buried in a small hillside cemetery overlooking his beloved Junction Pool.

By far, the largest trout ever taken from the Beaverkill was a brown, first reported on in the fall of 1903. On November 4, the *Walton Reporter* carried a story of a 38-inch German trout found dead near Cooks Falls. The enormous fish was taken to Leighton's store and tipped the scales at nearly 15 pounds! Other New York newspapers ran the article, and the story culminated in the pages of *Forest and Stream,* which published the following two letters on January 9, 1904:

A BIG BROWN TROUT OF THE BEAVERKILL

Middletown, N.Y.—Editor, Forest and Stream: About election time a squib went the rounds of the papers hereabouts that a large trout had been found dead in the Beaverkill at Cook's Falls, Sullivan County, which measured thirty-eight inches long and weighed fifteen pounds, and that it had died from fatty degeneration of the heart or starvation, or probably old age, nobody knew which. A whopping lie I said to my-

---

[5]*Forest and Stream,* September 1924, p. 536.

self, and let it go at that. On the 16th of November the Daily Press of this city again published another big trout found dead at Rockland. That made two big 'uns, and I thought I would investigate; so I wrote to my friend "Bill" Keener, the genial proprietor of the Roscoe House at Rockland, and, as luck would have it, I struck the right man and the same fish, as you will see by the enclosed letter. Friend Keener is an all-round sportsman, and is an authority on fishing, particularly in the Beaverkill and Willowemoc country. I am glad this big fellow has gone to the happy hereafter, the place where all big ones ought to go.

John Wilkin

Mr. Keener wrote: I can tell you about the big trout. I am the first one who saw it after the two small boys found it. On November 1, I was down the track about three miles below here and met the boys coming down with the trout strung on a cane, carrying it between them. I measured it, and it was plumb 3 feet 2 inches long. They took it down to Cook's Falls and it weighed 14¾ pounds. It was very poor; if it had been fat it would have weighed 20 pounds at least. This is no fish story. Lots of people saw it. It was a German brown trout. It was found down by the old stone mill between here and Cook's Falls. The time of the high water last month it ran up a little spring brook between the track and the river; when the water went down it could not get back, and I suppose starved to death. I don't think it was dead when the boys found it, but the boys were afraid of the law and said they found it dead. I had a hound dog with me and the trout's head was as large as the dog's. It does not appear possible that there could have been such a fish in the river, but it is true.

William Keener

I was so intrigued by this story that shortly after reading it, I decided to find the stream where this incredible trout's life came to an end.

The timing of the incident coincided with the spawning season for brown trout. What stream could entice such a grand trout? My interest increased when the topography map of the area did not show any streams in the vicinity described by William Keener: three miles below Roscoe, between the railroad and the Beaverkill.

On a summer day, I crossed the river opposite the Red Rose Motel and found the old railroad bed. Walking in the direction of Cooks Falls, I soon came upon the stream, which Keener described as a "little spring brook." Its source was a large spring, welling up in a partially hidden glen, less than a couple of hundred feet away. The little stream of springwater flowed to, and then alongside, the railroad for a short distance, then ran through a culvert to the opposite side. Here, between the railroad and the Beaverkill, there was a small plunge pool a foot or more deep and several feet wide, after which the stream flowed overland and shortly disappeared, hundreds of feet short of the river.

Only during floodwaters could any trout reach the spring run, and only during such high flows could they leave. Incredibly, this little stream, its total length only six to eight hundred feet, maintains an isolated population of brook trout. On this particular day there were more than two dozen nice trout trapped in the pool; and my approach sent them scurrying wildly, to and fro, seeking to get under anything that would give them shelter. This was, without a doubt, where the boys found the great trout, in a weakened condition, with no place to go and no place to hide; the fish could not escape them.

The small spring brook next to the railroad bed, where the largest trout ever to come out of the Beaverkill was captured.

No one knows which pool this noble trout called home, but my guess is that it moved up from the nearby Mountain Pool. Large and deep, it has long been a favorite of Beaverkill fishermen; combined with the Lower Mountain Pool, it forms some of the best-looking water on the lower river.

Louis John Rhead (1857–1926) was an Englishman who came to the United States in 1883. By profession he was an artist, and a good one, painting in oil as well as watercolor, exhibiting in American and European galleries. At expositions, Rhead captured gold medals for his artistic posters, but he is perhaps best known as an illustrator of books and magazines. Many of the books he illustrated were juvenile classics such as *Swiss Family Robinson, Gulliver's Travels, Robin Hood,* and *King Arthur and His Knights.* His work was so popular that it is still produced today by Children's Classics in New York.

Rhead began fishing in 1888 or 1890 and became a very enthusiastic angler. He wrote several fishing books and numerous fishing articles, many of which appeared in *Forest and Stream,* for which he also produced a number of magazine covers.

Local newspapers first reported on his visiting the Beaverkill in 1901. That summer, he stayed at the Campbell Inn, overlooking the Forks, and gathered material along area streams for a book he was editing and illustrating titled *The Speckled Brook Trout.* The book, which was well received, sported a unique cover design, with trout flies on imitation birch bark. It featured pieces by such well-known angling writers as William C. Harris, the editor of *The American Angler;* Charles Hallock, the editor of *Forest and Stream;* and A. Nelson Cheney; "An Angler's Notes on the Beaverkill," by Benjamin Kent, contained valuable information on fishing the Beaverkill at the turn of the century. *The Speckled Brook Trout* also featured excellent illustrations by Louis Rhead, depicting scenes on the Beaverkill, the Willowemoc, and Mongaup Creek.

Louis Rhead became a Beaverkill regular, spending more than twenty years fishing his favorite water, below the Forks on the Big Beaverkill. He frequently stayed at the Campbell Inn or the Roscoe House, where he enjoyed the friendship of William Keener. On occasion, he fished the Willowemoc and, like most anglers of his day, made his headquarters at DeBruce, at the Hearthstone Inn, hosted by Elizabeth Royce.

Rhead believed strongly in the theory of exact imitation; in 1914, he wrote a seven-part series for *Field & Stream* titled "The Entomology of American Trout Streams." While he would go on to write several books of his own, *American Trout Stream Insects,* published in 1916, was his most noted work. Some have hailed the book as "the first American work on trout stream insects,"[6] and others as "America's first angling entomology."[7]

---

[6]Wetzel, *American Fishing Books,* p. 202.
[7]Lynn Scholz, "Louis Rhead's First Career," *The American Fly Fisher,* Vol. 12, No. 1, 1985, p. 18–24.

In preparation for this ambitious undertaking, Rhead had spent three years studying and collecting the aquatic insects of the Beaverkill. Unfortunately, he lumped all aquatic insects together: mayflies, caddis, stoneflies, and so on were identified only by a monthly insect chart. While he included plates of naturals, they are not identified other than by names he devised, such as "Female Green-Eye," "Male Green-Eye," "Broadtail," "Greenback," or "Yellow-tip."

He may have started out to write an angling entomology, but his work was amateurish and fell well short of the goal. At the very beginning of the book, on page 5, Rhead made the impetuous remark, ". . . I deem it wise to brush aside the science of entomology. . . ." *American Trout-Stream Insects* is not an entomology and should not be considered one.

Louis Rhead went on to design almost one hundred different flies, but it is impossible to match these with the natural insects he set out to imitate. In fact, Rhead excluded the dressings of his "nature flies," as he called them, in an obvious attempt to control their manufacture and sales. He sold the flies from his home and through the New York firm of William Mills & Son, which had the ". . . exclusive rights to make and sell all my new patterns."[8] He often promoted these flies in fishing articles and advised his readers that they could be obtained by writing to his editor at *Forest and Stream*.

In Rhead's many articles on trout fishing, he was constantly discovering new flies that were more killing, and he had no qualms about making boastful claims about himself or the flies he invented. He created "nature flies," "metal bodied flies," "shining fly minnows," and so on; his flies, he told his readers, were better than all the rest.

American Trout-Stream Insects was not this country's first entomology; it was, however, the first book devoted to the theory of exact imitation. Louis Rhead believed strongly in directly imitating the more prolific aquatic insects trout feed upon, and he tied his flies as true copies of the naturals. He dubbed the standard flies of his day "fancy flies" and saw them as useless: "If an exact copy of the natural insect is offered to the fish, it is sure to entice and lure a trout more readily than a fancy fly." How ironic it is that not one of the numerous flies he designed and promoted is known by the fly fisherman of today, while many of those he saw as useless are still favored, seventy-five years later, by trout fishers everywhere.

One who fished with Louis Rhead, on the lower Beaverkill, was William Schaldach. Like Rhead, he, too, was an artist and an angling writer; his career with brush and pen were just beginning:

---

[8]Rhead, *American Trout-Stream Insects,* p. 99.

William Keener and Louis Rhead

Louis Rhead had a great devotion to the natural-imitation theory, and he tied lifelike replicas of crawfish, hellgrammites, nymphs and adult flies. He would fish these diligently, day after day, and the empty creel with which he often returned never dampened his spirits. Anglers called him a luckless fisherman and kidded him unmercifully; but usually, when things were at their worst, he would show up with a brownie or rainbow of prodigious size and silently slay his critics.[9]

---

[9]Schaldach, *Currents and Eddies,* p. 50.

21

Creating New Trout Waters

During the 1890s, two new fishing clubs acquired more than seven miles of the Beaverkill and, in so doing, made virtually all of the water on the upper river private and posted.

In 1895, a few avid fly fishermen from New York formed the Fly Fishers Club of Brooklyn and acquired a one-mile stretch of the Beaverkill that flowed through the farm of Ben Hardenbergh, at Craig-e-clare. The club bound itself to three rules: No trout under 7 inches would be creeled; members could fish only with flies; and the stream would be stocked with adult or yearling trout, "persistently and liberally."

A few years later, a small group of anglers from Binghamton began acquiring leases and strips of land bordering the stream, from Beaverkill Falls downstream to the Bonnie View. They made their purchases from farmers, sawmill operators, and boardinghouse owners; put together a holding of approximately six miles; and became known as the Beaverkill Fishermen's Association. In 1903, this group's holding was acquired by the Beaverkill Stream Club, which made its headquarters at the Bonnie View.

With more of the best stream water on the upper river becoming posted, serious attention was given to creating private trout preserves by constructing artificial lakes and ponds. During the 1890s, a number of these man-made impoundments made their appearance in the Beaverkill (and

© Jack Niflot

The Brooklyn Fly Fisher's Club.

Willowemoc) watershed; private trout hatcheries were constructed on their premises to replenish the lakes on a regular basis. A few became well-known trout-fishing resorts, adding to the history of the Beaverkill. The first trout hatchery to appear in the Beaverkill region was established in 1890, at Alder Lake.

ALDER LAKE

Actually, Alder Lake was at one time a natural body of water. When the region was first surveyed in 1809, by Jacob Trumpbour, the lake was quite small. In his field notes, Trumpbour wrote that lots 190 and 191 contained "about 14 acres of Aulder Pond, and [are] watered by its outlet on which is a fall of about 10 feet, a good mill site."[1]

As with most of the farm lots surveyed in the Beaverkill valley, the land was "steep and stony" and "a poor lot." These surveyor descriptions readily explain, in a few words, why the land was not settled for nearly a half century after being subdivided.

---

[1] Field Notes, Hardenbergh Patent Great Lot 6, 1809, Delaware County Clerk's Office.

It was not until 1856, when Asahel Bryant of Andes purchased "Aulder Pond" and lots 190 and 191, that the land became occupied. This pioneer settler constructed a log cabin and worked diligently to convert the wilderness into an "improved farm." Farming was never easy in the rugged mountainous country; winters were long and sometimes punishing. During the first spring, Bryant lost fourteen of his thirty head of cattle, due to a late snowstorm. A deep snow fell in April, catching him out of forage; far from any neighbors and surrounded by forest, it is a wonder he did not lose them all.

In 1861, Bryant's brother, William, took over the farm and continued making improvements. He constructed a sawmill at the falls and replaced the primitive log cabin with a more permanent dwelling. Learning, perhaps, from the hardships of his brother, he drained Aulder Pond and turned it into a rich meadow, which, in turn, provided his cattle with enough hay to last the long winters. The Bryants farmed the land successfully for many years before trading farms with Julius (June) Smith of Dunraven in 1889.

June Smith had a different vision of the farm carved out of the wilderness. He knew about trout, having been a guide in the area since 1866; but more important, he knew about trout propagation. Instead of a meadow, he saw a lake full of leaping trout. Many farmers on the nearby Beaverkill enhanced their incomes by boarding fishermen, and Smith decided to flood the farm, create a lake, and build a fishing resort, which would attract trout-fishing tourists.

He found the financial means to carry out his dream when he formed a partnership with Colonel Charles H. Odell. Odell was a wealthy Pittsburgh steel manufacturer with a Wall Street address. The two men were from vastly different backgrounds, and how their unusual alliance was formed is not known exactly. Perhaps it was their Civil War experiences that brought the two together; June Smith had seen plenty of action as a member of the Third New York Cavalry. It was said that he was a veteran of more than sixty battles before he was discharged. The two men also shared another bond: a love for trout and a desire to improve trout fishing.

A large dam was constructed and a new, larger, deeper Alder Lake now covered fifty-five acres. The lake was stocked with native brook trout taken from the Beaverkill. Placed in a new lake with cold, clean water and no competition, they grew large and plentiful. To enhance the fishery, June Smith constructed a hatchery below the dam, in a narrow ravine along the lake's outlet.

At the rear of the lake, where spring feeders flowed, shallow ponds were made by building small dams with fishways, which allowed spawning trout to enter. Once in the ponds, the trout were captured in nets and taken by buckboard to the hatchery, where ripe trout were stripped of their eggs, then returned to the lake. In time, when the fry were large enough, they, too, were placed in Alder Lake.

The old hatchery at Alder Lake.

The partnership between Colonel Odell and June Smith dissolved in 1891, and a corporation was formed with the name of the Alder Lake Club. Membership was limited to forty, and most members resided in Kingston. Samuel D. Coykendall, a millionaire railroad and steamboat company owner, was its most prominent member. A large clubhouse was constructed, along with a barn and icehouse.

While some members traveled from Kingston by wagon, and even on horseback, transportation to Alder Lake was generally provided by the Ulster & Delaware Railroad. The detraining point was Arkville; from there, members traveled the fourteen miles by carriage or buckboard.

The lake quickly developed a reputation as a great trout preserve. Its members regularly returned to Kingston with catches of large brook trout, some in the 2-pound class; occasionally, they would even bring back a trout of 20 inches. On May 28, 1892, the *Kingston Weekly Leader* reported:

> The finest mess of trout ever seen in this city was brought in town on Thursday afternoon by Abraham Hasbrouck, President of the National Bank of Rondout. He captured them in Alder Lake which is the property of a fishing club which he is a member. The catch weighed 15 pounds, and none of them weighed less than a pound and the largest weighed two pounds.

"Any luck?" is a question fishermen hear all the time. Most experienced anglers, however, will tell you that luck has little to do with catching fish. It is skill, or knowledge, or maybe even perseverance, they will say, that makes for successful fishing. An incident, though, that clearly demonstrates how luck—both good and bad—can be involved occurred on a day in June 1895.

Jansen Hasbrouck, an Alder Lake Club member, was fishing with two hooks on his line and caught what fly fishermen call a "double": two trout at once. Unfortunately, the pair of speckled beauties became snagged on the bottom and broke Hasbrouck's leader—an apparent case of bad luck. Later in the day, he hooked another trout, which fought furiously, swimming to and fro with seemingly increasing strength. When Hasbrouck finally was able to bring the fish to the net, he saw that the trout had become entangled with his lost double, and he landed all three! An obvious example of good luck.

When the trout season opened in the spring of 1899, Samuel Coykendall was the new owner of Alder Lake. He purchased the shares of the other club members and planned to create a stylish estate and fishing preserve. On a knoll overlooking the lake, Coykendall constructed a stately mansion of grand proportions. More than a hundred men were employed during its construction; all materials were hauled from Livingston Manor, sixteen miles distant.

By June 1900, the magnificent three-story building was completed. In addition, Coykendall added hundreds of acres of forest lands to his lake holdings and constructed a new road, mostly at his own expense, over Cross Mountain from Arena. While the road may have made the trip a little shorter and more pleasant, it also made it easier for poachers to find Alder Lake.

Once word had gotten out about how good the trout fishing was, poaching became a problem. There was always a resident caretaker; at times, the club employed as many as seven men to patrol the lake's shore. Confrontations were common and especially troublesome at night, when patrolmen were occasionally assaulted by determined poachers. But poachers, too, paid indirectly for their indiscretions. Old-timers tell of hasty escapes and injuries sustained while fleeing in the dark, tripping over rocks and logs.

The late Catskill fly tier Harry Darbee told the story of three poachers who were caught at Alder Lake with more than a hundred trout over the legal limit. The state police were summoned; the trespassers and their catch, which was in a burlap bag, were placed in the rear of the troop car for a trip to the judge in Livingston Manor.

All the way down the road leading out of the Beaverkill valley, on the way to the Manor, the men quietly and efficiently tossed their illegal catch out the car's rear windows. Upon arriving at the town justice, a red-faced trooper discovered that he had no evidence!

I can still see the glint in Harry's eye, and hear his laughter, as he finished telling the story with a slap on his knee. While he frowned on their greedy deed, Harry admired the poachers' ingenuity and their ability to outwit the law.

Samuel Coykendall owned Alder Lake for many years, enlarging his estate to more than sixteen hundred acres, which also included Beecher Lake. To reach Beecher from Alder, he improved a rough wagon road, which had been an ancient Indian trail, running between the two lakes.

The stewardship of Alder Lake by the Coykendall family ended in 1945, when the estate once again became a trout-fishing club. A new Alder Lake Club emerged; only this time, its membership came from Liberty, in Sullivan County. This club maintained the lake for fifteen years before conveying the holdings, in 1960, to the Nassau County Council of Boy Scouts.

Alder Lake.

© Ed Van Put

For the next twenty years, the lake and its woodlands were used as a summer retreat by the scouts from Long Island. In 1980, Alder Lake and the sixteen hundred acres surrounding it changed hands for the last time. The lands were acquired by New York State and added to the forever-wild Catskill Forest Preserve.

ORCHARD LAKE

During the 1890s, June Smith went on to construct other private trout hatcheries in Sullivan County. He became a well-known expert in trout propagation, pioneering, at least locally, an industry whose time, it seemed, had come.

In 1894, Smith established the Orchard Lake Hatchery at the headwaters of Sprague Brook, a Willowemoc tributary. This facility was owned by Stoddard Hammond, a tanner and acid manufacturer, who constructed a dam, creating a forty-acre lake he named the Orchard Lake Trout Preserve.

In 1911, the Hammond family sold the lake to a group of New York City sportsmen, who became known as the Orchard Lake Club. With a hatchery located on the premises to ensure a constant supply of trout, it was not long before Orchard Lake developed a reputation as a fine producer, especially of large brook trout. In 1915, one club member even captured the *Forest and Stream* contest prize for catching the largest trout on a fly.

Membership was about fifty, and while the lake's excellent fishing was the main attraction, another important activity was the club's clay pigeon shooting. In time, Orchard Lake Club amassed two thousand acres and changed its name to the Trout and Skeet Club of New York. In 1955, after a span covering more than forty years, ownership of Orchard Lake, too, passed on to the Nassau County Council of Boy Scouts.

WANETA LAKE

Another trout hatchery that began operations during this period was constructed immediately below Lew Beach, on a spring tributary of the Beaverkill. It was built by Bruce Davidson in 1895, the same year he created a trout preserve farther down the Beaverkill road. A year earlier he had purchased an "alder swamp" and employed a large force of men to cut trees and burn brush, clearing more than thirty acres. He then built a stone dam across the small stream flowing through the wetlands and created Waneta Lake.

Davidson stocked the waters with trout, constructed a fine boardinghouse, and, for many years, provided his paying guests with excellent trout fishing.

FOREST LAKE

Another trout preserve that made its appearance about this time was Forest Lake, located opposite the Salmo Fontinalis Club water. In 1894, William Bidwell built a small trout pond where a series of springs flowed over his property.

Searching for a place to enjoy trout fishing, Frank and Charles Andrus of Roxbury, Delaware County, purchased the Bidwell property, constructed a new dam, and enlarged the pond to twelve acres.

After a few years, the Andrus brothers sold their lake to a small group of anglers, mostly from Roxbury, who became incorporated under the name of Forest Lake Club. For many years, club members enjoyed trout fishing in their spring-fed waters. Individual catches of brook trout numbering in the hundreds were not unusual.

H O D G E   P O N D

One of the most bizarre attempts at creating a trout fishery occurred in 1899, when a Brooklyn contractor named Patrick H. Flynn attempted to "blow up" a lake in order to rid it of undesirable fish, and then restock its waters with trout. Flynn purchased more than two thousand acres surrounding a beautiful, mountaintop twenty-acre lake named Hodge Pond. The land was heavily forested; the lake, deep and cold, straddled the divide between the Beaverkill and the Willowemoc.

Flynn's goal was to have a game and trout preserve in the wilderness, and he began by importing deer from New Jersey and Wichita, Kansas, and turning them loose on his property. He built a road into Hodge Pond and constructed a large summer residence high on a hillside overlooking the lake. For transportation to and from his preserve deep in the forest, Flynn brought to Livingston Manor the first automobile ever seen there. A local newspaper reported, "It is a curiosity to the people living along the route, and is inspected most thoroughly by horses that chance to meet it."[2]

Hodge Pond had all of the physical requirements necessary to be an excellent trout pond, but it was populated by pickerel, perch, bullheads, and sunfish. Flynn was determined to wipe out the existing fish population by the very novel use of explosives. In preparation, he hired a dynamiter and acquired between twelve hundred and twenty-five hundred pounds of explosives.

In the early spring of 1899, a crew of men worked for a week, drawing off water to lower the lake by three feet. As it was still covered by more than thirty inches of ice, they drilled two hundred holes, fifty feet apart. Each hole was wired with dynamite, which was lowered to within four feet of the lake bottom. From five to thirty-five sticks were placed in each hole, and connected to three circuits, which were timed to explode seconds apart.

On the day of the big event, a crowd of nearby residents gathered at the lake to witness the unusual occurrence. They made their way by horse and carriage or buckboard; and, as they gathered along the lake's shore, speculation among the multitude was varied. Some believed Hodge Pond would "go heavenward," others "didn't think it would budge an inch," and a few were "absolutely sure it would blow the whole bottom out."

At the sound of a pistol shot, the electric spark was sent, discharging the explosives. The earth shook, and the detonation was accompanied by a roar similar to "a hundred claps of thunder":

---

[2]*Roscoe-Rockland Review,* August 15, 1901, p. 4.

With the first plunge of the batteries fifty-four holes were exploded, and a sight as grand and awe inspiring as one could wish to see met the eager eyes of all. There is nothing with which to compare it, and description will not avail. From fifty-four holes as many columns of ice and water ascended simultaneously to a height of one hundred, to one hundred fifty feet, each column being ten to fifteen feet in diameter.[3]

Within a second of the first explosion, there was another, and then a third equally as large. The result was "one of the grandest spectacles ever witnessed."

Several days later, when an assessment of the experiment could be carried out, it was discovered that though the lake bottom was covered with dead fish, many remained alive: "While the experiment was an underwater pyrotechnical success from a spectator point of view, so far as exterminating the finny tribe is concerned it was a gigantic failure."[4]

PUNCH BOWL POND

One other noted trout preserve was developed during the 1890s; it was constructed by Jeronimus S. Underhill, the Brooklyn sportsman who had gifted the Roscoe railroad station with the famous trout weathervane. In 1892, he built a dam across Meadow Swamp Brook, a spring tributary of Abe Wood Brook, which flows into the Willowemoc just upstream of Junction Pool. The pond he created was small, a little over six acres; unfortunately, shortly after it was constructed, the dam sprang a leak and drained. After reconstruction, continuing leakage problems caused the oval-shaped pond to maintain a half-full appearance, similar to a punch bowl, and it thus became known as the Punch Bowl, or Punch Bowl Pond.

Underhill also built a large, rustic, three-story clubhouse overlooking the valley and the village of Roscoe, providing a "bird's-eye view for miles around."[5] Alongside the building, high in a hemlock, flew an enormous American flag. It measured thirty feet by eighteen feet and was suspended from a huge tree more than one hundred feet high that had been trimmed for the purpose. The glorious flag could be seen for miles, capturing the attention of fishermen and travelers. Atop the mountainside, it could be spotted from the veranda of the Beaverkill House, opposite the railroad station, where curious travelers marveled over who lived in such a wonderful location.

---

[3]*Liberty Register,* April 14, 1899, p. 2.
[4]*Roscoe-Rockland Review,* April 20, 1899, p. 1.
[5]*Walton Reporter,* October 5, 1895, p. 2.

Punch Bowl Pond.

© Ed Van Put

When the pond was completed, it was stocked with twenty-five hundred trout; that July, it received another fifteen hundred fish, from 7 to 15 inches in length. The following spring, several thousand trout from the Alder Lake hatchery were added to its waters. With so many fish crammed into such a small pond, Underhill found it necessary to feed them artificially. An ingenious method was devised, in which a small "trolley tub" ran across a wire suspended over the water. Seeing thousands of trout crowded together, one visitor remarked, "You take out the trout and there would be very little water left."

For all intents and purposes, the Punch Bowl was similar to a hatchery rearing pond, only larger. In fact, trout at the pond were even stripped of their eggs, by state workers, for use at the newly constructed Beaverkill Hatchery in Rockland.

The Punch Bowl has been known to New York anglers as the place where the New York State record brook trout was caught. For many years, among the list of record game fish was the entry of an "8 pound, 8 ounce brook trout, *Salvelinus fontinalis,* captured by William Keener in 1908, in Punchbowl Lake, Sullivan County."

Having extensively researched all available Catskill newspapers, prior to and following the date of capture, and, in addition, volumes of sporting journals and magazines, I have been unable to turn up any evidence that William Keener ever caught such a trout. During his lifetime, never once was it reported that Keener himself, or anyone who wrote of his prowess as an angler, ever claimed he caught a brook trout of such proportions. The big trout never appeared in print, not in his lifetime or, for that matter, for many years afterward.

Keener was an unpretentious man; but he was a well-known trout fisherman with a reputation. As was frequently the case, when he caught a large fish, it made area newspapers. Would not a sizable brook trout, especially the largest ever taken, have made the newspapers?

Brook trout were revered by the trout fishermen of Keener's generation; in the small mountain communities it would have been impossible to keep the capture of an incredible 8½-pound fish a secret! William Keener knew and fished with the outdoor writers of his day; it is incomprehensible that such an extraordinary trout would escape their attention and go unnoticed or unmentioned while the man was alive.

The first mention of the brook trout does not occur until 1935, when Clayton B. Seagears of Middletown, New York, published an attractive map of Sullivan County titled *The Anglers Guide*. The map featured trout streams, including the Beaverkill and Willowemoc, with drawings of large fish, along with notes on their capture. The map depicts the Punch Bowl and states, "Brook Trout caught in the Punch Bowl by Wm. Keener, W 8½, L 23″, G 19½″, Old Rec." (The proportions alone make one suspicious.)

Although Seagears referred to the trout as an old record, there were no official state records at the time. The first official list of game fish was compiled in 1941, by Conservation Department biologist Cecil Heacox of the Rochester office. Heacox relied on, and made an extensive search of, records compiled by *Field & Stream,* which sponsored fishing contests; entries were supported by evidence made under affidavit, and contest records went back to 1911.[6]

In my efforts to learn more about the record brook trout attributed to Keener, I telephoned Cecil Heacox, who had long since retired from the Conservation Department. He searched his files, and, much to my delight, mailed me the original list of record game fish he had compiled, along with the news release!

Interestingly, the 8½-pound brook trout caught in the Punch Bowl was not listed. Instead, the record brook trout was a 6-pound, 12-ounce fish caught in 1913 by Herman B. Christian. The big trout was caught in Sand Pond, the same Sand Pond located at the headwaters of the Willowemoc, where the Willowemoc Club was founded.

---

[6]New York State Conservation Department, news release, September 17, 1941.

Surprisingly, the large brook trout allegedly caught by William Keener surfaces as the official state record in 1946, in the August issue of the *Conservationist*. For some unexplainable reason, the Division of Conservation Education, through its magazine, became "a clearing house for future records" and the "custodian of New York State angling records."

Why this responsibility was removed from the Bureau of Fisheries is questionable. But there is a connection concerning the insertion of the Punch Bowl trout as the new record. The director of the *Conservationist* was Clayton B. Seagears, who had first reported the fish on his *Anglers Guide* map, years before.

There was one very large brook trout that did come out of Punch Bowl Pond. In the fall of 1898, the big fish was found dead along the shoreline. The *Roscoe-Rockland Review* reported that J. S. Underhill had hooked, but not landed, a large trout, which was later found dead; it measured 24 inches in length and weighed 4¾ pounds: "The specimen was of the brook trout variety and estimated to be about 5 or 6 years old, dating from the time the lake was first stocked."[7]

There are rumors that this grand trout was mounted and found a home over the bar in the Roscoe House, owned by William Keener. Is it possible, considering its final resting place, that over the years it grew, and became the state record?

---

[7]*Roscoe-Rockland Review,* October 20, 1898, p. 1.

22

The Falls Lot

A year after dissolving his partnership with June Smith and building a preserve at Alder Lake, Colonel Charles H. Odell decided to make a trout preserve at Beaverkill Falls.

One of the most picturesque portions of the Beaverkill is the high falls, located two miles upstream of Turnwood. A hallowed landmark, it attracts large trout and, in their pursuit, some of the legendary names of fly fishing.

Waterfalls are naturally beautiful gifts of nature. They have the ability to exalt the mind and lift our spirits. Beaverkill Falls is notable in that it offers an impressive, vivid scene of great natural beauty and combines this harmony with some of the best trout fishing on the Beaverkill.

At times, large numbers of trout congregate at the falls pool, seemingly drawn there by the sound of the roaring water. More likely, though, what has happened is that trout migrating upstream find the falls an impassable barrier; and the plunge pool is so large, deep, and inviting that they choose to stay.

The Falls Lot is a 151-acre parcel also known as Lot No. 225 of Subdivision No. 3, Great Lot No. 6, of the Robertson Tract. The first recorded owner was Gulian Verplanck. Born in New York in 1698, Verplanck was a descendent of Dutch merchants and ship owners from New York and New Amsterdam. In 1741 he began investing heavily in the Hardenbergh Patent; and, when it was divided into Great Lots in 1749, Verplanck had acquired 281,000 acres, including Great Lot No. 6.

Upon his death, the greater part of his lands passed on to his two sons, Gulian and Samuel. In 1793, Samuel Verplanck sold to Alexander Robertson, a New York merchant, 35,000 acres of Great Lot No. 6, including the falls and thousands of adjoining acres.

Robertson subdivided the land into three parcels, conveying 8,138 acres to his son, John A. Robertson. This land was surveyed and divided into farm lots in 1809, with the falls being designated as Lot No. 225. These lands, like most of the lands in the Catskills, were steep and stony—generally poor for farming; and so they remained vacant, wild forest for many, many years.

In an attempt, perhaps, to lure others and develop the land, Alexander Robertson's two sons-in-law constructed homes along the Beaverkill. They were said to be men of wealth who were not accustomed to the rigors of life in the wilds. Eager to return to a more civilized environment, they sold their fine homes and their contents for almost nothing. The properties were acquired by Philo Flint and James Murdock, who turned them into celebrated trout-fishing resorts.

As fishing resorts became established along the Beaverkill in the 1840s and '50s, Beaverkill Falls became a special attraction not only for trout fishermen but for many visitors who found the falls, in its splendor, an inviting site where they could picnic or enjoy nature in an untamed setting.

What was it like to visit and fish the falls during this period? Let's look back in time and read the words of one early angler, who plied his skills in 1855:

> From thence, we went about one fourth of a mile through the woods, to what is called the high falls. A spot well known to many who visit this stream, as being one of its best fishing places. The falls are about thirty feet high, formed by irregular ledges of rock, receding as it rises, upon which the water falls successively until finally buried in the deep dark basin of water below. On the whole, a scene is here presented that the most fastidious novelist might envy. The mountains rise abruptly upon either side, presenting to the eye an unbroken wilderness. The entire stream in falling upon the rocks, is converted into a white foam, producing a noise that is almost deafening, and throws off a watery mist handsomely illustrating in miniature, the great Niagara.
>
> The rain had now ceased, and I was soon lost in contemplating the grandeur of the scene around me. Wild flowers bloom upon either bank in rich profusion, imparting their fragrance to every breeze that sweeps through the valley. Ever and anon, the joyous song of some feathered warbler near me, would mingle with the war of the

Beaverkill Falls.

waters, as he flitted from bough to bough among the giant hemlocks that skirt the banks of the stream, while a glance over the dark blue waters of the basin beneath the fall, discovered to the eye, numerous trout leaping from their watery element after flies that were skimming over its surface. Stopping short in my musings, I commenced fishing. As in imitation of the real, I drew my artificial fly lightly over the water. It was eagerly seized, and one fine trout after another, came floundering upon the bank near me.[1]

Historically, the fishing experience described above is important, since this Delaware County angler was certainly not fishing wet flies in the traditional style. His description borders on dry-fly fishing at a time when the method was not known or practiced in this country. He appears to be fishing one fly on top of the water. While he does not mention it, he most assuredly had to false cast or dry the fly in order to have it at or near the surface, especially after catching a trout.

In the years that followed, the Falls Lot, like other portions of the Beaverkill, was despoiled, its appearance debased by a sawmill and forest exploitation. In 1874, John and Robert Jones constructed a sawmill, dammed the water above the falls, and began manufacturing lumber, shingles, and wooden trays.

While the mill destroyed the scenic aspects of the falls and affected its trout resources, anglers still flocked to its waters. One of Beaverkill Falls' most dedicated users was the famous Ned Buntline.

Whenever his large American flag was flying at Tripp's, Ned was sure to be found fishing at the falls pool. It was his favorite, and he was a familiar figure there, standing midstream with his cherished Orvis, casting a pair of wet flies straight upstream into the foamy water at the base of the falls.

He liked to use a Coachman, Black Gnat, General Hooker, or Seth Green. However, if flies were not working, Ned would not be opposed to using worms and split shot to reach the large trout that lived in the depths of the "grand pool at the foot of the Big falls."[2]

The Jones brothers halted their mill operations in 1891, when they sold the Falls Lot and all of their stream holdings to Colonel Charles H. Odell.

Odell intended to make a trout preserve, and he began by constructing a summer residence he called Troutholme. The first trout fisherman to own the falls, Colonel Odell was determined

---

[1]*Bloomville Mirror,* July 17, 1855, p. 1.
[2]*The American Angler,* May 26, 1883, p. 327.

One of Colonel O'Dell's habitat-improvement structures, originally built using work oxen one hundred years ago.

to restore the fisheries. Under his stewardship, the Falls Lot began to recover from the effects of the mill and nearby forest degradation.

In 1892 he improved the fishery by stocking brown trout above the impassable waterfall and initiating a program of stream or habitat improvement. Colonel Odell employed Robert Jones, who had operated the sawmill for many years, to supervise the construction of in-stream structures of logs and stone.

Jones knew the power of the Beaverkill; he had seen the damage its high flows were capable of. The stream work, done with oxen, proved to have created the most durable and effective improvement structures placed in the Beaverkill. They were sensible, stable, long lasting, and not only pleasing to the eye but appealing to the trout as well. With only minor repairs, these structures have withstood countless floods and ice-outs, and they have lasted for more than a century—a remarkable achievement!

The next owners of record were the Snedecors: Jordon L., Abraham, and Eliphadeth. They were a family of fly fishermen, very much involved with every aspect of the sport, and were known socially by most of New York's large fly-fishing community. During the years the Snedecors owned the falls, one of their guests was the legendary Theodore Gordon. At the time, Gordon was using the dry fly but had not yet perfected his famous Quill Gordon. One thing is for certain, though: He made an impression on his hosts:

> J. L. Snedecor and his two sons owned for a number of years the famous high falls stretch of the Beaverkill (now the Jenny Henderson water) above Turnwood, and I remember Abram Snedecor telling me of Gordon stalking and catching a very large trout with one fly tied on the end of his leader and cocking it beautifully.[3]

In 1912, the Falls Lot changed hands, as the Snedecors sold their interests to Gifford A. Cochran, a famous yachtsman and wealthy Yonkers carpet manufacturer. Two years after acquiring the property, Cochran conveyed the falls to the Beaverkill Stream Club, which owned the adjoining downstream water.

Later that same year the Beaverkill Stream Club sold the falls back to Cochran, and in an obvious attempt to preserve Beaverkill Falls, placed a series of unique restrictions in the deed. In addition to barring every known form of manufacturing or establishment, the list protected the falls from "any place for public amusement, circus, theatre, menagerie, or other store of any description, or any trade business or calling whatever."

The deed restrictions further safeguarded the falls by not allowing the owner to "throw or allow to run into any waters in the premises herein conveyed and above described any dyestuffs, coal tar, refuse from a gas house, sawdust, shavings, tanbark, lime or other deleterious or poisonous substance whatever injurious to fish life."[4]

In 1921, Gifford Cochran relinquished title to the falls to Malcolm D. Whitman of Manhattan. During Whitman's tenure, the Falls Lot was leased, in 1954, to a small group of fly fishers who mostly came from Connecticut. Inspired by the finding of a framed card giving guest privileges to

---

[3]Guy R. Jenkins, "Theodore Gordon: Random Recollections," *American Trout Fishing,* by Theodore Gordon and a Company of Anglers, p. 25.
[4]Deed 449, Ulster County Clerk's Office, p. 436.

Theodore Gordon, the men decided to call themselves Quill Gordon Associates. The card was dated May 17, 1902, and had been used by Gordon while the Snedecors owned the falls.[5]

The Quill Gordon Associates' lease of the water ended in 1984, when the Whitman family sold the Falls Lot and its adjoining lands to Larry Rockefeller. The noted environmentalist added the property to his Beaverkill valley holdings. From 1749 to the present, a period of nearly 250 years, ownership of Beaverkill Falls has been limited to just seven families. It is comforting to know that the falls will be preserved, in its present state, for years to come.

---

[5]John D. Leggett Jr., "The Quill Gordon Water," *Anglers Club Bulletin,* Spring–Summer 1990, p. 22.

23

"Dancing Feather Creek"

Mongaup Creek may be the most beautiful and best-known tributary flowing into the Willowemoc. The stream flows out of Mongaup Pond and travels four miles through forest lands, entering the Willowemoc at DeBruce. Along the way, many large springs add their icy-cold waters, creating excellent habitat for native brook trout.

The stream begins at an elevation of 2,139 feet; at first, its gradient is rather moderate, but after a short distance the Mongaup descends rapidly, plummeting more than three hundred feet in the next two miles. Its swift current carries the stream through a series of cascades over solid bedrock, falling wildly, swirling and churning, agitating the water into a foaming, hissing body that culminates in a beautiful waterfalls encircled by emerald ferns, hemlocks, and moss-covered ledges. After the falls, the stream settles down and continues on its way at a more gentle, less hurried pace.

The Mongaup is an excellent trout stream, with good habitat and cold, clean, well-oxygenated water; its riffles and pools are capable of holding the largest trout. The stream's reputation as a fishing ground was founded during the earliest days of Catskill trout fishing, and its abundance of native brook trout caused anglers to stray from the Willowemoc and work their way up the Mongaup, assured that in doing so they would return with a heavy basket.

The naturalist John Burroughs fished its waters, and while he was enamored with the name of the Willowemoc, he found the Mongaup more productive: "When fishing in the Willowemoc, the beauty of that lovely stream's lovely name enhanced for him its charm: 'Thy name casts a spell upon me, Willowemoc, Willowemoc!'—but we take more trout from the Mongaup!"[1]

The stream's beauty and the abundance of trout attracted many fishermen and other pleasure seekers—too many, it seems, as early on local anglers fabricated a story to frighten away visitors. A tale was told of a huge panther, or mountain lion, that frequented the Mongaup in search of tourists; one story even went so far as to state that the monster panther was seen in the act of eating a fisherman!

At the beginning of the trouting season of 1882, the *Hancock Herald* reported:

The rapid descending waters of Dancing Feather Creek.

It is about time to hear something about that DeBruce panther. The animal generally puts in an appearance in April or May, just about the time the trout up the Mongaup are aching to be caught. The last time seen by a reliable correspondent up that way the animal had a pair of fishermen's boots dangling out of his mouth.[2]

In time, angling was restricted along the Mongaup, as its waters became private and individuals acquired large portions of the stream, turning them into fishing preserves. The first to establish private water was O. M. Cleveland of Newburgh, who purchased a couple of miles in 1895.

In 1922, Robertson Ward constructed a rustic fishing lodge and trout hatchery along its banks. Guests attracted to Ward's preserve included celebrities of the day, such as the famous world heavyweight champion Gene Tunney and Irvin S. Cobb, a noted American humorist, nov-

---

[1]Barrus, *The Life and Letters of John Burroughs,* p. 13.
[2]*Hancock Herald,* April 27, 1882, p. 2.

elist, and short-story writer. Both men enjoyed fishing and found the trout and pleasant scenery of the Mongaup much to their liking.

One other large landowner of note was John Karst, who moved to the Mongaup in 1907. Karst was the premier wood engraver of school texts in the country, and he enjoyed a nationwide reputation as an artist who raised the standard of textbook illustrations.

Considered a man of culture, he collected rare prints, old books, antiques, weapons, paintings, clocks, and historical furniture. His home was described as a museum, crammed full of priceless relics, including a number of books from the library of Henry Ward Beecher.

John Karst lived in retirement with his daughter Esther, and when he died in 1922, she inherited his estate. In the early 1930s, Esther Karst became embroiled in a controversy that caused a barrage of letters to appear in area newspapers. At issue was her desire to change the name of Mongaup Creek, an idea that incited not only local residents, summer residents, and former residents but even nonresidents.

Esther wrote to the *Livingston Manor Times,* suggesting the stream be renamed because it was confused with the Mongaup River, which had branches that began in the nearby town of Liberty. She invited readers to think of a new name.

A month later, the newspaper reported that the state historian recognized that "some change seems advisable" and suggested that interested readers who desired to submit new names should address the editor.

Esther Karst began to circulate a petition for the renaming and again urged readers to send in their suggestions. One of the first to write and object was Ada Cooper. Her grandfather had been a pioneer settler of the area, and for many years she had owned and operated the Homestead, a popular fishing resort at DeBruce.

> From the earliest days of De Bruce and vicinity, it has been known to sportsmen as Mongaup Creek.
>
> As long ago as when the fishermen came from Ellenville with three-seated buckboard wagons, before the O &W RR was built, it was known all over the country by sportsmen as Mongaup Creek, the outlet of Mongaup Pond.
>
> It grieves me, to think anyone would want to change the old Indian names which have come down from the history of the early days of this part of the country.
>
> Mongaup means "Dancing Feather." What better name could be selected.[3]

---

[3]*Livingston Manor Times,* February 1, 1934, p. 4.

Another letter, signed "A Lover of the Forests and Streams," favored a name change and even suggested Esther Creek, in honor of Miss Karst. This letter was followed by many others opposing a name change. A writer from New York City stated:

> To change the name now to a surname or nondescript female name would be most confusing; would lose this stream its identity among trout fishermen as a picturesque trout stream and would not be in keeping with the other Indian and historic names of the neighborhood.[4]

Esther retaliated with another letter in defense of her petition. She suggested calling the stream "Hunter Creek" or "Mountain Creek" and proposed that "as wild orchids have been found near it, the name Wild Orchid Creek would be appropriate."[5]

Another writer with an opposing view replied:

> It is difficult to understand how anyone can conceive of changing the name of one of the beautiful trout streams flowing through that valley.
>
> It is not difficult to imagine the soft shod Indian wandering through our woods and coming upon the babbling Mongaup and calling it by a name that its ripples suggest, despite the fact that another river many miles away is called by the same name. Certainly this is no argument to deprive that river of its beautiful name and us trout fishermen of something very near and dear to our hearts. We don't call it the Mongaup River nor the Mongaup Creek, but just plain "Mongaup."[6]

Esther Karst lost out on her bid to alter history and change the name of the Mongaup; and while she stirred up the ire of many, there was never any lasting ill will directed toward her. Indeed, in a circuitous way, her name is honored; she is remembered, perhaps immortalized, by the beautiful waterfalls of the Mongaup, which is still known today as Esther Falls.

---

[4] *Livingston Manor Times,* February 15, 1934, p. 4.
[5] *Livingston Manor Times,* March 1, 1934, p. 4.
[6] *Liberty Register,* March 8, 1934, p. 4.

© Ed Van Put

Esther Falls.

24

Acid Factories

Beaverkill anglers of the 1890s had a couple of reasons to celebrate. The stream and its tributaries were finally beginning to recover from the abuses of the fading tanning industry, and the introduction of brown trout was proving extremely successful. But any celebration was to be short-lived: Just as the tanneries were closing down, a new, larger, and even more destructive industry developed in the watershed.

Like the tanneries it, too, exploited the forest, fouled the air, polluted the water, and destroyed trout fisheries. This new industry was the manufacturing of chemicals from wood, by hardwood-distillation plants, known locally as "acid factories."

These forerunners of today's chemical industry were well suited to the Catskills. They required an abundance of hardwood, large quantities of water to cool their distillation machinery, and unskilled labor to harvest the forest and work in the plant.

There were many more acid factories than tanneries, and while the tanner laid waste to the hemlock, the acid men were not as selective and cut down whatever was standing. Thousands of acres of beech, birch, maple, oak, and chestnut were felled, cut, and split into four-foot lengths. Mountainsides were devastated by clear-cutting; a single plant consumed up to thirty cords of wood in a single day, and between five thousand and ten thousand cords per year. (One cord is a stack $4 \times 4 \times 8$ feet.)

Cordwood was placed in retorts, or ovens, and subjected to heat by a coal fire. Approximately 60 percent of the wood was converted into a liquid, called pyroligneous acid, from which wood alcohol, acetate of lime, and wood tars were obtained. Wood alcohol (methanol) was used as an antifreeze and solvent. The rest of the wood was reduced to charcoal, which was removed and sold.

The first plant appeared along a Trout Brook tributary, at Acidalia, in 1878. In time, as the industry grew, there were sixteen wood chemical plants operating in the Beaverkill watershed, with many being constructed during the 1890s. Along the Willowemoc, there were acid factories on Sprague Brook at Willowemoc, Livingston Manor, and Hazel, a tiny hamlet located between Roscoe and Livingston Manor. On the Beaverkill, factories were located at Cooks Falls, Horton, Elk Brook, and Peakville and along Spring Brook, Horton Brook, Russell Brook, and Trout Brook.

From the beginning, the wood chemical industry proved it was not compatible with trout streams. Reports of fish kills followed the construction of plants, and many people believed they caused more injury to trout fishing than the tanneries and sawmills ever did.

Fish kills became a regular occurrence downstream of virtually all acid factories. They generally occurred when streamside tar pits, or cesspools, which were filled with residue wastes such as insoluble wood tar, known as "oil of smoke," overflowed or leached into nearby waters. They were also caused by carelessness and incompetent laborers; valves were left open, and vats of acid overflowed into the stream. Some plants constantly discharged their lethal poisons directly into the stream and did not kill trout or other fish, simply because there were no trout or other fish life located below them; their wastes kept the stream permanently depleted of all aquatic life.

Streams below acid factories were smelly from their putrid discharges, and samples taken near them often recorded that the water contained "zero" oxygen. The bed of the stream generally contained a "vigorous growth of gray, slimy organic matter."[1] One angler who spent a week

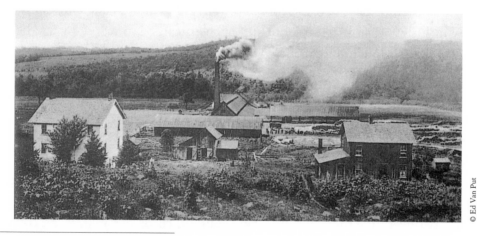

Willowemoc
Acid Factory.

© Ed Van Put

---

[1]*Liberty Register,* February 14, 1924, p. 4.

fishing the Beaverkill, in the area of Cooks Falls and its acid factories, complained bitterly of his lack of success in the pages of *Forest and Stream:*

> I caught a few California trout in the Russell brook about two miles above the Beaverkill River and ruined a pair of boots from the refuse of a wood alcohol factory that empties its chemical filth into, what otherwise has the natural condition for a good trout stream. The Beaverkill is a great stream for chubs, bass, wood alcohol and lemons.[2]

Prior to 1890, laws pertaining to pollution were relatively weak and rarely enforced. In 1892, however, a new law prohibiting pollution was passed:

> No dye-stuff, coal tar, refuse from gas houses, saw dust, shavings, tanbark, lime or other deleterious or poisonous substance shall be thrown or allowed to run into any of the waters of this State, either private or public, in quantities destructive to the life of, or disturbing the habits of fish inhabiting the same.

All mills and factories were given notice of the new law, and time to correct any discharge problems.

But the new law did little to halt pollution. Most of those discharging into streams continued to do so, as game protectors found it difficult to enforce laws of this nature. Fish kills were the most obvious evidence that deleterious or poisonous substances were dumped into the stream, but often by the time a game protector was notified, and drove the many miles by horse or wagon to the site, the fish kill would be over, and the discharge long gone.

Those who did undertake to sue acid factory owners met with stiff resistance. Factory owners were generally influential men who might ask, "Would you have us throw all these men out of work because we kill a few fish that some rich fisherman might otherwise catch?" Cases against them sometimes took years, as they would repeatedly be knocked off court calendars. When they were tried, the fines were so small that owners continued doing business as usual, as it was cheaper to run wastes into the streams, and kill fish, than to remove the cause of the pollution.

Letters deploring stream conditions in the vicinity of wood chemical plants appeared in local weekly newspapers and in sporting journals. A. Nelson Cheney, a state fish culturist, was appalled at conditions he found when he visited the Beaverkill, especially in the area of Spring Brook.

---

[2] *Forest and Stream,* September 1, 1906, p. 341.

Only a few years earlier a tank at the Spring Brook factory had burst, dumping acid into the Beaverkill, killing "a ton" of trout—by estimate, more than four thousand trout, of between 2 and 18 inches in length. In an article titled "Trout and Acids" Cheney let it be known that the state would discontinue stocking trout in any stream receiving acid factory wastes, and he reported:

> On a recent visit to the region of which I am writing, I found it infested with acid factories that were running their refuse into the streams and thus killing the fish.
>
> One of the factories was on Spring brook, one mile from the point where it empties into the Beaverkill, and the brook is two miles above the State hatchery. I sent a man to procure some of the water and put a trout of known size into it and note the result. He reported that a 6 inch trout placed in the bucket of water lived four minutes, and when I saw the sample of water, I was surprised that the fish lived as long as it did.[3]

The problems associated with the Spring Brook acid factory continued, and it was but a few years later that a veteran Beaverkill angler wrote to the local newspaper:

> I saw and smelt something that made me feel very sad, namely, the condition of Spring Brook. . . . It was covered with some stuff from the acid factory, making it full of soapy bubbles, and on getting out the smell was very perceptible all along the main stream. Is there no way to stop it? There are few enough fish in the river now, and if this continues there will be less.[4]

It continued, and six months later there were less, many less fish in the Beaverkill. In the middle of the spawning run, when adult trout moved up into Spring Brook, a chemical spill caused the stream to be strewn with dead fish. One man alone picked up twenty trout that weighed twenty pounds; every trout below the factory perished.

Writing in *Field & Stream,* the noted fly fisherman George M. L. La Branche deplored their stream-discharging practices:

> There is another condition over which no control is exercized, but which might and should be brought under strict regulation: I refer to the pollution of these waters.

---

[3]*Forest and Stream,* September 1, 1900, p. 166.
[4]*Sullivan County Review,* May 11, 1905, p. 1.

Chemical companies, or "acid factories," as they are called, pour their refuse into the stream in direct defiance or contempt of the law which is supposed to prohibit it. These men tell you, if remonstrated with, that running water purifies itself every hundred feet or so, which may be true, but not when sludge is incorporated with it—and trout are actually prevented from negotiating many stretches from this cause, which bars them from reaching the spawning beds in the fall. One day some courageous man will be placed at the head of the Forest, Fish and Game Commission, and these offences against public health and privilege will cease.[5]

But it was not just trout and streams that were the victims of the wood chemical industry. Thousands of acres of forest lands were sacrificed, as woodchoppers marched through, cutting virtually every tree greater than three inches in diameter. What they left behind looked like a wasteland, and the devastation caused by the clear-cutting did not go unnoticed.

In one of the most remote and heavily forested areas of the watershed, the Willowemoc correspondent to the Livingston Manor *Ensign* asked:

> What will this country look like in ten years from now if the axe and saw, six steam saw mills and an acid factory continue on in their destruction of our beautiful forests? To see the hillsides denuded and laid bare by the woodsmens axe spoiling the watersheds and drying up the streams and the damage done by freshets in time of heavy rains is a sad thing to many of us.[6]

And downriver, the editor of the Roscoe newspaper lamented on the same subject:

> The forests of the Town of Rockland are disappearing into the acid factory retorts of that town like water into a rat hole. Each factory is a whirlpool around which the forests are eddying in a constantly diminishing circle finally to forever disappear in its ever hungry vortex. . . . Surely the forests of Rockland cannot long service this careless demand.[7]

---

[5]*Field & Stream,* June 1912, p. 136.
[6]*The Ensign,* January 26, 1905, p. 7.
[7]*Sullivan County Review,* June 22, 1905, p. 2.

It was generally not profitable to haul wood long distances; acid factories harvested their wood from nearby areas. When their wood supply was exhausted, some factories were dismantled and moved to a new location, where wood was again abundant.

Just prior to World War I and the peak period of the industry, the Arthur Leighton Company announced plans to revolutionize the wood alcohol business by cutting thousands of acres at the headwaters and floating the logs down the Beaverkill to its factory at Elk Brook. Until this time, deforestation had taken place only in the immediate areas of the acid factories, and the upper Beaverkill had been spared massive clear-cutting.

The company owned more than eight thousand acres of timber along the headwaters of the Beaverkill and Willowemoc and intended to remove ten thousand cords of wood each year. The wood was to be cut and left to season in the woods; in the winter it would be hauled to the stream bank and piled; in the spring it would be floated downstream to Elk Brook, where a giant boom placed across the Beaverkill would catch it.

© The Wood Chemical Industry in the Delaware Valley

Weir stretching across the Beaverkill, constructed by the Arthur Leighton Co. to catch logs floated downriver from the headwaters.

156

In anticipation of its "inexhaustible supply" from the headwaters, the Leighton Company made a test run by floating a large quantity of logs from Roscoe downstream to Elk Brook. Even with a crew of men who followed along after the logs, freeing those that got washed on shore, the experiment met with only moderate success.

This, however, did not alter the company's plans to cut and float timber from the headwaters of the Beaverkill. In fact, they were halted only when stream owners became alarmed over the effect clear-cutting and floating logs would have on stream habitat and trout populations.

In an attempt to stop the acid men, landowners and clubmen united and obtained an injunction, restraining the Arthur Leighton Company from floating logs down the Beaverkill. This was the first major conflict in which trout fishermen joined their efforts in order to preserve the integrity of the Beaverkill. And while it may have involved a private portion of the stream, it was important to the preservation of the entire river.

The action was headed by the Beaverkill Stream Club, which owned four miles of the stream between Lew Beach and Turnwood. The club members were joined in their efforts by Gifford A. Cochran, who owned Beaverkill Falls, Jay Gould, the Salmo Fontinalis Club, and the Balsam Lake Club.

Reporting on the case on March 28, 1914, the *Walton Reporter* stated that the trout clubs believed that the Leighton Company had no right to use the Beaverkill to float logs, because it is not a navigable river, and that the logs would destroy stream banks, streamside vegetation, and trout habitat.

It was the Arthur Leighton Company's contention that state and federal laws allowed the public the right of navigation of all streams, that the Beaverkill was navigable, and that the company had the right to transport logs downriver but was not liable for any damage.

The Beaverkill Stream Club was granted a permanent injunction in the summer of 1915, and the Leighton Company took the case to the Appellate Division of the Supreme Court. On January 8, 1916, it was reported that the court unanimously affirmed the injunction.

The Arthur Leighton Company took the case to the Court of Appeals, which dismissed the appeal in favor of the Beaverkill Stream Club.

This was a long and costly fight, and while trout fishermen were victorious in keeping the wood chemical plants from destroying the habitat of the upper Beaverkill, the industry continued its destructive practices elsewhere in the watershed.

For more than seventy years (1878–1950), acid factories had a negative impact on the trout resources of the region. Due to the remoteness of some plants and the fact that most of the year no one was on the streams, it can be assumed that many fish kills went unreported. Fish kills and the ruination of trout habitat, though, were a large part of the history of the industry. Here are but a few samples of the effect it had on the watershed:

June 22, 1893: The *Hancock Herald* reports that the acid plant on Horton Brook spilled two hundred gallons of crude wood alcohol into the stream, killing hundreds of trout.

August 23, 1901: The *Liberty Register* reports that a game protector investigated a complaint of acid refuse flowing into the Willowemoc. "He found that from De Bruce to Willowemoc, about four miles, thousands of fish have been killed. In fact between the points mentioned no living thing had been left in the waters."

September 8, 1914: The *Narrowsburg Democrat* states, "The Luzerne factory has resumed operations after an idleness of over six months. As a result about 150 trout varying in size from 7 to 14 inches in length were picked up dead below the factory the next day after it started."

August 16, 1923: Two newspapers report on two separate fish kills on the Willowemoc. The *Liberty Register* reports, "Thousands of trout and other fish have died within the last week in the Willowemoc Creek above De Bruce." And the *Sullivan County Review* notes "many trout poisoned," as hundreds of fish were killed following the dumping of acid at Livingston Manor.

May 22, 1930: The *Livingston Manor Times* tells its readers that thousands of fish, mostly trout, were killed in Cattail Brook and Willowemoc Creek when an acid vat foamed over and a large amount of "buttermilk tar" escaped into the stream.

August 24, 1944: The *Sullivan County Democrat* reports a fish kill on the Beaverkill, below the acid factory at Horton.

Acid factory sites were often small communities within themselves. One site might contain horse barns, wagon sheds, blacksmiths, a woodworking shop, company houses, and a company store. Laborers at the plant were formed into three groups: factory men, teamsters, and woodchoppers. Factory men unloaded and piled the four-foot logs, fed the retorts, and sacked the charcoal. Teamsters brought the wood from the forest to the factory, in drays or wagons. Woodchoppers downed the trees, cut them, and split them into cordwood. They used a four-and-a-half-pound double-bladed ax, entered the woods at dawn, and did not leave the mountainsides until dark, when they returned to the factory settlement.

The work was hard and the hours long, and worst of all, there was no hope that conditions would improve. Acid factory workers often worked twelve hours a day, seven days a week, some for $1.60 per day! Most of the workers chewed tobacco to keep their throats moist in the acrid, smoke-filled factories.

As with the tanneries, the acid factories exploited not only the environment but the spirit and strength of the men as well:

> For the woodchopper there were no holidays, paid or otherwise. He had to keep
> the raw material—the wood—going to the factory. A blizzard might slow the tempo of

the rhythmic chopping of the cutters but the work went on as usual, for there were children to be fed and clothed—all on three to five dollars a week plus a shack to live in.[8]

Such low pay kept woodchoppers destitute; a Saturday night in town could take all of a worker's money. By Monday, he would be back at the company office seeking an advance to purchase groceries at the company store:

> Slavery was illegal in the country, and no acid factory owner ever asked the courts for the right and title to any of his workers. Instead, he ran the company store or commissary—ran it in such a manner that few workers would have a dollar left to take home after the store bill was deducted from their paltry pay. The workers were simple and so was the method. It kept overhead down and labor turnover to a minimum.[9]

It was said that woodchoppers could not afford to get sick; when one did and then did not appear at work the next day, his neighbors began to polish their boots in anticipation of a funeral.

The industry was always an up-and-down business; plants tended to overproduce, causing frequent shutdowns and closings. At times, acid factories deliberately overproduced; they would stockpile huge amounts of wood to create a surplus, then lay off woodchoppers and rehire them later at lower wages:

> The shutdown of the chemical factory at Willowemoc makes times dull in that vicinity. The company are not having any wood cut and have reduced wages all around to one dollar per day. Part of the men are working on the Pole road near De Bruce and part of them are hunting woodchucks, which are worth 50 cents fresh and 75 cents smoked.[10]

One of the peak periods of employment in the industry was due to the war in Europe in 1914; acetate of lime was used in the making of smokeless gunpowder, and there was a great demand for other products needed for the manufacture of explosives and for embalming. However, throughout the life of the industry, even in the good times, conditions for workers seemed never to improve. A series of articles appearing in local newspapers in 1935 revealed that even after thirty-five years of operation, life at the Hazel acid factory remained not much more than an existence.

---

[8]Gerow, *Alder Lake,* p. 13.
[9]Gerow, *Alder Lake,* p. 14.
[10]*Hancock Herald,* September 7, 1893, p. 2.

HAZEL FAMILIES IN DIRE STRAITS, read one headline; NEAR RIOT AMONG HAZEL ACID FACTORY EMPLOYEES, read another. The plight of the workers surfaced when a woman who had recently become a woodchopper's widow was taken to the hospital delirious from pain, suffering from malnutrition and blood poisoning. Welfare officials found the woman living in a primitive cabin, unable to care for herself or her young son. While making their investigation, they found other families running low on food.

One week later the *Roscoe-Rockland Review* reported:

> A near riot took place in town Saturday afternoon when a group of men recently
> employed at the Hazel factory came to town to get aid for themselves and families and
> insisted that they would remain here until aid was given. The welfare officer was called
> and orders for supplies were given the unfortunates who left town shortly afterward.[11]

Demand for the products of the wood chemical industry declined steadily as newer synthetic ones, equally good and cheaper to manufacture, came into existence. The plant at Livingston Manor halted operations in 1943, the Hazel plant in 1945. Undoubtedly, a cheer was heard up and down the river in 1950, as fishermen witnessed the last wisp of black smoke escaping from the factory at Horton.

© *The Wood Chemical Industry in the Delaware Valley*

Horton Acid Factory, one of many in the watershed. Note the pipe leading into the Beaverkill and the desecrated streambanks with tar pits next to the river.

---

[11]*Livingston Manor Times,* February 14, 1935, p. 1.

25

Fish Hatchery Folly

ROSCOE GETS IT, read the headline of the Livingston Manor *Ensign*. The weekly newspaper was referring to a new trout hatchery the state had decided to construct along the Beaverkill. Ever since 1889, when rumors of the hatchery surfaced, the two rival communities had worked hard at persuading the legislature to place the facility near their village. With a trout hatchery nearby, their streams would not be neglected; more fish in the stream, it was reasoned, meant more fishing tourists.

There were strong arguments made that a hatchery was needed in Sullivan County; its nearness to New York and its excellent, inexpensive railway accommodations brought trout fishermen to the Catskill streams in record numbers. The New York Ontario & Western had more than forty miles of streams contiguous to its line and employed a liberal policy of stocking them. The Fish Commission report for 1890 revealed that more than a million trout were placed in the streams of Delaware and Sullivan Counties, and the railroad alone had distributed 200,000 of them in nearby waters.

In March 1891, Assemblyman Beakes introduced a bill that stated:

> Section 1. The Commissioners of Fisheries are hereby authorized as soon as possible after the passage of this act, to erect a fish hatchery establishment at some conve-

nient point, to be selected by said Commissioners at such point on the "Willowemoc," in the County of Sullivan, in the State of New York, for the purpose of restocking the lakes and streams in that locality with trout and other fish, and stocking such other streams and lakes as the Commissioners may deem necessary.

Hardly had the bill been introduced when it was urged that it be amended to bring the hatchery nearer the railroad, making it more convenient to access. Any site chosen on the Willowemoc would place the hatchery near Livingston Manor; Roscoe, it was pointed out, was a better location.

Not wishing to get embroiled in a dispute over which community, Livingston Manor or Roscoe, should secure the hatchery, Assemblyman Beakes dropped his insistence on a Willowemoc site and amended the bill, leaving the selection of a hatchery location to the Fish Commission. Besides, it was reasoned, the commission had experience in such matters and was free of all local prejudices and, therefore, would choose the best possible site.

The Hatchery Bill was vetoed by Governor Flowers, who did not see the need for another state hatchery. Two years later, however, a similar bill introduced by Assemblyman U. S. Messiter of Liberty was signed, authorizing the construction of a hatchery in Sullivan County.

Once again, the issue of where it should be located caused division between the residents of Livingston Manor and Roscoe. Manor people claimed to have the best water on earth, and plenty of it. Roscoe countered that all the Manor water flowed through Roscoe and as much again flowed down the Beaverkill.

In August 1893, representatives of the state Fish Commission arrived at Livingston Manor, where they were met by a delegation of citizens who drove them to a location along the Willowemoc. While the site itself was considered excellent, water temperatures taken at several places were found to be 70 degrees Fahrenheit. The officials then proceeded to Roscoe and were met by a group representing the Roscoe-Rockland area.

Members of the Fish Commission made a point of telling everyone that great attention would be paid to the temperature of the water; this new hatchery, it was stated, had to be just right: "It will not be located in water that stands above 60 degrees and the volume must be such as will fill a 10 inch pipe under 10 foot pressure when the water is at its lowest."[1]

These officials, some of whom represented the Ontario & Western, arrived on the railroad president's private car. The Roscoe residents escorted them up the valley and urged that the hatchery be located on Darbee Brook, a low-gradient stream composed of large, unfailing springs. The

---

[1] *Walton Reporter,* August 5, 1893, p. 8.

water was clear and cold and suitable for trout; the water temperature was found to be 58 degrees. Though it was impossible to measure the flow, it was believed the stream did not contain sufficient volume.

The party then turned its attention to the Beaverkill, which was found to be 59 degrees and suitable for trout in every way. The reputation of the Beaverkill no doubt had some influence on its decision, as can be seen in its report to the legislature:

> In the opinion of many experts, men like W. C. Harris, of "The Angler," and others, the Beaverkill is the finest trout stream in the world. In a pool, partly formed by the dam before mentioned, your committee saw one school of at least 100 trout. These fish were in a very healthy condition and have an abundance of food. There is no doubt that at this point an abundant supply of the best possible trout water could be obtained.[2]

The site was again visited in November, this time by Commissioner Huntington, an employee of the Cold Spring Harbor hatchery, and railroad officials. They selected a 4¾-acre parcel adjoining the Beaverkill at the north end of the Rockland Flats, on the farm of Alonzo Dodge. The Ontario & Western contributed $200 toward the purchase price of the land, and the balance of $750 was paid by the citizens of Roscoe and Rockland.

That a poor site had been chosen became obvious almost immediately. During construction, in the summer of 1894, the hatchery was visited by members of the Fish Commission, who found the new buildings satisfactory but were dismayed and disappointed to find the Beaverkill at 80 degrees! Not only was the water too warm, but the twelve hundred feet of glazed sewer pipe bringing it from the stream to the hatchery leaked so badly that it had to be replaced.

When the facility was completed, it was officially designated the Beaverkill Hatchery, and Herbert E. Annin, who had worked for years at Caledonia, was named superintendent. He moved his family into the second story of the main building and began operations in January 1895. By the middle of the month more than a million eggs were on trays, including 150,000 lake trout and 100,000 brown trout; the balance were brook trout that had been taken from fish in the vicinity of the hatchery.

Applications began to arrive, and when the eggs were hatched, the trout fry were sent out to area streams. Hardly had these operations commenced when troubles were renewed; in April, a devastating flood overwhelmed the hatchery, killing thousands of trout.

---

[2]New York State Fisheries Commission, annual report, 1893, p. 288.

Unfortunately, the Beaverkill Hatchery's problems continued, as water temperatures this far downstream were often too warm. Only one year after operations began, the Fish Commission publicly admitted to the legislature, in its annual report, that the hatchery was having great difficulties with water temperature and flooding, and that maybe it should never have been constructed at its present location:

> Up to the first of April we had every reason to believe that this hatchery would turn out nearly a million fish of all kinds, but about the first of April occurred one of the worst freshets that had visited that section in twenty-five or thirty years, and the Beaver Kill River, from which the hatchery takes its water supply, rose beyond all precedent, so that the hatchery was completely surrounded. The troughs were filled nearly full with sediment, so that it took a full week for Foreman Annin and his assistants to separate the eggs and fry from the mass of dirt. This is liable to occur at any time, and it is with great reluctance that I send or gather any eggs for hatching to this hatchery. It is simply impractical to build any breeding ponds at this hatchery. During the spring they would be in danger of freshets, and the lay of the land is such that it would be almost impossible to guard against it. During the summer the temperature remains for weeks above the limit that would sustain trout life. It is very unfortunate that this hatchery was ever located where it is. To be a success, the location must be changed. There are sites within a short distance that are far better, and where spring water in abundant supply could be obtained to run the hatchery to its full capacity, and where I think sufficient could be obtained also to carry a number of stock fish.
>
> The people in this section have done everything in their power for this hatchery, but a large majority of them never favored the present location.[3]

As stated in the report, adult trout could not be raised in holding ponds; nor, for that matter, could trout fry be kept past the middle of May, or they would perish. Operations were soon limited to only seven months of the year. While continuing to stock large numbers of fry, the commission, in 1896, began a policy of distributing fingerlings and yearlings as well. This change was received favorably by the angling public, and from all over the state came encouraging reports of better fishing.

---

[3]New York State Fisheries, Game and Forest Commission, annual report, 1896, p. 70–71.

But this policy created more doubt about continuing operations at the Beaverkill Hatchery. In an attempt to increase production, a small spring was piped a quarter of a mile in, and about five thousand fingerlings were raised. This, too, failed, however, when the pipes froze and the project had to be abandoned.

The Fish Commission ceased operations in 1902 and leased the premises to private interests, who were also unsuccessful at running the hatchery. No one was more disappointed in the Beaverkill Hatchery's failure than the residents of Roscoe and Rockland. They had worked diligently to bring it to their area, believing the facility would become a real asset to their community. They had put their trust in public officials to select the proper site, and had even put up their own money to acquire it.

Finally, in 1904, less than ten years after it opened, the governor announced the abandonment of the Beaverkill Hatchery and signed a bill to permit its discontinuance. He then presented the building to the citizens of Rockland, who used horses to move it across fields to the main road, where it served for many years as the home of the Rockland Hose Company.

The last words written on the folly of the Beaverkill Hatchery were put forth in the *Middletown Mercury* by William Cairns, a popular columnist who wrote under the pen name of Rusticus:

> For some years before it was built, your humble servant worked hard for a fish hatchery at some point or other on the line of the O. & W.—I did not care where it was. The powers that were decided to locate on the Beaverkill River at Rockland. There was plenty of water to be sure as it was, and at times it was too plenty and the workmen and their families had to be taken out in boats. The whole thing was a failure, and a blind man could have told what would happen before the first shovelful of dirt was thrown out.
>
> Were it not for the fact that my old pen is about worn out it would make some who, in the past, were interested in the propagation of trout tremble. . . . In fact, the whole business of the State hatcheries is like its life insurance—more for the benefit of those who run it.[4]

The Beaverkill Hatchery was a sham from the very beginning, and while the people of Roscoe were deeply disappointed by the Fish Commission's bungling, the citizens of the Manor

---

[4]*Walton Reporter,* November 25, 1905, p. 2.

never gave up their quest for a hatchery. Though it would be many years before their efforts would be rewarded, one of the finest trout hatcheries in the state would be built on a Willowemoc tributary at DeBruce.

The story of this hatchery begins when Robertson S. Ward, a well-to-do sportsman from Newark, New Jersey, established the Willowemoc Creek Hatchery in 1928. Actually, Ward's facility was located along Mongaup Creek but kept the name of the location where it had begun operations downstream, at the present site of the DeBruce Fly Fishing Club.[5]

Along with his trout hatchery, Ward constructed a rustic fishing lodge, which he used as a summer residence. Though he raised trout only as a hobby, his establishment had a manager and was a profit-making business. The Willowemoc Creek Hatchery became well known not only for its picturesque surroundings but for the fact that it employed the latest scientific methods of breeding and raising trout.

Early in its operations, Ward adopted a policy of raising only brown trout, and every two years he purchased eggs from other sources so that new stock would prevent inbreeding. One of his largest customers for brown trout was the state of Pennsylvania, which stocked its waters with New York fish. He sold trout all over New York as well, to local private fishing clubs and to sportsmen's groups that stocked public waters.

During the 1920s, sportsmen in the region began to join together, forming clubs and organizations that would effectively pursue their special interests, especially with state legislators, who made laws pertaining to fish and game. Rod and gun clubs became the order of the day, and while both Livingston Manor and Roscoe-Rockland had such an organization, the most active and vocal was the Liberty Rod & Gun Club. A club with more rod than gun, it could boast of some very skilled anglers among its membership. Roy Steenrod was the president; other members included Rube Cross, William Chandler, and George W. Cooper, all of whom would find their way into the pages of fly-fishing literature.

---

[5]In 1903, Charles B. Ward, Robertson's brother, acquired the old tannery and acid factory flats along the Willowemoc, below DeBruce; and it was at this location that the Willowemoc Hatchery was formed. In 1918, he purchased the fishing-resort property of Elizabeth Royce (Hearthstone Inn), and the following year, he acquired the Homestead resort from Ada Cooper.

Ward consolidated these holdings into a 1,300-acre estate, which included 2½ to 3 miles of the Willowemoc and Mongaup. For many years, he operated a popular fishing hotel known as the DeBruce Club Inn.

In 1946, he sold his holdings to Walter Kocher; at present, the DeBruce Fly Fishing Club leases these waters from members of the Kocher family.

The Liberty Rod & Gun Club engaged in a variety of outdoor activities, including stocking streams and lakes, feeding deer during hard winters, and lobbying for changes in fish and game laws, public fishing, and the erection of a state hatchery in Sullivan County. Similar clubs cropped up in most small communities, while in some larger towns Izaak Walton League chapters were formed.

When Robertson Ward died in 1932, these organized sportsmen, resort and hotel owners, and local politicians made an all-out effort to have the state purchase the Willowemoc Creek Hatchery. They were joined by the *Livingston Manor Times* and the *Liberty Register,* which also saw the need and stated so in editorials: "It is a model facility, ideally situated for economic transportation," reported the *Times.*

The *Register* argued that increasing fishing pressure was emptying the famous trout waters of the region, forcing area sportsmen to stock the streams at their own expense, while trout from the Ward hatchery were shipped out of state to Pennsylvania.

In 1934, rumors surfaced of the state's interest in a site above Ward's hatchery, known as Toad Basin Spring, which was said to be one of the largest and best springs on the headwaters of the Beaverkill and Willowemoc. There was no move by the state to acquire the spring, or the Ward hatchery, and trout for area streams continued to be brought from the Rome hatchery, 150 miles away.

Times were changing. In 1935, the governor recommended to the legislature that they enact a law empowering the conservation commissioner to make regulations governing season and bag, or creel, limits in the taking of game and fish. A year later, the individual fish and game clubs united into a more politically powerful organization, which came to be known as the Sullivan County Federation of Sportsmen's Clubs. The federation, it was believed, would give outdoorsmen a louder voice in decisions made by a changing Conservation Department. It was also hoped that the sometimes duplicated efforts of clubs stocking the same stream could be avoided.

William Chandler became the federation's first president and immediately began calling for a hatchery in Sullivan County. His efforts intensified in 1937, when he was elected to the state assembly. For years, the federation, with Chandler as its president, pursued the idea of a state hatchery located near the famous trout streams of the county.

Finally, on July 16, 1946, the state took title to the Ward property, including all fish-hatching equipment; in addition, it also acquired, from George H. Treyz, 243 acres, including Toad Basin Spring. While the rearing ponds of the Ward hatchery would be utilized, the state also constructed a modern facility half a mile upstream. With its new ponds filled with brook and brown trout, the Catskill Mountain Fish Hatchery began operations in the fall of 1949.

The summer previous, the Division of Conservation Education had renovated the Ward buildings and begun operating a summer conservation education camp for boys, who were instructed by department experts in forestry, game management, fisheries biology, fire fighting, fly tying, casting, and the use of firearms.

26

From Sunken Fly to Floating Fly

The impact that brown trout had on the Beaverkill and other Catskill streams cannot be overstated; the fish reproduced and thrived, especially in the lower river environments, those sections too warm for native brook trout. These were the areas where silt and vegetative matter accumulated, where gradients were less, and where an abundance of aquatic insects could be found—particularly mayflies, including burrowers as well as those that preferred slower water. Here, insect life was much richer than upstream, where hatches were more varied but not nearly as plentiful.

Waters like the Beaverkill were known as excellent producers of surface-riding mayflies; now, the long, deep pools were full of rising trout, and trout fishermen soon observed that floating flies were needed. This coming together of brown trout and the magnificent mayfly hatches would change forever the way men would cast their flies.

During the 1890s and early 1900s, trout fishing changed significantly. Fly-fishing tackle improved, and a new angler was emerging. This new era saw fly rodders adopt the practice of using floating flies; and the Beaverkill and Willowemoc played a leading role in the development of dry-fly fishing in America.

Floating, or dry, flies were not unknown at the time, but their use was limited to but a few of the more knowledgeable fly fishermen. The technique of fishing a dry fly had its origin in England. While at a much earlier date flies were purposely floated on the surface to lure a wily trout, the English fly-fishing historian John Waller Hills has suggested that the invention of the dry fly was not complete until there was "intentional drying of the fly" (false casting). In his *A History of Fly Fishing for Trout,* Hills went on to state that the first mention of drying the fly occurred in 1851, and from this date on "the dry fly has a continuous history, but its use did not become common until 1860"—and even then, on but a few streams in the south of England.

In America, fly-fishing historians have long acknowledged that the first reference to fishing dry flies in this country appears in Thaddeus Norris's *The American Angler's Book* (1864), which described an incident on Willowemoc Creek. As will be seen, the incident described by Norris met Hill's criteria for dry-fly fishing. The flies were false cast for the purpose of "intentional drying of the fly":

> If it could be accomplished, the great desideration would be, to keep the line wet and the flies dry. I have seen anglers succeed so well in their efforts to do this . . . by whipping the moisture from their flies, that the stretcher and dropper would fall so lightly, and remain so long on the surface, that a fish would rise and deliberately take the fly before it sank.
>
> One instance of this kind is fresh in my memory: it occurred at a pool beneath the fall of a dam on the Williwemock, at a low stage of water—none running over. The fish were shy and refused every fly I offered them, when my friend put on a Grannom for a stretcher, and a minute Jenny Spinner for a dropper. His leader was of the finest gut and his flies fresh, and by cracking the moisture from them between each throw, he would lay them so lightly on the glassy surface, that a brace of Trout would take them at almost every cast, and before they sank or were drawn away. He had tied these flies and made his whip especially for his evening cast on this pool, and as the fish would not notice mine, I was obliged to content myself with landing his fish, which in a half hour counted several dozen. Here was an exemplification of the advantage of keeping one's flies dry. . . .[1]

---

[1] The experience described by Norris most likely took place behind Cottage Street, in Roscoe, near the mouth of Stewart Brook, at the site of the old Cochran & Appley tannery dam.

Thaddeus Norris informed his readers of a very useful tactic—and undoubtedly, anglers did, on occasion, employ his lesson; however, it was many years before Americans would take dry-fly fishing seriously, and not until the establishment of brown trout.

In England its popularity soared when Frederick M. Halford became a militant advocate of the dry fly and wrote extensively of its use during the late 1880s. Halford fished and studied the entomology of aquatic-insect-rich English chalk streams: waters that were low-gradient and slow flowing and waters with stable flows, weed beds, and flat glassy surfaces. On these streams, fly fishermen did not enter the water but cast from the stream banks at individual rising trout.

Halford stressed exact imitation of the natural insect and made a series of dry-fly patterns. He copied the major hatches occurring on the waters he fished, paying strict attention to form, size, and color. He was devoted to perfecting and improving dry-fly fishing and is credited with establishing the dry fly as we know it today.

In 1886 he produced *Floating Flies and How to Dress Them* and in 1889, *Dry-Fly Fishing in Theory and Practice*. These two books were instrumental in spreading the practice of dry-fly fishing beyond England, to other countries around the world and, importantly, to America.

Theodore Gordon at age thirty-one.

© *New York Herald Tribune, April 1, 1964*

In this country, one of the first to take a serious look at dry-fly fishing was Theodore Gordon. Introduced to fly fishing at a very young age, Gordon maintained a lifelong love of the sport. He studied *The American Angler's Book* and, from Norris, learned the fundamentals of fly tying while only thirteen.

He became an ardent and expert fly fisherman, fly tier, and fishing journalist. Theodore Gordon was one of those individuals who possessed that rare combination of being a good angler as well as a good writer. His writings first appeared in 1890, in England, in the *Fishing Gazette,* edited by R. B. Marston. In 1902, he began contributing articles to *Forest and Stream,* and he wrote for both publications until his death in 1915.

While he did, at times, write articles on hunting, Gordon wrote primarily about the habits and preferences of trout, tackle, flies, techniques, and tactics. He had great powers of observation and description, and he wrote intelligently. He was well known as an authority on fly fishing throughout this country and England, and he was greatly admired by those who read his work. Theodore Gordon was as knowledgeable an angler as any of his generation, yet his writing was neither pretentious nor boastful.

171

Born in Pittsburgh, Pennsylvania, on September 18, 1854, Theodore Gordon learned to fish on the trout waters of that state. However, his favorite streams were in the Catskills, and he spent the greater part of thirty-five years on or near the Beaverkill, Esopus, Neversink, and Willowemoc. He was fishing these streams as a very young man in the 1870s, and he spent the last years of his life along the banks of the Neversink, in Sullivan County. It was on these streams that he experimented with floating flies, and he shared with his readers his personal experiences and his love of the Catskills.

Gordon first became interested in dry flies soon after Halford published *Floating Flies and How to Dress Them*. In 1889 or '90 he imported an English rod, line, dry flies, and fine silkworm gut and began corresponding with Frederick Halford. In 1890 he received from Halford an assortment of forty-eight dry-fly patterns; Halford urged him to use them and to determine which worked best on American waters.

Most Americans were slow to adopt dry flies; they associated their use with those conditions found on placid English chalk streams. In this country, the more popular trout waters were mountain streams of rapid descent, with conditions, they reasoned, that favored wet flies. When some of the better American fly fishermen did begin to take up the dry fly, they limited its use to summer, when the water was low and clear, with conditions closer to those found on English chalk streams.

R. B. Marston made a selection of the best English flies and sent them to Gordon; and for a few years, Gordon carried fifteen dozen dry-fly patterns, trying them whenever he saw a good trout rising. He adopted the English tradition of fishing only to trout rising to natural insects, and while he found the English rod and line unnecessarily heavy and tiring, he did catch a few trout.

After a while, his enthusiasm began to wane; until an incident occurred that renewed his interest:

> I had been fishing the rapids up stream with two flies when I came upon a fine reach of smooth, gliding waters, and sat down at the tail end to smoke a pipe and rest. While sitting there I spotted three good trout rising at the lower end of the pool, and taking off the stretcher fly, replaced it with a small floater. I did not bother to remove the dropper, which happened to be a favorite fly of my own tying. Changing the tail fly occupied a few minutes and in approaching the fish I naturally kept the flies in the air by a series of false casts. These dried the dropper so much that it floated quite as well as the orthodox dry fly, and the result was that all three trout rose at it and were killed one after another. It seemed that they moved out of position to get it, and passed by the tail fly. This was an eye opener. It showed that a good wet fly pattern, if properly

172

dressed with sufficient hackle was also a good dry fly pattern, and that my own flies could be made to float well. This gave me a great start and added interest to the floating fly.[2]

Halford was dogmatic about exact imitation, and until this experience Gordon had been trying to match English flies to American naturals. The fact that all three trout passed on the English fly and took his floating wet fly proved to Gordon that he need not be so dependent on English imitations. Now, with his interest renewed, he began tying and experimenting with dry-fly patterns he designed to imitate the more abundant hatches he found on Catskill streams.

During the 1890s Theodore Gordon spoke at angling club dinners on the merits of the dry fly. And while he may not have been alone in his promotion of dry-fly fishing, very little was written on the subject in American sporting publications. The few articles that did mention fishing with dry flies generally referred to it as an English method, not practiced, to any extent, on this side of the Atlantic.

In fact, as late as 1898, the noted angling author and fish culturist Fred Mather stated, "In America as far as I know dry fly-fishing is not practiced." He went on to describe its use in England and summed up the feelings of the majority of American anglers at the time when he wrote, "Somehow the dry fly has not tempted me to try it. It looks like hard work to little purpose and where I fish there seems to be no necessity for it."[3]

Gordon did not view dry-fly fishing as particularly difficult; nor, for that matter, did he see its use as a radical development in fly fishing:

> If you have fished up stream on a low, clear water with a single fly, or even two, you have practically put in practice about all you will require in dry-fly fishing, except guarding against the drag. You have not dried and floated your fly, otherwise the difference in method is not extraordinary. No great revolution in fishing.[4]

Through his writings, Theodore Gordon encouraged others to adopt the dry fly as a part of their fly-fishing tactics. From 1906 on he gave explicit and accurate instructions on dry-fly fishing in the pages of *Forest and Stream* and was recognized as this country's leading authority on its use.

---

[2]*Forest and Stream,* April 27, 1912, p. 529–530.
[3]*Forest and Stream,* April 16, 1898, p. 809.
[4]*Forest and Stream,* April 27, 1912, p. 530.

Yet the dry fly continued to have few American advocates. Some still believed floating flies were meant to be used only on slow, clear, placid streams with smooth, flowing waters. Others were waiting for someone to identify American trout-stream insects and devise exact imitations of them, as Halford had done for English streams.

Royal Coachman dry fly, tied
by Theodore Gordon.

Another early advocate of the floating fly was Emlyn M. Gill, who in 1911 wrote a series of introductory articles on dry-fly fishing for *Field & Stream*. In 1912 he produced *Practical Dry-Fly Fishing*. Just as Norris had enshrined Willowemoc Creek with his early references to dry-fly fishing, so, too, would Gill celebrate its waters in the first American book devoted to the subject.

Gill began using floating flies in 1905 or 1906 and became an expert angler, learning his skills fishing Willowemoc Creek. Writing fondly of his Willowemoc experiences, he modified the methods of the English purist to fit the different conditions found on American streams. He advised readers to fish fast water as well as pools, and he gave concise, accurate information about dry-fly fishing. His well-written book also urged readers to carry a little "bug net" and copy the natural with an "artificial counterpart" from their fly box. At this time, the vast majority of dry flies sold commercially were imported English patterns.

In June 1912, the *New York Times* published a full-page article titled "Veteran Angler Urges Dry Fly Fishing in America." Complete with photographs of Emlyn Gill, the piece began with the question, "What is dry-fly fishing?"—an obvious indication that the method was still relatively unknown.

Gill was quoted throughout the article, giving his opinions and advice on technique, definitions, flies, and so on. He advocated the use of dry flies and urged Americans to adopt the English method.

While the article concentrated on the merits of the floating fly, Gill deviated from the subject with a noteworthy comment on releasing trout. He persuasively told fellow anglers:

> He alone deserves the title of sportsman who returns carefully to the water all
> trout that he does not need for food; as soon as the fish is taken into the net, all the sport

to be had with that particular fish is over, and when killed and put into the creel it has become simply meat.[5]

A second book on the dry fly appeared a year later. In 1913, the Outing Publishing Company produced *Fishing with Floating Flies,* by Samuel G. Camp. Yet visitors to tackle shops in New York were still being openly advised that dry-fly fishing was a fad, "destined to pass quickly."[6]

George M. L. La Branche was another early dry-fly advocate. In 1914, Charles Scribner's Sons published his *The Dry Fly and Fast Water*—the book that finally provided the spark that ignited interest in dry-fly fishing.

© *Forest and Stream,* Oct. 20, 1906

George M. L. La Branche.

La Branche, who began using the dry fly in 1899, was an excellent fly fisherman. He prided himself on casting accuracy and fly presentation, and he was known as a champion caster who participated in fly-casting tournaments.

One of his trademarks when fishing was his "meticulously well groomed appearance on the stream."[7] While he fished extensively on the Beaverkill and was, at one time, a member of the Beaverkill Trout Club and the Balsam Lake Club, he was familiar with all Catskill streams and knew the waters of Kaaterskill Creek equally as well as the Callicoon or the Neversink. However, it was along the Willowemoc that he honed his skills, and once again this tributary of the Beaverkill was the focus of early dry-fly experiments.

La Branche began writing about dry-fly fishing before Emlyn Gill. In an article titled "The Evolution of a Dry Fly Fisherman" (1904), he related to his readers how he first tried a floating fly on the Willowemoc, on a pool formed where Mongaup Creek enters the stream.

He "doctored" a wet Beaverkill into an imitation of a dry fly by tying the wings upright and, on his very first cast, delightedly caught a foot-long rainbow! In thirty minutes of fishing, he managed to net four trout, all between 12 and 14 inches—three rainbows and one "native" trout.

---

[5]*New York Times,* June 9, 1912, p. 14.
[6]*New York Times,* July 6, 1913, p. 9.
[7]Ives, *Seventeen Famous Outdoorsmen,* p. 28.

In 1912, La Branche also wrote a series of articles for *Field & Stream,* titled "The Dry Fly in America." The articles were a prelude to his book, and in them he reminisced about his favorite pool on the Willowemoc:

> The Junction Pool, the meeting of the waters of the Willowemoc and Mongaup, a beautiful spot, and one famous among fly fishers—to me, it is the loveliest water in the whole world, not alone because it is beautiful, not because it holds many fine fish, nor because I have taken many fine fish from it; but on this very water, though it has changed in character since that day many years ago, I rose my first fish to a floating fly.[8]

La Branche fishing the dry fly on the Willowemoc.

© Recreation, July 1909

[8]*Field & Stream,* June 1912, p. 133.

When he first began experimenting with dry flies, George La Branche, like others, believed they could only be used successfully on smooth, slow water. He used them only on water he believed Halford would approve, and he cast only to rising trout. Through experience, though, he learned dry flies could be fished on any part of swift-flowing streams. However, he remained uncomfortable doing so, being very much influenced by English writers, who insisted it was "practically impossible" to fish dry on mountain streams: "It seemed to me that by continuing to use the dry fly on them I was profaning the creed of authority and inviting the wrath of his gods upon my head."[9]

He continued to apply the dry fly to Catskill streams and, in addition, abandoned the idea of fishing only to rising trout. He was a true "presentationist," believing he could get by the whole season with just a few patterns. In fact, he became known for his ability to *make* a trout rise by creating an "artificial hatch." This he did by repeatedly casting a floating fly flawlessly, without drag, where he expected a good trout to be.

After he had fished one of the more famous chalk streams of England, the *Fishing Gazette* praised his casting skills:

> His fishing is smooth and entirely effortless, line, cast and fly all under perfect control of brain, eye, muscle and sinew, in the air as well as in the water.
>
> His flies go where he wishes them to go and act as he directs them when they get there. Briefly, Mr. La Branche is a very beautiful fisherman.[10]

While La Branche disagreed with his English mentors on where and when to use the dry fly, he did choose to abandon the wet fly altogether. In England, Halford and his followers had adopted the dry fly to the exclusion of all others, and Halford believed "that those who thought otherwise were either ignorant or incompetent."[11]

George La Branche knew Theodore Gordon; they corresponded and saw one another socially on occasion. Reviewing *The Dry Fly and Fast Water,* Gordon wrote:

> I know Mr. La Branche by reputation, and his ideals are high. He fishes the floating fly only, and kills a few of the largest trout. All the rest are returned to the water.

---

[9]La Branche, *The Dry Fly and Fast Water,* p. 8.
[10]Ives, *Seventeen Famous Outdoorsmen,* p. 24.
[11]Hills, *A History of Fly Fishing for Trout,* p. 131.

His point of view is original, and there is not a dull page in this book. He has no great faith in the imitation of the natural insects and gives a very short list of artificial flies.[12]

La Branche was an excellent fly fisherman who saw little value in exact imitation. He proved to American anglers that they need not be locked to English traditions, especially about where and when to fish a dry fly; and the theory that to be successful with dry flies one had to use an exact imitation of the natural.

In *The Dry Fly and Fast Water,* he stated, "I give the dressing of eight patterns, although I rarely use over six. If I were compelled to do so, I could get along very well with one—The Whirling Dun."

While Gordon, Gill, and La Branche were pioneers in the use of the dry fly, and while all three encouraged others, through their writings, to adopt the method, it was Theodore Gordon who was at the forefront of developing America's dry flies.

---

[12]*Forest and Stream,* June 27, 1914, p. 858.

27

Catskill Style

Until the late 1800s, Americans generally fished with English flies—flies that were not imitations of the aquatic insects found in this country. Most were imported, but even those tied here professionally were copied from English patterns. For many years, the best tiers in New York and Philadelphia were former Englishmen and Irishmen.

It was not uncommon for American anglers who did not know the name of an English pattern to rename the fly; even the famous Beaverkill, a fly archetypically American, was of English origin. Some flies were tied anew with alterations, a good example being the Royal Coachman. First tied in 1878, by John Haily of New York, it is a modification of the well-known English Coachman.

The first tied standard American trout flies were wet-fly patterns, classified as "fancy flies." They became popular in the 1880s and employed various color combinations aimed at capturing the eye of the purchaser. A few of the better-known patterns were named Rube Wood, Holberton, Abbey, Imbrie, and Seth Green; as can be seen, they appealed not only to the eye but to the vanity of anglers as well.

One of the most popular early wet flies was the Parmachene Belle, tied prior to 1885 specifically for the large brook trout then found in Maine. Flies tied for Adirondack waters were equally gay, brilliant patterns. Since these flies were not imitations of any natural insects, they were considered "lures." They were, nonetheless, effective at taking native brook trout, which seemed to have a preference for bright, gaudy flies.

With the advent of brown trout and dry-fly fishing, patterns changed dramatically. Fancy flies gave way to a more impressionistic interpretation of the naturals found along trout streams. During the 1890s, when the attention of fly fishermen became focused on surface or floating flies, Theodore Gordon began creating America's earliest dry-fly patterns.

Gordon learned to tie flies as a youngster, through the pages of *The American Angler's Book*. His knowledge of the craft grew as he read everything pertaining to fly tying he could lay his hands on. As an adult, he dissected English floating flies, purchasing dozens from Holland & Son, master fly tiers, who were the first to dress all of Halford's patterns. He learned all of the methods described by Halford in *Floating Flies and How to Dress Them*.

Gordon became a skilled and innovative fly tier; shortly after learning about the dry fly, he began imitating the natural flies he found along Catskill streams. Writing on his success during the 1889 season, *Forest and Stream* reported:

Trout Valley Farm.

He thinks that we are all wrong on the subject of artificial flies, and believes we ought to discard various foreign fancy patterns, and copy our own natural insects and flies as closely as possible. He carries out his theory in practice. On the Neversink last season no one brought in better baskets of trout than Mr. Gordon whether they used fly or bait.[1]

On the Beaverkill, one of his favorite stretches was the water around the hamlet of Beaverkill, where he stayed at Jay Davidson's Trout Valley Farm.[2] Being an excellent observer, he often tied at streamside, creating imitations of the hatches found there.

---

[1] *Forest and Stream,* November 27, 1890, p. 877.

[2] Trout Valley Farm was one of the most famous fishing resorts on the Beaverkill. It opened its doors in 1887 and catered to fishing guests for the next seventy-six years. Jay Davidson sold his interest in 1922 to Fred Banks, who successfully ran the resort until 1963, when the property was purchased by the state of New York; it is now a part of the Beaverkill Campgrounds.

While he did tie copies of naturals, he was not an exact imitationist. He preferred using a number of patterns that were typical of certain species: "By making them a little darker or lighter in color one is able to cover any fly of that species."[3]

A fly that typified his belief was the Quill Gordon, one of the first and finest purely American dry flies ever conceived. He first tied it in 1903, and from the beginning he made Quill Gordons in three different shades, ranging from a silvery water color to a dark smoky blue dun. Gordon did not tie the fly to imitate one specific hatch but dressed it to represent a variety of early-season blue-gray flies. He was adamant in his belief that size and color were the two most important requisites of a successful fly.

He acknowledged that the Quill Gordon was a troublesome fly because of the rarity of the dun hackle required to tie it. As with professionals today, he was very particular about the color and quality of the dry-fly hackle; and he experienced, early on, the problems associated with obtaining it: "No one but a fly-maker can realize the difficulty in getting hackles fit for trout flies. Not one cock in twenty is worth examining."[4]

He, like other fly tiers who would come after him, believed the best way to obtain the elusive dun shades, so necessary in tying his favorite patterns, was to raise the roosters himself. He did so on a friend's nearby farm, learning the crossbreeding methods necessary to produce blue dun hackle.

Gordon was a highly original fly tier who had a major influence on American fly tying. His flies differed greatly from English flies, which tended to be overdressed and, to Gordon's displeasure, often incorporated soft hen hackles. He favored using cock hackles, which had less web to absorb water as well as stiffer fibers, which enabled the fly to ride the surface film more buoyantly. He learned that flies tied sparser floated better and were more killing than those with a bushy appearance. While he did, at times, tie his wood duck wings in a solid upright position, he is best known for splitting the wings and securing them with a figure eight, to make them cock and float better. Theodore Gordon created what came to be known as "Catskill style." Years later, his contribution to fly tying was noted by Catskill fly tier Harry Darbee:

> He actually changed the anatomy of the fly. He set the wings with the butts toward the rear and placed his hackle at right angles to the hook. He was smart enough to use nonabsorbent materials, which made a big difference. English dry flies at the time were nothing more than modified wets.[5]

---

[3]Letter from Gordon to Steven Wager, August 15, 1913.
[4]*Forest and Stream,* March 14, 1903, p. 212.
[5]McClane, A. J. "Feather Merchant," *Field & Stream,* July 1955, p. 36.

Gordon created the first American dry-fly patterns accepted as standards. He purposely created a style of dry fly that would float in the rapid, descending streams found in the Catskills. His unique style propelled the craft into an art form that became regional, and his disciples were set apart from the rest and known as the Catskill School of fly tiers.

A Catskill-style fly has a generally sparse appearance; a fine, tapered body of spun fur or quill; a perfectly matched, divided wing of wood duck flank feathers; and a sparse, incredibly stiff, glossy cock hackle—most often, blue dun or ginger, in various shades. The tails of Catskill-style flies were tied with wood duck, and were tied at an upward angle to the hook shank. Later, they were replaced by stiff hackle barbules, tied evenly with the hook shank, to support the fly in the surface film.

It has been alleged by some present-day writers that Theodore Gordon was secretive about his fly tying; yet far more evidence exists to the contrary.

First of all, the very idea or concept of fly-tying "secrets" is highly overrated. There are certain basics of fly tying that, once learned, apply to all flies. Tying can be, and often is, learned from books; and books describing the art have been around for centuries. Second, fly makers need only look at a pattern to make a reasonable assessment of the materials needed to copy it. Additionally, one can easily take apart—as Gordon did—the work of others to determine how the fly was constructed.

What makes one person's flies superior to another's is often that person's inherent skills or craftsmanship—nothing secret, just the ability to use materials and do the job more skillfully. The dressing of a pattern may be a secret, but a fly tier with experience can determine, within reason, the materials used to make a particular fly.

In his letters and articles, Theodore Gordon often described his tying techniques and gave the dressings for his favorite patterns. When the firm of William Mills & Son had difficulty copying his popular Quill Gordon, he sent it samples of the fly—hardly the course of a man who was secretive.

It is also a fact that Theodore Gordon's very nature was that of a kind and giving man. His friends were frequently given gifts of flies, materials, hard-to-get fishing items, and, on occasion, even a quality fly rod. The famous English angler G. E. M. Skues said of Gordon, "I think he must have been one of the most generous of men, for seldom did I have a letter from him that had not some little gift in it. . . ."[6]

---

[6]McDonald, *The Complete Fly Fisherman,* p. 547.

Theodore Gordon spent the last ten years of his life in the Catskills. He stayed year-round at modest boardinghouses and fishing resorts, mostly in or near the village of Neversink. He died on May 1, 1915, at the age of sixty, while boarding at Anson Knight's farmhouse, overlooking the river he loved.

Gordon had devoted a lifetime to the sport of fly fishing, and in his day he was its most beloved authority. He wrote about fly fishing for more than twenty-five years, and he was widely read not only in this country but in England as well. He made the Beaverkill a familiar stream to English fly fishermen, who read Gordon's praise of the stream in the *Fishing Gazette*.

"Beloved" is truly the proper term to apply to the man, for he had a following unequaled in the realm of fly fishing. As a writer, Theodore Gordon had a unique ability to endear himself to his readers. Upon his death, the highest praises came from those who read his work; they took his passing as a personal loss and said so, in letters to *Forest and Stream:*

> Mr. Gordon was unknown to me personally. His writings were his means of keeping me interested and filled with pleasure, and pleasure of the righteous and noble sort. Those who knew him intimately in life have lost much indeed for there can be little doubt as to the fact that he was a figure of endearing charm as much personally, as was shown in his writings.[7]

And another angler who had never met Gordon but was saddened by his death wrote:

> If it be sometimes true, according to Mark Anthony, that "the evil that men do lives after them, the good is oft interred with their bones," it is also true, and on higher than Shakespearian authority, that the good that men do "follow after them." Theodore Gordon is dead, but he left behind him a legacy worthy of our highest and long continued appreciation.
>
> So farewell, Brother Gordon. Our admiration and affection goes with him, and when on the streams he loved so well and with such skill portrayed the "gentle art," we will think of him.[8]

---

[7]Robert Page Lincoln, "An Appreciation of Theodore Gordon," *Forest and Stream,* October 1915, p. 607.
[8]Charles D. Davis, "In Memory of Theodore Gordon," *Forest and Stream,* November 1915, p. 676.

As a tribute to the relationship Gordon had with his readers, the editors at *Forest and Stream* extracted from their files previously unpublished manuscripts, dusted them off, and printed them, years after his death.

One of the last articles he wrote "dealt with the subject near to his heart—the fishing of the future." Titled "Good Fishing Near Large Cities," the article was about one of Gordon's "pet projects." He encouraged New York officials to allow public fishing on the newly completed New York City reservoir at Ashokan. He urged that the new body of water be made into a trout lake and that the city, if necessary, sell seasonal "fishing tickets":

> We must do all that we can to maintain free trout fishing in our streams, but this new lake affords an extraordinary opportunity to bless the everyday hard working man. The small salaried man and the workman can take a day off now and then, and the value of the fish taken will, by supplying his family with a perfect food fish, defray the cost of his railway and fishing tickets.[9]

There were not many unpublished articles in the files, but *Forest and Stream* got the most from what they had, publishing the last, titled "Some Trout Fishing Memories," in March 1921! This may have been the last written word by Theodore Gordon, but his spirit and memory were kept alive by disciples who continued tying his unique flies and using his tying style.

Fly fishermen learned quickly, through the pages of *Streamcraft* (1919), by George Parker Holden, that they could still obtain flies tied in the Gordon style. In the late 1890s, Holden lived and practiced medicine in Kingston. In addition to being an avid fly fisherman, he had been a customer of Gordon's, and he delighted in telling his readers:

> While no one may fill Theodore Gordon's unique place as a writer specially beloved of all American anglers, the reader may be interested to learn that flies tied in the exquisite Gordon fashion are still obtainable from Gordon's friend and neighbor, Mr. H. B. Christian of Neversink, N.Y. Mr. Roy Steenrod of Liberty, N.Y. likewise is familiar with the patterns, and we understand that to those gentlemen was bequeathed the bulk of Gordon's tying materials.[10]

---

[9]*Forest and Stream,* December 1916, p. 1238.
[10]Holden, *Streamcraft,* p. 112.

Featured on the pages of *Streamcraft* is a black-and-white photo of a Quill Gordon tied by Herman Christian. *Streamcraft* became a favorite of many, and the informative little book included good, practical information on tackle, fly casting, trout habits, stream entomology, and fly tying. It also contained drawings of aquatic insects by Louis Rhead and attractive color plates of flies tied by William Mills & Son of New York, including a few of the earliest American dry flies.

Holden had met Theodore Gordon the summer before his death and considered him a "super angler." *Streamcraft* was the first book to praise Theodore Gordon and his contributions to American fly fishing.

Although Theodore Gordon tied and created flies along the banks of the Beaverkill, he was not the first professional tier to do so. The earliest professional fly tier of note to live in the Beaverkill watershed was a blacksmith from DeBruce by the name of George W. Cooper (1859–1932). Cooper was born in Napanoch, Ulster County, and when he was but six weeks old his parents, Mathias and Elizabeth Cooper, traveled the bridle paths through the forest and settled at what is now DeBruce. They were one of the first families to settle in that area, and it was truly a wilderness.

Just three years earlier, in 1856, Cooper's grandfather had built the Hammond & Benedict tannery nearby, along Willowemoc Creek. The little settlement grew, and George Cooper became the village blacksmith. His shop was located along Mongaup Creek, a short distance from its famous junction with the Willowemoc.

As the tanning industry began fading out of existence in the late 1880s, the citizens of DeBruce focused on trout fishing and summer tourists. George Cooper enlarged his blacksmith operation to include a post office and general store, in which, for many years, he sold flies, baskets, boots, and fishing tackle.

His two sisters, Ada Cooper and Elizabeth Royce, became pioneer summer boardinghouse keepers. They owned and operated two of the best-known trout-fishing resorts on the Willowemoc, the Homestead and the Hearthstone Inn. Old stocking records reveal that the sisters and Cooper were very active in replenishing the Willowemoc and Mongaup with trout fry. Each season they would order fish from Caledonia and place them in nearby waters.

George W. Cooper, early DeBruce fly tier.

George Cooper was an avid outdoorsman; he was a fine angler and fly tier. Exactly when he began tying commercially is not known; however, there is evidence that suggests he was tying in the 1870s. The rugged physical demands placed on a blacksmith do not seem compatible with the patience and gentle hand needed to tie delicate trout flies; the occupations appear to be at odds with each other. Cooper, though, had a reputation for being a skillful tier who raised his own hackle, possessing prize Rhode Island Reds.

He was known to tie an excellent fly, and his notoriety spread with his creation of the Female Beaverkill (another early American dry fly), developed in the Beaverkill watershed. The fly was a very popular turn-of-the-century pattern. It is uncertain as to exactly when Cooper devised the Female Beaverkill, but it was being used as early as 1913.

Today's imitationists believe the fly George Cooper tied was created to imitate the female Hendrickson spinner *(Ephemerella invaria),* the most prolific hatch on the Beaverkill. Anyone who has fished the stream during this hatch can see the resemblance and, by noting the distinct yellow egg sac of the natural, can understand why Cooper added this feature to his fly.

In 1923 George Cooper sold his store to Mahlon Davidson. Davidson was born in 1890 and grew up along the Beaverkill, in the Lew Beach area, where he hunted, fished, and trapped. Like Cooper, he was an avid fisherman and fly tier who raised his own roosters for hackle. He continued operating the post office and general store, which became a regular stopping place for fly fishermen who visited the upper Willowemoc. In addition to selling groceries, Davidson sold flies and other assorted fishing tackle, and he was one of the last to make solid wood fly rods out of bilberry or shadbush.

Among the more popular patterns he sold was a fly he devised, similar to the Light Cahill, known as the Davidson Special, which he first tied in the 1920s.

DeBruce Post Office and General Store, a popular rendezvous of fly fishermen who purchased flies from George W. Cooper and later Mahlon Davidson.

© Emerson Bouton

Part

III

28

"The Kettle That Washes Itself Clean"

The Indian name for the Beaverkill translates to "The Kettle That Washes Itself Clean." It is supposed that the name came about because of the river's spring freshets, which sweep away debris and scour the river bottom.

Flooding can be devastating to trout habitat; it can erode stream banks, change watercourses, and scour streambeds. This scouring can destroy essential aquatic food supplies found in the bed of the stream and, if flooding takes place shortly after spawning, can eradicate redds or nests.

Trout populations on the Beaverkill have always been affected by natural disasters, particularly floods and droughts. The Beaverkill and its tributaries are steep-gradient; and runoff from rains and melting snow causes them to rise quickly and overflow their banks frequently.

The stream's history is filled with incidents of droughts, floods, and the ravages of ice jams. These occurrences continue to be common and unpredictable. Their circumstances lead to rising water temperatures, scoured spawning beds, erosion, and, at times, degradation of trout habitat.

The climate of the Beaverkill region is one of long, cold, often snowy winters. The mean annual snowfall in the Balsam Lake area is 100.3 inches. Temperatures below zero in winter are quite common, with a mean annual extreme being −18 degrees Fahrenheit. The coldest temperature ever recorded was −36 degrees, and was taken at a weather station in nearby Walton.

© The American Fly Tyer

Old timer Gus Bailey fishing the Beaverkill during the high flows of spring.

Each winter, the waters of the Beaverkill and Willowemoc freeze, with ice thicknesses of a foot or more. Following a midwinter thaw, this ice usually breaks up and, depending on stream flow, temperatures, and weather, can accumulate in areas, forming ice jams.

Great amounts of broken ice can be backed up for a half mile or more; the severity of the ice jam varies with how long these stream blockages remain in position. Ice jams often divert stream flows into new channels, leaving the normal channel dry of water, causing havoc to aquatic insects and trout, which are left stranded.

If the ice jam gives way suddenly, there can be great damage, as this mass of moving ice uproots trees, relocates boulders, scours the streambed, and rips and tears at stream banks.

Erosion is an ongoing process. Generally, it occurs slowly, almost without notice; but in times of freshets, or high flows, it can be dramatic. Banks formed of glacial till tend to erode easily. Although the root systems of trees along the banks hold the soils, they still become undermined, and there are times when the weight of mature trees alone is enough to collapse a stream bank. The gravel removed, or eroded, from one area deposits in another; some pools or riffles fill in, while others may deepen.

Perhaps one of the most memorable instances of stream erosion occurred on September 18, 1863. In less than twenty-four hours, Shin Creek went from being unusually low to a raging torrent. Early in the morning, the stream jumped its banks and swept away over an acre of adjoining lands, which happened to be the entire cemetery where early settlers of the Beaverkill Valley had buried their dead.

The *Delaware Gazette,* on September 30, reported that as many as sixty bodies were taken downstream, "some of them with broken coffins lodged along the stream."

During times of drought, water temperatures often rise above those preferred by trout. Fish populations become concentrated, as great numbers gather at spring holes and off cooler tributary mouths. At these times, trout are in distress, become more vulnerable to predation by animals and birds, and are easily exploited by man. With insufficient flows, nursery streams (those containing young-of-the-year trout) that are not spring-fed may dry up entirely.

In summer, stream flows on the Beaverkill are dependent on rainfall; and while approximately fifty to fifty-two inches of rain falls annually near the headwaters, it is rarely distributed evenly. A dry summer can be followed by a year of devastating floods, as it was in 1894 and 1895.

Reporting on stream conditions on the Beaverkill in July 1894, the *New York Times* stated:

> The stream is low now and the water is warm, and the trout, especially the Fontinalis, seek spring holes in the pools, and the mouths of brooks and the spring rills.
>
> Last week, taking an opera glass along, the writer saw between 4,000 and 5,000 trout, all beyond the catching limit, between the pool above the Suckerback and Shin Creek bridge, as he passed at least a dozen places where trout school at this season, without looking for them. At the Suckerback pool were between 300 and 400 trout luxuriating on the gravel bar at the mouth of the little mountain brook that aerates this large sweep of water.
>
> At the Second Docking, just above in a deep spring gully, was a school of 400 or 500 nice trout running from six inches in length to a pound and a half. At the head of

Davidson's Pool were hundreds of smaller trout in a spring run, and there was school after school in the back waters at Sprague's. At the Rocks at Sprague's was a school of uniformly large fish not less than ten inches; some of them were fourteen-inch fish. At Hardie's Pool, just below the bridge, were several schools of nice trout off the mouth of the little spring brook which "keeps up" better than any other in this neighborhood.[1]

These warm-water conditions were found not on the lower river but far upstream, on a section of the upper Beaverkill just below Lew Beach. The following year, a major flood destroyed much of this very critical habitat:

> The great rush of water that flows every few years in the Beaverkill causes many changes in the bed of the stream. One of these big "freshes," as they are called, occurred about the year 1895 and it made great havoc, especially between Shin Creek and Ellsworth's. Just below Shin Creek there was a large pool on Abel Sprague's land that we called the swimming-hole; this was completely filled up with stones and a flat rift above was hollowed out into a deep pool. At Voorhess's great changes took place. The big pool called the "Second Docking," one of the most enchanting places for fly-fishing, was entirely turned about, the pool filled up, and a new channel formed back under the hillside. "Little Pond Brook," another pool, beloved by all oldtimers, was ruined. At the "Big Bend," about midway between Jersey's and Ellsworth's there was a great upheaval of rocks and stones, piled up fifteen to twenty feet high, and the entire character of the stream changed.[2]

One river-related industry that may have been beneficial to the Beaverkill was the operation of sawmills. Sawmills were not generally compatible with trout streams; sawmill owners constructed dams, which prohibited the upstream migration of fish. Most mills discharged their unwanted sawdust directly into the water, which not only fouled the stream but made fishing below them an unpleasant experience. Writing in *Forest and Stream,* the legendary fishing journalist Theodore Gordon stated:

---

[1] *New York Times,* July 29, 1894, p. 17.
[2] Benjamin Kent, "An Angler's Notes on the Beaverkill," *The Speckled Brook Trout,* ed. Louis Rhead, p. 107.

> How we detest a sawmill on one of our favorite streams. The sappy, heavy saw-
> dust not only floats on the surface, but sinks to the bottom and permeates the entire
> river. The trout will not rise; in fact, I do not believe that natural flies would be noticed,
> even if they would come up through the trash, and hatch out on the surface.[3]

There were, however, some positive tradeoffs associated with the industry. The in-stream
ponds its high dams created often provided some of the best habitat found along a stream section.
For years, many of the biggest trout taken from the Beaverkill were caught in the large pools above
and below these structures.

At the turn of the century, all of the old water-powered sawmills had been going out of business, and by 1900, only one remained—the Wamsley & Davidson Mill, located below Shin Creek.

The last of the dams were gone from the Beaverkill in 1910, and even Theodore Gordon
seemed to lament their passing. In a letter to the *Liberty Register* in which he urged that something
be done about the destructive erosion taking place along Catskill streams, he stated:

> The old dams and water powers that were so numerous thirty years ago have
> vanished. Except for a tumble-down structure here and there, weakened by neglect
> and time, they have yielded to the battering of floods and ice. They would have pro-
> tected the streams to some extent and made them less torrential in character.[4]

---

[3]*Forest and Stream,* March 2, 1907, p. 340.
[4]*Liberty Register,* March 28, 1913, p. 6.

29

"Day Trippers"

Another event that occurred at the turn of the century was a new and improved form of transportation. The automobile, like other, previous forms of travel, had an immediate impact on the Beaverkill and the Catskill region. (In 1901, the year mass production began, there were approximately 8,000 autos in the United States; a dozen years later, ownership of automobiles skyrocketed to 1,194,261!)

The very first auto seen in Roscoe arrived in 1902. A local newspaper reported, "The machine had run up from New York . . . and was on its way up the Beaverkill."

The automobile created "day trip" fishermen, who no longer found it necessary to plan ahead for a few days' stay at local resorts.

Early on, confrontations arose between automobile owners and area residents. Autos were forced to drive on roads ill adapted to their travel; at times, they caused horses to bolt, overturning wagons and injuring people. "Day trippers" also disrupted the customs of the country people, especially along the Beaverkill:

> The residents of the sections where fishing is most popular are becoming enraged over the automobile parties who come on Sundays and spend the day fishing, taking fine strings back with them.

"Day Trippers"

There is a law against fishing on Sunday which the residents of the counties obey. To have outsiders come in and take away fine catches every Sunday during the season goes against the grain.[1]

Early automobile anglers.

---

[1]*Sullivan County Review,* May 6, 1915, p. 4.

Laws prohibiting fishing on Sunday had been enacted as early as 1853. A fine of twenty-five dollars was imposed, with one-half going to the informer. In general this law, designed to enforce morality, was adhered to, especially in the days before automobile travel and "day trip" angling. Previously, trout fishermen tended to stay at a boardinghouse, hotel, or fishing resort for an extended period of time, and were more willing to relinquish recreation on Sunday.

To be sure, not everyone obeyed the law; regional newspapers often cited arrests and fines paid, reminding readers that a law existed prohibiting fishing on Sunday. Local people claimed that they obeyed this law, while visitors from the city did not. Undoubtedly, it was, on occasion, ignored by both sides. This humorous item appeared in the *Delaware Gazette:*

> You can buy a cane fish pole for 25 cents and catch just as many fish with it as you can with a jointed one that costs $17; but you can't take it apart and slip it under your coat when you go fishing Sundays as you can a jointed one, and a religious outside appearance is worth $16.75 to most men.[2]

With the advent of the automobile, complaints against Sunday fishing became much more frequent. Locals grumbled that new state roads brought "hordes" of fishermen who disregarded the law, particularly along the Beaverkill. Residents found the stream lined with cars belonging to city visitors, and they were indignant at the lack of enforcement.

During these initial years of auto travel, the rift over Sunday fishing generated many letters and editorials. One example of the exchanges that appeared in local newspapers occurred in the summer of 1914. The editor of the *Sullivan County Review,* based in Roscoe, reported that the law was being "flagrantly violated on the Beaverkill," and that local residents along the stream should put a halt to it. A correspondent who signed his letters "Waltonian" took issue with the editor:

> I have several times observed such fishermen, generally city men, and invariably found them men of the highest character, enjoying an opportunity to get close to nature but at the same time respecting the feeling of others who preferred to spend the day in church.
>
> With conditions as they are today, for most men Sunday is the only day for relief from the cares of business or labor, and if they occasionally take advantage of this day to spend a few hours fishing, I cannot see that it harms anyone. It is proposed to arrest

---

[2]*Delaware Gazette,* June 2, 1876, p. 2.

fishermen, the cost will finally fall on the town as surely no one will return to a place where visitors are treated in such a manner. The best crop today along the Beaverkill is the summer boarder brought there through the fishermen.[3]

© Louis Rhead, *Forest and Stream*, Oct. 1916

Complaints against Sunday fishing continued well into the 1920s. Times were changing, though, and eventually such blue laws were eliminated, and fishing on Sunday became an accepted practice.

"The American Trout Fisherman."

[3]*Sullivan County Review,* June 4, 1914, p. 8.

30

The Best of Times

Even though the automobile made the Beaverkill more accessible to a larger number of persistent anglers, the excellent trout fishing that existed at the turn of the century continued into the 1920s and '30s. Up and down the Beaverkill, monster-sized brown trout continued to be caught.

On July 31, 1926, the *Walton Reporter* announced that Fred Shaver of Turnwood had caught one of the largest browns ever from the upper river, just below Beaverkill Falls; "the trout measured 28 inches in length, 15 inches in circumference and weighed 10 pounds."

In July 1929, Al Romer of Livingston Manor caught a 24¾-inch, 6½-pound brown from Decker's Eddy on the Willowemoc.

A year later, in 1930, another impressive 10-pounder was taken from the lower Beaverkill; this trout, however, caused considerable controversy. Arthur Tyler, also of Livingston Manor, caught the huge brown near Cooks Falls, claiming he took it on a light stone dry fly. Many doubted a trout of such proportions could ever be taken on a dry fly; others claimed the big fish was seen several times; that it was blind, injured, and probably found dead.

One thing is certain: Arthur Tyler caused quite a commotion when he walked into the Roscoe House carrying the 30-inch brown, which weighed slightly over 10 pounds! It was the largest most people had ever seen, and the owners of the Roscoe House sent the fish to New York to be mounted. For years it was displayed in the lobby, where all agreed it was a beautiful specimen.

A few years later, in May 1935, Art Jennings of Livingston Manor did find a 30-inch German brown, dead, at the Vantran covered bridge; it would have tipped the scales in the 10-pound range. Downriver, a week later, at Ferdon's Eddy on the Beaverkill, Charles Volke of Roscoe caught a 25½-inch, 5½-pound brown.

Fred Shaver with a huge brown measuring 27″ and more than 8 pounds that he caught on the upper Beaverkill.

© Sherry Bellows

Another big brown was taken in June 1937: Ed Young of Liberty captured a 25¼-inch 6½-pounder, near Horton. And in June 1939, Fred Shaver again made the local newspapers when, downstream of the falls, he took another huge trout, which measured 27 inches in length and weighed in at more than 8 pounds!

The 1920s and '30s were a time when increasing numbers of trout fishermen began motoring to and from the Beaverkill. A great following of regulars began fishing the big river every weekend, developing a familiarity and love for its waters not readily found on other streams. Its most loyal disciples were fly fishermen, who recognized that the lower Beaverkill was special and that its broad, deep pools, abundant fly hatches, and eager-to-rise trout offered classic dry-fly fishing.

It was a new era in fly fishing; the popularity of the dry fly now exceeded that of the more traditional wet fly, and to a great many fly fishers, it was the best of times. It was a time of changing tactics, steadily improving tackle, and greater experimentation with dry flies. A new breed of Beaverkill angler advanced the sport of dry-fly fishing by becoming familiar with the river's major fly hatches, learning where and when the best trout fed, and determining which flies should be used to take them. Many of these Beaverkill regulars recognized their fishing as unique and developed an intimate relationship with the river that was to last a lifetime.

One man who influenced many Beaverkill fishermen during these years was Richard "Pop" Robbins. Robbins experienced, firsthand, the significant changes brought about by the introduction of brown trout. In his more than fifty years of fishing the Beaverkill, he had seen it all. As a young man, he fished the stream when it contained only brook trout and dry flies were unheard of. He became a master at fishing two wet flies, earning a reputation with the dual combination by taking numerous trout, up and down the Beaverkill.

When browns came along and filled the waters of the lower river, he was one of the first to recognize the need for surface flies—and he successfully changed tactics and adopted the dry fly. Robbins believed brown trout were the salvation of the Beaverkill; their excellent fighting qualities, combined with their habit of surface feeding, made for exciting fishing in the heavy flows of the big river.

Richard Robbins was an expert fly fisherman who spent a considerable amount of time fishing and learning about a river he loved; by the 1920s, he was the acknowledged "dean" of the Beaverkill. While he was exceedingly popular with all anglers along the stream, he became a great favorite of the younger, beginning fly rodders, to whom he was especially helpful. Knowledgeable and kindhearted, Pop, as he became known, knew the ways of trout and passed along what he learned, influencing generations of fly fishermen, fly tiers, and angling writers.[1]

Robbins was originally from New York and had traveled back and forth from the city as a wealthy club fisherman. A founding member of the Fly Fishers Club of Brooklyn, he retained membership for many years. However, poor health led to dwindling finances and forced him into early retirement.

Pop Robbins.

As a frequent visitor, Pop had developed a special relationship with the Beaverkill, and he decided to spend his remaining days living near the waters he had come to love so well. He settled in Roscoe and adopted a simpler life, renting a room in a boardinghouse just a short walk from the Forks—and the stream he "always stoutly maintained was the grandest trout river on earth."[2] Pop eked out

---

[1]Forty years after Robbins's death, Harry Darbee dedicated his book *Catskill Flytier* "To the one fisherman who has meant more to me than any other in my life—Pop Robbins."
[2]Schaldach, *Currents and Eddies,* p. 47.

a living guiding fishermen, waiting tables, and working at odd jobs. All of his free time he spent fishing the Beaverkill.

The physical ailments that had reversed the fortunes and lifestyle of Richard Robbins worsened, and he became crippled with arthritis. The joints in his hands and feet grew grossly swollen, and his fingers became fixed in distorted positions. It was difficult for him to perform simple tasks, but although the old man could barely get around, he would not give up fishing his beloved Beaverkill.

He could force his rod into his twisted hand, and it would stay there; but his gnarled fingers would not let him tie on a fly. In his last years, whenever he could get to the river, Pop would sit along the banks of Ferdon's Eddy or the Forks, wait patiently for someone to pass by, and ask them to tie on a fly. Most likely it would be a big bivisible or a fanwing floater, something his fading eyesight could pick up on the mirrored surface of the big river.

Even with a body wracked by constant pain, Pop Robbins never lost the kind and generous disposition that endeared him to so many. Before he died, in January 1937, Pop expressed a desire to be buried in the cemetery overlooking the Forks, "so I can look up the Willowemoc, down the Big Beaverkill and across to the Little River."[3]

His wish was carried out; however, for many years, this "great angler and fine gentleman" lay buried in an unmarked grave.

Those who regularly fish the Beaverkill are, at times, drawn together; most often they rally to protect the stream from would-be despoilers. In 1953, though, a small group of its faithful decided to meet each year, in the dead of winter, to enjoy one another's companionship and to reminisce. They were led by Ray Church and John Trainer of New York and Frank Foster of Pennsylvania. They called their little get-together the Angler's Reunion Club, and they met each January, for three days, at the Antrim Lodge in Roscoe, to be near the Beaverkill. The group dined, talked of big trout that got away, the fly hatches, new rods, and old friends who were no longer with them. They were "dedicated to conservation and protection of the historic Beaverkill." Over the years, the annual pilgrimage to the Antrim drew noted wildlife photographers, outdoor writers, and nationally known fly-fishing experts and fly tiers.

In 1956, the reunion numbered about eighty, and a small group journeyed to River View Cemetery to pay homage to Pop Robbins. They placed a wreath at his grave and read a poem; and right then and there, they decided to start a fund for a proper headstone to mark the site.

---

[3]*Liberty Register,* July 7, 1938. Letter from Sparse Grey Hackle (Alfred W. Miller) to *New York Herald Tribune,* p.7.

Today, visitors to the little cemetery overlooking Junction Pool will find that the plans of the group were fulfilled. There, on an open hillside, is a headstone etched with a leaping trout chasing a mayfly, and the inscription DICK "POP" ROBBINS, 1863–1937.

If indeed Pop's spirit can look up the Willowemoc and down the Big Beaverkill, then he can view generation after generation of fly fishers who are also lured and charmed by these waters, wading and casting their flies, just as he had done so many years before.

Another of the big river's most devout regulars was Ted Townsend. Townsend was a fabled game warden from Westchester County and was known as "a true artist with the dry fly."[4]

T. Edward Townsend became a game warden in 1915 and was considered "one of America's best-loved outdoorsmen—and certainly its best known Game Protector."[5] It was said that he hunted and fished with Teddy Roosevelt; however, on the Beaverkill, he was often in the company of Melly Rosch or Les Petrie.

Ted Townsend tied his own flies, often at streamside, and carried a butterfly net, which he used to capture hatching mayflies. With a natural as a model, he would fashion an imitation while sitting along the banks of Ferdon's, Barnhart's, or one of the other popular pools along the big river.

His friend Les Petrie also tied his own flies and was known as a great experimenter with fly patterns, tying dozens of his own creations. One pattern that became very popular for many years was a dry fly known as Petrie's Green Egg Sac. The fly was viewed as an early caddis imitation, although its shape or form was of the traditional Catskill style—sparsely tied, with upright wings of wood duck and blue dun hackle.

Petrie was an old-time Beaverkill fisherman who knew, and who purchased flies from, Theodore Gordon. In the spring of 1907, Petrie received an order from Gordon that included, as was Gordon's custom, extra patterns for him to experiment with. In this shipment was a Royal Coachman tied with white breast feathers taken from a wood duck. A huge success among dry-fly advocates, this innovation became known as the Fanwing Royal Coachman. The fly was a very killing pattern that enjoyed popularity for more than thirty years. It was a favorite of many, with entire articles being devoted to its success, and was known to take trout when everything else failed.

During the 1920s and '30s, many of America's most renowned fly fishermen called the Beaverkill their home waters. A number were influential in the world of outdoor writing; and

---

[4]Wright, *The Fly Fisher's Reader,* "The Best-Loved Trout Stream of Them All," Corey Ford, p. 231.
[5]*Conservationist,* April–May 1950.

Fanwing Royal Coachman tied by Rube Cross.

© Judy Van Put

through their written works in newspapers, magazines, and books, they enshrined the Beaverkill to yet another generation of trout fishermen. The river always enjoyed a special relationship with outdoor columnists and angling writers; its proximity to New York City and other major population centers, along with its excellent trout fishing, made the Beaverkill their favorite. The fame and reputation of the river continued to grow, at a pace exceeding that of the fast-growing brown trout, which thrived in the deep pools from Roscoe to Cooks Falls and beyond.

A few of the better-known fishing writers, during this time, were Corey Ford, William J. Schaldach, the talented John Taintor Foote, Foote's fishing partner Ray Holland, who edited *Field & Stream* from 1921 to 1941, Eugene V. Connett, and Sparse Grey Hackle (Alfred W. Miller).

These men all knew one another and often fished together, sharing pools, flies, and the good fellowship that develops between stream mates. After the fading light of day gave way to the evening rise, and then darkness, the men retreated to the Antrim Lodge, Roscoe House, or Ferdon's River View Inn. On the verandas, or at the bars, they gathered with others and reviewed the day's fishing experiences. There was tackle talk and discussion over which flies were hatching. Theories were exchanged, along with fly patterns and the good-natured ribbing that exists between close friends.

Frank Keener owned the Antrim Lodge, a fisherman's hotel, which enjoyed a valued relationship with angling writers, who would visit the bar and mix with the colorful characters who fished the Beaverkill. The bar, with its mounted trout lining the adjoining walls, became known as Keener's Pool. This is understandable, as it was a famous watering hole for anglers, who often stood three and four deep, waiting for a drink to take away the river's chill. At the bar, stories were told of fish caught and lost, and big trout tended to increase in size in proportion to the number of drinks consumed. And it was part of local lore that some of the biggest trout ever taken from the Beaverkill came out of Keener's Pool!

The River View Inn was the favorite of Ted Townsend and Corey Ford, who for years wrote a *Field & Stream* column known as the "Lower Forty." Ford had a special fondness for the Beaverkill, having learned to fish dry flies in Barnhart's with Ted Townsend as his teacher. Years later, he would capture, warmly, the happy years he spent on the river in an article titled "The Best-Loved Trout Stream of Them All."[6]

William J. Schaldach was a writer and artist well known to several generations of outdoorsmen; his fine artwork of fish and wildlife is still sought after by those who appreciate his easily recognizable style. In the early 1920s, he wrote and illustrated for *Forest and Stream;* he later became an associate editor at *Field & Stream*.

Bill Schaldach began fishing the Beaverkill in 1922. During the 1920s and '30s, he spent anywhere from two weeks to three months each season at the stream, making Roscoe his headquarters. During his many years on the river, he enjoyed the friendship and camaraderie of the regulars who fished the Beaverkill. He fished with the colorful Louis Rhead, who passed on to Schaldach his knowledge of the river and its trout and aquatic insect life. But it was the venerable Pop Robbins who was his mentor, and with whom he spent his happiest days. Pop's vast experience and wealth of Beaverkill lore were absorbed by Bill Schaldach, who came to love the river, much in the manner of the older man. He would go on to write extensively of its charms, its trout, its anglers, and its natural beauty. His delightful *Currents and Eddies* included a chapter titled "The Bountiful Beaverkill."

Currents and Eddies was one of the first books to mention the famous pools on the lower river; Schaldach listed them in order, along with brief comments on their appearance, how they fish, their characteristics and beauty. In his *The Wind on Your Cheek* was a drypoint drawing of Barnhart's Pool, done in 1929, along with a drawing of the Conklin covered bridge pool on the upper Willowemoc.

John Taintor Foote (1881–1950) was a well-rounded fly fisherman, of a generation that generally fished wet flies in pairs, downstream, and then turned around and fished a dry fly back upstream. He purchased property along the Beaverkill in 1924, and while he was a member of the Fly Fishers Club of Brooklyn, he often fished the big water below Roscoe.

Though he was trained as an artist, John Taintor Foote made his living by writing, and by these means he also furthered the reputation of the Beaverkill. He was an author of popular sporting classics, and he wrote humorous stories and articles for such publications as *Colliers,* the *Saturday Evening Post,* and *Field & Stream*. In addition, he was a playwright and successful Hollywood

---

[6]Wright, *The Fly Fisher's Reader,* "The Best-Loved Trout Stream of Them All," Corey Ford.

John Taintor Foote, circa 1922.

screenwriter; he did particularly well with movies about horses, such as *Kentucky* and *Sea-Biscuit*. John Taintor Foote wrote seventeen books, including such favorites of fishermen as *A Wedding Gift* (1924), *Fatal Gesture* (1933), *Broadway Angler* (1937), and *Anglers All* (1947).

Eugene V. Connett III (1891–1969) is best remembered as the founder of Derrydale Press, which specialized in printing limited editions of sporting books. Derrydale flourished in the 1930s and '40s, and its books are popular today with collectors, who regularly pay several hundred dollars or more for copies. The first book to carry the Derrydale imprint was written by Connett in 1927 and had the fanciful title of *Magic Hours Wherein We Cast a Fly Here and There*.

Gene Connett contributed fishing articles to various magazines; as early as 1916, he promoted the use of the dry fly on the pages of *Forest and Stream*.

A well-traveled, veteran fly fisherman, Connett wrote several books on angling—perhaps his most popular being *Any Luck?* (1933). The book contained practical information on equipment, casting, personal experiences, and flies and an introduction by his friend and angling companion George M. L. La Branche. Connett recalled memorable days spent on the Beaverkill and devoted an entire chapter to the Willowemoc, which he seemed to favor. His chapter on flies had high praise for the tying talents of Rube Cross, and he wrote glowingly of Catskill dry-fly patterns. *Any Luck?* was also the first book to extol the tying skills of Walt Dette, who was in the early years of his professional fly-tying career.

Alfred W. Miller (1892–1983) wrote under the pseudonym of Sparse Grey Hackle; and by that name, he was well known to fly fishermen, who read his classic fishing stories.

By profession he was a writer, beginning his career as a reporter for the *Wall Street Journal* and then running his own financial public relations business. For many years he contributed fishing articles to publications such as *Outdoor Life, Sports Illustrated,* and the *Anglers' Club Bulletin,* of which he was also the editor.

© Patricia M. Sherwood

A. W. Miller (Sparse Grey Hackle), circa 1940s, with a friend.

He was friends with many of the syndicated outdoor columnists of his day, and it was common to find his work on the sports pages of New York's leading newspapers; where he served as guest contributor to Ray Camp, Don Stillman, and the great Red Smith.

An excellent writer, Sparse, as he was best known, was fascinated by the Catskills and spent many years fishing their storied streams, especially the Beaverkill and Willowemoc. While he wrote of his personal experiences along these streams, he also preserved Catskill history when he chronicled, in his popular book *Fishless Days, Angling Nights,* the intimate relationship Herman Christian and Roy Steenrod enjoyed with Theodore Gordon.

As a member of the nearby De-Bruce Fly Fishing Club, he would visit with his good friends Harry and Elsie Darbee. Those fly fishers who gathered at the Darbees' popular fly shop often had the good fortune to meet Sparse, as his visits were frequent. He and Harry would reminisce about the good old days along the Beaverkill, and of Pop Robbins, and Louis Rhead, and the old-time fishermen who met at the Antrim Lodge or Roscoe House.

Sparse had a habit of including everyone in the conversation, even total strangers. While anyone was perfectly free to join in the lively discussion, most would just listen, as Sparse was vividly expressive in his speech and had a world of experience, wisdom, and knowledge about a river they were just beginning to know.

Alfred W. Miller was a great friend to the Beaverkill, and widely respected among his peers. Fly fishers today still delight in reading his ever-popular *Fishless Days, Angling Nights.*

31

A. J. McClane and
"The Turnwood Years"

Another writer who fished with Pop Robbins and contributed significantly, through his writings, to the popularity of the Beaverkill was Al McClane. He began fishing the river in the 1930s, and although it is difficult to think of him as a Beaverkill angler, he fished its waters over a span of six decades and lived along its upper reaches for many seasons.

As the longtime fishing editor of *Field & Stream,* Al McClane traveled the world, sampling the game fish of 140 countries and building a reputation as a sophisticated, polished master angler with international credentials.

For more than forty years he globe trotted, sharing his angling experiences with a loyal readership that knew him to be at home whether trouting on the Test or Itchen, wading the grayling streams of Austria, or angling for bonefish in the Bahamas.

Al McClane enjoyed an enviable career as a fishing journalist and a savant of fish cookery. His reputation as a superb writer on the world's game fish overshadowed his modest beginnings; his angling roots can be traced to a tiny Catskill mountain stream flowing through a rocky hillside dairy farm, in the town of Hardenbergh.

Rider Hollow is the stream where his trout-fishing education began. It is a steep, stony, icy-cold feeder that was home to an infinite number of showy brook trout, whose brilliant colors and delicious flavor remained forever in McClane's memories of his childhood. Like other boys who spend their youth along mountain streams, he enjoyed the pleasure of cooking his catch on an open fire at streamside:

> At the top of the mountain, there was an infant waterfall that formed a deep greeny pool shouldered by gravel bars where I could build a fire and cook my trout. . . . Nature designed them for the frying pan; three little trout could be tucked in my skillet, allowing room to curl and sizzle until the crisp skin popped, exposing moist, pink flakes. After a half-century fishing career in over a hundred countries, I admit to more superlative fish at table, but the flavor of a wild brook trout in its prime foamy with butter, hits the synapses of my brain like that two-dollar Big Ben alarm clock on a school morning.[1]

Albert Jules McClane was born in Brooklyn in 1922. At a remarkably early age he decided to abandon city life, and so when he was only thirteen he left his family behind and hitchhiked to the Catskills, seeking work. The year was 1935, deep in the Great Depression. That his parents would even allow such an odyssey is testimony to the hard economic times and the demands placed on working people.

He made his way to the Margaretville area and found both employment and a place to live on a dairy farm. He learned the basics of farm life, and when chores were caught up with, or he received a rare day off, he followed the example of many country boys and found adventure exploring nearby trout streams.

Rider Hollow was a favorite. It is a tributary of Dry Brook, a stream that many of the earliest fishermen traveled to reach the upper Beaverkill and Balsam Lake. Margaretville, the town that Al more or less adopted, was the nearest village. It is located on the East Branch of the Delaware and is central to some of the best trout fishing in the Catskills.

Not surprisingly, the area was home to a number of veteran anglers, most of whom plied their piscatorial skills on the East Branch, below the village, where the river meandered through flat and fertile farmlands. This was "big water," with large, deep pools and lengthy insect-rich riffles and runs.

---

[1]McClane, *The Compleat McClane,* p. 274.

Those men who knew the river and worked hard at their fishing took trout in the 5- to 7-pound range each season, often after dark, with large wet flies or bucktails. Big browns decorated the walls of many of the bars, taverns, and hotels in and around Margaretville.

This was trout country. The young McClane became an avid student of fly fishing and sought out local experts, eager to learn their fishing secrets. He said, ". . . I was the 'kid' who was allowed to tag along."[2]

That he had a natural talent for the sport surfaced early. He was just fourteen years old when he stunned local veterans by taking a huge brown, weighing 7 pounds and 2 ounces, from the East Branch, on a nymph.

Eager to learn more about fly tying, he traveled over to the Beaverkill valley the following winter to visit the legendary Rube Cross. Rube had only recently set up shop in Lew Beach, yet he found the time to teach the youngster a few tricks of the trade. He must have seen the boy's keen interest and enthusiasm for learning everything about fly fishing; before Al left, Rube inscribed a copy of his *Tying American Trout Lures*. The two established a friendship that would last for life.

Al McClane had good teachers, and he thoroughly enjoyed his learning years in the Catskills:

> But these were truly wonderful years for me. I met and fished with many of the great Delaware anglers: Ray Neidig, Dan Todd, Mike Lorenz, John Alden Knight, Doc Faulkner and, sometimes, Pop Robbins and Reub Cross when they came over from the Beaverkill.[3]

His love for fishing and his talent for writing both surfaced early in his life, and it seemed inevitable that he would find a career as an angling journalist. In 1939 he entered Cornell University, as a fisheries major. While in Ithaca, he worked in state fisheries programs, as a junior aquatic biologist, on lake and stream surveys, and on migration studies on Finger Lake tributaries. And it was during his college years that he actually began freelancing, selling his first fishing article, at the age of nineteen, to *Outdoor Life*. One year later, he sold another to *Field & Stream*.

Just as his career looked promising, it was interrupted by World War II. In 1942, Al joined the U.S. Army. He saw combat in France and Germany; by the time he was discharged, he had received the Bronze Star and the Purple Heart.

---

[2]McClane, *Fishing With McClane,* p. xiii.
[3]McClane, *Fishing With McClane,* p. xiii.

Shortly after the war ended, *Field & Stream* began publishing his work regularly, and by June 1947 he was fishing editor. His official byline was "A. J. McClane"; and in no time at all, he developed a large following of loyal readers, who discovered that he possessed unlimited angling knowledge, was unpretentious, and wrote honestly. His writing was precise, very descriptive—the best of modern fishing journalism. For more than forty years, his was the most familiar and respected byline in angling literature.

A. J. McClane became a good teacher; he presented his knowledge and experiences clearly, often combining fisheries facts and science with angling techniques. Like Theodore Gordon, he had a style so original that if, by chance, his byline was ever absent, his work would still be easily recognized.

Travel and writing assignments for *Field & Stream* kept him busy, yet Al managed to continue fishing the Catskills and the Beaverkill. He wrote often of the stream, its people, and even individual trout that challenged his angling skills. Though he wrote several books on angling, A. J. McClane is best known for *The Practical Fly Fisherman* (1953) and *McClane's Standard Fishing Encyclopedia* (1965; revised and expanded, 1974).

The Practical Fly Fisherman is considered a classic, comprehensive work on fly fishing. It contains many references to the Catskills and to experiences on the Beaverkill and Willowemoc. Also featured in the book are the tying skills of Walt Dette, whose fine examples of Catskill-style dry flies are depicted in color plates, along with wets, nymphs, streamers, and bucktails.

McClane's Standard Fishing Encyclopedia, a tremendously popular book, has sold nearly one million copies. It is a premier reference source for writers, editors, anglers, and fisheries professionals across the country. This book features decorative color plates of flies tied by Harry and Elsie Darbee, showing all of the Catskill classics as well as the standard patterns of the day. Also included are excellent illustrations of the Darbees' tying instructions, drawn by the noted Catskill wildlife artist Francis Davis.

Except for the period of time he spent in the military, Al McClane regularly found the time to fish the Beaverkill. He knew all of the famous pools on the lower river as well as anyone; and he learned how to fish the tricky currents and eddies of Junction Pool as intimately as he did the swirling waters of the deep plunge pool at Beaverkill Falls.

In 1954 Al McClane returned to the Catskills, seeking a place to write and relax and enjoy good fishing. He chose the upper Beaverkill, and for the next half-dozen years he leased the mile of water that flowed through the Arthur Marks estate, above Turnwood. (The land had originally been settled by Ransom Weaver in the 1870s. His farm was said to be the most beautiful on the Beaverkill and was a regular stopping place for fishermen, who found his boardinghouse accommodations and trout fishing to be among the best.)

On one side of the Beaverkill, the property was open fields or meadows and contained a large farmhouse, barn, and beautiful Norman-style chateau, which remained the residence of Margaret Marks, following the death of her husband, Arthur.

Hidden behind a knoll, among towering hemlocks on the opposite side, was a fishing lodge, originally built by Jay Gould, who had bought the property in 1912. Though rustic in appearance, the building was designed for comfort and solitude, and was constructed right on the bank of the Beaverkill, in a very attractive setting. During the days of wagon roads and buckboards, it was visited by many famous men—heads of industry and politicians, including, it was said, President Grover Cleveland.

It was the Gould cottage in which Al and his wife, Patti, made their home each summer and where he wrote many of his articles. For a fishing writer, the surroundings were ideal. The stream was literally at his doorstep. Its sounds were a constant reminder that if he needed a break from his typewriter, or more inspiration, he had only to walk to the Beaverkill, tie on a fly, and test his skills against the craftiness of the trout that were his neighbors.

When not at the typewriter, Al McClane mixed his interest in fisheries with his love of fly fishing by conducting his own fish-tagging experiments. He studied the trout on his water: how, where, and when they were caught, as well as the frequency of their capture and their movements. He caught a few of his tagged trout three miles downstream, at Beaverkill Falls; but his biggest surprise came when a couple of his trout turned up in the Delaware River, fifty to sixty miles downstream!

Over the years, Al and Patti frequently had fishing guests, and one of the earliest was Arnold Gingrich (1903–75). Al and Arnold met in 1955, and they became instant friends. That the two took a liking to each other is not surprising; they shared a love of travel, fly fishing, and angling literature, and they had many friends in common.

At the time, Arnold Gingrich was the well-known publisher and vice president of *Esquire*. One of the founders, as well as the editor, of the literary publication, he is credited with making the magazine an instant success. He persuaded Ernest Hemingway to write for the first issue, and then he used Hemingway's name to lure many other noted writers, including William Faulkner, F. Scott Fitzgerald, John Steinbeck, and Sinclair Lewis.

A warm, friendly man, Arnold was well spoken and gracious, and he had a passion for fly fishing. A year after they met, McClane invited him to share the Marks water with him, and for the next five seasons the two often fished the Beaverkill together, sharing knowledge, experiences, meals, and companionship.

211

An excellent and widely respected writer, Arnold Gingrich wrote several books on fly fishing, including *The Well-Tempered Angler* (1965), in which he recalled their Beaverkill experiences in a chapter titled "The Turnwood Years."

These were wonderful years for Arnold. The fishing on the upper Beaverkill was superb; the stream, with its pristine waters flowing through the unspoiled wild forest, teemed with native trout. He became a short-rod enthusiast, his favorite a 6½-foot Midge, which, more often than not, was bent by the straining of one of the hefty brook, brown, or rainbow trout he caught with great regularity:

> The fishing on that stretch of the upper Beaverkill was so good, for all five of those seasons I fished it, that if I were condemned to go utterly fishless from here on out until I pass ninety, I would still figure that I was ahead on points. There were days when I would take and release better than forty fish, fishing from early morning until night. . . .[4]

At the time, Arnold maintained a diary of his fishing experiences, recording the number of trout hooked, landed, and released, and which flies the fish had taken. While he was opposed to any competitive form of angling, he devised an updated version of the old practice of fishing for count. He urged anglers to throw away their creels and adopt bookkeeping methods instead of fish-keeping: "I did not begin to approach my present level of enjoyment of angling, however, until I began carrying a notebook instead of a creel, and started thinking of angling as an interesting game rather than as an uncertain meat-substitute."[5]

Arnold's meticulously kept records reveal that throughout the years he fished the upper Beaverkill, he averaged 21.6 trout per day!

Credit, in part, for the excellent fishing found on the mile of water Arnold Gingrich shared with Al McClane must go to Ellis Newman (1913–65), who carefully managed the stream.

Ellis came to the Beaverkill valley in 1930, taking a position with the Marks family as their caretaker. As with most of the private water on the upper Beaverkill, the Marks water contained in-stream structures aimed at improving trout habitat. While Beaverkill fishing clubs were engaged in habitat improvement as far back as the 1870s, structures along the Marks stretch were

---

[4]Gingrich, *The Well-Tempered Angler,* p. 122.
[5]Gingrich, *The Well-Tempered Angler,* p. 140.

rather original. Ellis designed a unique type of pool digger: He drilled holes through a series of large boulders and then ran a steel cable through them, thus constructing a "necklace" rock dam.

While Ellis Newman was a proficient fly tier and skilled fly fisherman, he earned his reputation through his expertise with a shotgun and his talent for casting a fly rod. Commenting on his abilities, Al McClane once called Ellis "the greatest wing shot and fly-caster who ever lived—bar none. Ellis regularly threw measured casts of over 200 feet, and his entire style of delivery—particularly the long, slow backcast—was breathtakingly beautiful."[6]

A stocky man with enormous strength and extraordinary casting skill, he was famous for his ability to cast a standard HCH (DT-6) double-tapered fly line ninety feet—with his bare hands!

While he did not have the inclination to compete in fly-casting tournaments, Ellis demonstrated his casting skills many times before large audiences at National Sportsman's Shows in New York. For years, Al McClane hosted the *Field & Stream* fishing clinics; he would have Rube Cross demonstrate fly tying and Ellis Newman teach fly casting. Usually, when a crowd had gathered, Ellis would suddenly dispense with the rod entirely and astonish onlookers by casting with his right arm only!

Ellis Newman enjoyed teaching and helping others. In the 1950s he started a shooting and fishing school on the Marks estate, and while most of his students were able-bodied, he was a pioneer in the concept of providing hunting and fishing opportunities for the handicapped. At his own expense, he experimented with and designed wheelchairs and tractor-driven devices that enabled the physically challenged to fish and shoot. One such contraption was a bucket that hoisted a wheelchair-bound angler out over the stream, giving him the opportunity to place his fly in areas he would never be able to reach otherwise. While his inventions were not very refined—some would even say crude—they were, nonetheless, much appreciated by their users.

Unfortunately, Ellis Newman's life ended prematurely; in the summer of 1965, he met with a tragic accident. Though he had taught hundreds to cast and shoot and was an expert with rod and gun, he inexplicably shot himself. He had apparently slipped on a log, discharging his rifle and shooting himself in the chest. A coroner's investigation ruled the death accidental.

Ellis Newman was also a good friend of Al McClane's; they fished the Beaverkill together often, at times "just for the pleasure of each other's company." One of the best articles ever written by Al is titled "Song of the Angler." It is a philosophical, thought-provoking essay in which McClane explained why he enjoyed fishing. He made it clear that a large portion of his pleasure

---

[6]McClane, *Fishing With McClane,* p. 95.

was derived from the company he kept on the stream. He fondly recalled several of his angling companions and reflected on their camaraderie, noting in particular their overall goodness and moral quality. One of his recollections was of the years spent on the Beaverkill, at the old Gould cottage, and of the kindness and sensitivity of Ellis Newman:

> One day, when the mayflies were on the water, Ellis caught and released several good browns below the dam, one going about 3 pounds. At the top of the next run we met a young boy who proudly displayed a 9-inch brook trout. Ellis admired it so much that I thought we were looking at the biggest squaretail captured since Cook hit the jackpot on the Nipigon in 1914. When the lad asked Ellis if he had any luck, he looked very serious: "Oh, I caught a few, but none were as pretty as yours."[7]

© Francis W. Davis

While Ellis Newman paddles, A. J. McClane fishes Forest Lake, located on the Marks estate.

---

[7]McClane, *The Compleat McClane,* p. 386.

32

A Siren Along the Beaverkill

There is a section of the Beaverkill, located midway between the hamlets of Beaverkill and Rockland, known as Craig-e-Clare. Today, it is not much more than a name on a map, at a bridge crossing. But there was a time when it was more populated, when it had its own post office and a stately stone castle—in which, it was rumored, lived a beautiful and seductive woman who enticed fishermen from the stream into her extravagant fortress.

Known as Dundas Castle, the building with the mysterious past sat high on the bank overlooking the Beaverkill. It sits there still, though through neglect, mature trees and other forest vegetation now shield it from public view.

In 1891, Bradford L. Gilbert, a noted New York City architect, began acquiring land in the area. He amassed several hundred acres and constructed a beautiful summer home, known as Beaverkill Lodge.

Gilbert's wife was a native of Ireland, and the steep hillsides and rapid flowing stream so reminded her of home that in 1876, when the new post office at the tiny hamlet was to be named, she selected Craig-e-Clare. This was the name of her small Irish village, and translates to "Beautiful Mountainside."[1]

---

[1]*Roscoe-Rockland Review,* September 24, 1896, p. 1.

In 1915, Gilbert's estate was purchased by Ralph Wurts-Dundas, and it was Dundas, an eccentric millionaire, who constructed a replica of a French Burgundian castle on the banks of the Beaverkill.

Construction took more than eight years, with most of the building materials being imported from Europe. The roof and turrets were of slate, brought in from England; the marble floors, stairs, and fireplaces for the nearly forty rooms came from Italy; and the huge iron gates were from an old French château. The Beaverkill provided the only native construction materials, as tons of gravel and stone were removed from the streambed and used for the outer facing of the beautiful building.

Entrance to Dundas Castle.

© Ray Pomeroy

Ralph Wurts-Dundas died just before the castle was completed. Shortly after his death, in 1921, his wife was committed to a sanatorium and his estate, including the castle, was left to his daughter. Supposedly, the castle was never occupied, not by Dundas, his wife, or his daughter, yet the grounds were carefully guarded by police dogs. Visitors were never allowed access to the elegant estate.

In time, the daughter was also placed in an institution and declared by the courts to be mentally incompetent to manage her own affairs. This event, coupled with the excessive precautions taken to protect the privacy of the estate, caused local residents to ponder the unusual circumstances surrounding Dundas Castle. One rumor claimed that the young woman was confined to one of the castle's rooms.

In the 1930s, those who fished the water at Craig-e-Clare heard various stories about the majestic castle overlooking the Beaverkill. Perhaps none were more bizarre than that reported by the sharp-witted Corey Ford:

216

Another favorite poaching preserve of mine, as I recall, was the deep run just below a forbidding stone mansion on the Little Beaverkill, known as Craigie Clair. . . .
Rumor had it that the sole occupant was a beautiful but demented young girl, who
used to let down her golden hair from an upstairs window and lure unwary anglers
into her granite castle, for what probably amounted to nothing worse than an afternoon's pleasant seduction. I fished past Craigie Clair, hopefully, a number of times, but
I never got lured.[2]

---

[2]Wright, *The Fly Fisher's Reader,* "The Best-Loved Trout Stream of Them All," Corey Ford, p. 237.

33

Pools and Eddies

A unique characteristic of the Beaverkill is the long-established custom of handing down, orally, generation to generation, the names of the river's pools and eddies, riffles and runs. The tradition of naming points along the river began in the rafting days and was picked up again in the 1920s and '30s, as the popularity of the lower Beaverkill increased and more pools were recognized.

These designations are important; they enable even first-time visitors the pleasure of becoming immediately familiar with the pools along the lower river. And they allow all anglers, neophyte and veteran, the opportunity to converse about the Beaverkill intimately and intelligently. These are hallowed landmarks, the most written about pools in angling literature.

The best-known stretch of the lower Beaverkill is the first five-mile run, from Roscoe downstream to the hamlet of Cooks Falls. It is big water; pools are large, deep, and plenty wide for a back cast.

THE FORKS (JUNCTION POOL)

At the junction of the Beaverkill and Willowemoc is a deep pool with strange and mystifying currents and eddies. Legend has it that the confusing currents caused migrating trout to linger for days, trying to decide which stream to enter. This indecision causes delay, which, in itself, is the reason many of the largest trout taken from the Beaverkill are caught here.

Historically known as the Forks, the name change to Junction Pool did not begin until the 1940s. Long a favorite swimming place for local youngsters, the introduction of brown trout into the lower Beaverkill caused conflicts between its users:

> A city fisherman is having a hot time with the boys of Roscoe at the forks of the rivers. This place has been the town "swimming hole" for generations, and the boys are not inclined to give it up. This man entertains the strange notion that the boys must get out of the water as soon as he appears, and when they refuse to obey his commands he chases them with a club and uses abusive language. Some day the fathers of the boys will give this man a good ducking.[1]

One of the last truly large trout to come out of Junction Pool was caught on May 26, 1949, by

Howard Lindsley of Livingston Manor. Lindsley took a 27-inch brown that weighed an impressive 8 pounds, 2½ ounces. In an interview years later he recalled, "the water was just right"—a term used by local fishermen that means the river was beginning to rise and discolor from a rain, marking a time when big trout leave their hiding places and begin to feed heavily.

Howard Lindsley, Livingston Manor, with a 27", 8 pound 2½ ounce brown from Junction Pool.

---

[1]*Sullivan County Review,* July 9, 1908, p. 1.

FERDON'S EDDY

Named after an early river raftsman named John S. Ferdon (1822–1908), the eddy was used as a docking—a place where rafts were assembled. It was much larger than it is today. About 1900, after experiencing a washout of its tracks, the railroad placed rock fill in the pool, diverting the river from its original course into a split channel. For a few years following the fill, the pool was known as Carpenter's Rocks.

Old-timers cherished Ferdon's, especially the head of the pool, just before dark. It was here, in 1901, that Irving Finch of Roscoe captured a huge brown that measured 26 inches and weighed 6½ pounds.

John Ferdon owned and operated the Hillside Summer Home, which later became the popular River View Inn and was successfully run by his son Edwin for a number of years. A. E. Hendrickson made his headquarters at the River View whenever he fished the big river with his longtime fishing companion Roy Steenrod. It was at Ferdon's that Roy Steenrod first tied his famous Hendrickson dry fly:

> One day in 1916, while we were fishing the Beaverkill below the Junction Pool at Roscoe, a hatch of flies came on. We had never seen the fish rise so freely for any fly as they did for this hatch. I caught one of the flies and put it into my fly box, and after lunch that day at Ferdon's I tied some patterns of the fly as nearly as I could. We took fish with that fly day in and day out, and for years it proved to be a killer and is so today. One day, while sitting on the bank of the stream perhaps two years after I had tied the first patterns, the matter was brought up as to what I would call or name the fly. Looking at A.E., the best friend a person could ever wish to have, I said "the fly is the Hendrickson." I saw at once that A.E. was pleased.[2]

BARNHART'S POOL

The pool was named after the Barnhart family, who farmed both sides of the river for many years; the ford used to cross back and forth in the tail of the pool can still be seen. Barnhart's is long, approximately two thousand feet in length, and has good depth, curving along the foot of a steep mountainside.

---

[2]Quoted in Smedley, *Fly Patterns and Their Origins,* p. 68–69.

It is a "big fish" pool, and one of the largest was caught in the summer of 1936 by William Sandstrom of Highland Falls, New York. Sandstrom, fishing a bucktail, hooked and landed a 25½-inch brown trout weighing 6 pounds.

Trout fishers today can all be thankful that, in 1939, Claude Barnhart conveyed a public fishing easement to the state, guaranteeing that future generations can walk the banks, wade the waters, and cast their flies in the same pool John Taintor Foote, Ted Townsend, and Corey Ford called their favorite.

H E N D R I C K S O N ' S   P O O L

Hendrickson's Pool, like the famous dry fly, is named after Albert Everett Hendrickson. Hendrickson was a frequent Beaverkill angler, and the large, flat rock that lies in the middle of the pool was his favorite place to fish from.

H O R S E   B R O O K   R U N

A long stretch of fast water that includes a collection of every type of cover or habitat a trout could desire describes Horse Brook Run. Large boulders are found throughout its length, and the river flowing against, over, and around them creates shelters and pocket water capable of harboring even the largest browns.

The run takes its name from a small tributary named Horse Brook, which enters the river about halfway down the right bank.

C A I R N S   P O O L

Named after William Cairns (1844–1911), who lived in a neat hillside farmhouse overlooking the Beaverkill, Cairns was also a docking area for rafts—and William Cairns was known as a hardy steersman on many a raft.

He came from Scotland with his parents in 1851, and when his rafting days were over he became a successful newspaper columnist for the *Middletown Mercury*. Cairns wrote under the name of Rusticus, and was widely read and respected. He wrote on a variety of subjects, but mostly about rural life, and many Catskill newspapers carried his column.

Cairns is a long, deep pool. Along its entire length, large rock covers the far bank, protecting a long-abandoned railroad bed from erosion. Over the years, rocks have slipped into the pool, providing shelter for some of the most fished over trout on the Beaverkill.

Hendrickson's Pool.

Cairns flows alongside the old highway running between Roscoe and Cooks Falls, and access is easy—too easy, some say, as its location and numerous trout make it the most fished pool on the river. Even in the 1930s, "The biggest objection to Cairns Pool was its popularity."[3]

© Ed Van Put

Cairns Pool.

---

[3]Schaldach, *Currents and Eddies,* p. 41.

WAGON TRACKS

Wagon Tracks Pool was named by Sparse Grey Hackle, prior to 1938. Chester Cairns used the shallow, wide tail of Cairns Pool to ford the river and get his tractor and mowing machinery to the fields on the opposite bank. Sparse, in *Fishless Days, Angling Nights,* described the tractor "leaving white wheel marks on the algae-covered brown stones. The present writer therefore christened the hitherto anonymous pool below the ford 'The Wagon Tracks.'"

Wagon Tracks is one of those rare pools that can be fished equally well from either side or bank.

SCHOOLHOUSE POOL

Schoolhouse Pool was named after the tiny, one-room Sprague schoolhouse, which sits high on the roadside bank, overlooking the Beaverkill.

RUBBING MILL POOL
(RED ROSE POOL)

Rubbing Mill Pool was named after an old stone-cutting mill that was located along the left bank, between the railroad and the river. Water was diverted from the Beaverkill to power the mill, which cut stone and rubbed it down smooth. The mill was in operation as early as 1868, and its ruins can still be found along the riverbank. At the present time, fishermen refer to this pool as the Red Rose Pool, after the Red Rose Motel and Restaurant, which is located opposite the old mill ruins.

BROWN'S RACE,
JANE'S GUT

Brown's Race and Jane's Gut are located just downstream of the railroad bridge, below the Rubbing Mill Pool. In rafting days, the river split into two channels, with the somewhat shallow lesser flow running to the left. A man named Brown and his wife, Jane, ran a sawmill along the side channel and lived in an unpretentious house on the riverbank. This channel was known as Jane's Gut, and steersmen favored it over the main flow, which ran straight into a steep-sided cliff of ledge rock. Those taking the latter course often had their rafts "smashed to smithereens."

MOUNTAIN POOL, LOWER MOUNTAIN POOL

Mountain Pool and Lower Mountain Pool combine excellent trout habitat with the loveliest scenery found on the Big Beaverkill. One of the best physical descriptions of this stretch and its natural beauty comes from the pen of William Schaldach:

> A gravelly beach with gently sloping bottom—ideal wading conditions—forms one shore. There is ample room for the back cast.
>
> The opposite shore is almost theatrical in effect. Rising steeply from the shadowed water, a great ledge of rock looms over the river. It is heavily clothed with lichens, moss, oxalis and other woodland plants. Pine, hemlock and young hardwoods cling to the shallow top soil and ascend the slope to apparent infinity; the space they do not occupy is filled with an intricate network of laurel and rhododendron. Half a dozen varieties of ferns add accents of lighter green. Mountain Pool is beautiful at any time, but to see it at its best one should be there when the rhododendron is in bloom.[4]

PAINTER'S BEND

Located upstream of Cooks Falls, Painter's Bend is recognized by a lengthy stretch of stone wall that protects the banks of Old Route 17. This point in the river was known in pioneer days as a crossing place for panthers, or mountain lions. Large boulders occupied the river, and the big catamounts were said to leap from boulder to boulder, crossing the Beaverkill without wetting their feet. In rafting days, the rocks were removed with dynamite, to facilitate the floating of rafts.

Painter's Bend is an old Beaverkill name, the area having been known by that name at least since 1880. Over the years, the old-time raftsmen's "twang" corrupted "panther's" into "painter's."

---

[4] Schaldach, *Currents and Eddies,* p. 42–43.

C O O K S   F A L L S   P O O L

Cooks Falls Pool is a large, deep pool with water cascading over a large mass of ledge rock, creating a plunge pool of excellent trout habitat. In 1873, the rock ledge that made up the falls was altered with dynamite, to make raft navigation safer.

Throughout the years, an occasional big trout would make this pool its home for a while and capture the attention of the village; the bridge crossing the river gave an excellent view of the waters below.

Cooks Falls Pool.

34

The Dry Fly Takes Off

The theory of tying artificial flies that directly imitate the natural flies trout feed upon is possibly as old as fly fishing itself. This speculative idea appears, even in the earliest of times, to have caused a division in the ranks of American fly fishers.

The Reverend George Washington Bethune, considered America's foremost angling scholar, discussed the theory in an essay in 1847. Bethune edited the first American edition of Izaak Walton's classic, *The Compleat Angler,* and in his edition he included a lengthy footnote describing the fly fishing of his era:

> . . . the anglers of our day are divided into two schools, which may be conveniently distinguished as the *"routine"* and the *"non-imitation."* The former hold that the trout should be angled for only with a nice imitation of the natural flies in season at the time, and that, therefore, the flies seen on the water, or found in the belly of the fish, are to be carefully imitated. . . . The *non-imitation* school hold that no fly can be made so as to imitate nature well enough to warrant us in believing that the fish takes it for the natural fly; and, therefore, little reference is to be had to the fly upon which the trout are feeding at the time.

Thad Norris, too, was well aware of the direct-imitation theory, and did not find it essential to taking trout on a fly. Many years later, in his classic *The American Angler's Book* (1864), he would write:

> For the theory of "strict imitation," there is some show of reason, but I cannot concede that Trout will rise more readily at the artificial fly which most closely resembles the natural one, for the fish's attention is first attracted because of something lifelike falling on the water, or passing over the surface, and he rises at it because he supposes it to be something he is in the habit of feeding upon, or because it resembles an insect or looks like a fly, not that it is any *"particular"* insect or fly; for we sometimes see the most glaring cheat, which resembles nothing above the waters or beneath the waters, a piece of red flannel, for instance, or the fin of one of their own species, taken greedily.

It would be many years before fly fishers would practice the theory of direct imitation, or "match the hatch"—even after years of using dry flies and the introduction of brown trout.

It is supposed, by some imitationists, that Theodore Gordon's Quill Gordon was tied to copy the natural *Epeorus pleuralis.* But Gordon was, at best, a moderate believer in exact imitation. While his Quill Gordon is an excellent naturalistic pattern, it was designed to imitate, in Gordon's words, a "group of species."

In 1916, with *American Trout-Stream Insects,* Louis Rhead made an attempt to convince fly fishermen that the exact-imitation theory should be followed. While it was the first book devoted to the theory, the work, as mentioned previously, was amateurish, and not well received.

As late as 1919, a poll that appeared in *The American Angler* revealed that the majority of fly fishermen were still fishing with nonimitative patterns. Readers were asked to vote on their favorite flies, and out of the top twelve, only two were American in origin. The Royal Coachman finished at the top, and the Parmachene Belle placed third.

Even with the growing use of surface flies, it was not until the 1930s that a few anglers began to take a serious look at exact imitation. Prior to this date, the overall philosophy was that matching the hatch was not an important aspect of successful trout fishing. It was rarely written about, or even mentioned, in books, periodicals, or outdoor magazines.

The first book to accurately identify the primary aquatic fly hatches of American trout streams was *A Book of Trout Flies* (1935), by Preston Jennings. Jennings's work was a thorough effort to correlate artificial flies with aquatic insects. A good portion of his research was done in the

Catskills; and the Beaverkill, in particular, played an important role in this first serious work on exact imitation.

Roy Steenrod collected specimens of natural flies from the Beaverkill and reported on their emergence dates to Preston Jennings. *A Book of Trout Flies* included traditional Catskill favorites, such as the Quill Gordon, Light Cahill, and Hendrickson.

It was during the 1930s that the dry fly experienced a renaissance, as Catskill fly tiers sharpened their skills, improved their knowledge, and advanced the art of fly making. Fly fishers took another look at the old theory of direct imitation and began adopting a more scientific approach by correlating their artificials with the naturals they found along trout streams. New dry-fly patterns emerged yearly, as floating flies soared in popularity.

35

The Catskill School

The first mention of the Catskill School appeared in print not very long after Theodore Gordon's death. In an article titled "The Evolution of the Trout Fly," Louis Rhead stated:

> In the Neversink region of the Catskills there has lately grown up a small school of expert fly dressers, formed under the leadership of the late Theodore Gordon, who wrote so delightfully in the columns of *Forest and Stream*. Of the several patterns now being tied the one most widely known is called Gordon's Quill, and different varieties under other names.[1]

Herman Christian, Reuben R. Cross, and Roy Steenrod were among the first in a succession of Catskill fly tiers who continued to tie in the style of Theodore Gordon. Both Roy Steenrod and Rube Cross claimed to have learned to tie directly from Gordon. All three were professionals who not only preserved Gordon's methods but improved upon them, and advanced the development of American dry flies, creating new patterns of their own in the same Catskill style. In time, other

---

[1]*Forest and Stream,* November 1922, p. 504.

tiers were added to the Catskill School—most notably, Walt and Winnie Dette, Harry and Elsie Darbee, and Art Flick.

These men and women tied in haylofts and basements, or set aside a portion of their home as a fly shop. Their flies were always in great demand and were generally purchased by fishermen through mail order. From the tiny mountain villages of Lew Beach, Livingston Manor, Neversink, Roscoe, and Westkill, boxes of trout flies were mailed across the land, to cities and towns, distant states, and faraway countries.

ROY STEENROD

The Hendrickson is the most famous dry fly ever developed along the banks of the Beaverkill. Its creator was Roy G. Steenrod, who was born on August 15, 1882, about fifteen miles south of the Beaverkill region, in the adjoining town of Liberty.

As a youngster, he loved trout fishing, and the middle branch of the Mongaup was one of his favorite streams. He would walk from his home to the nearby stream, carrying a frying pan, bread, butter, salt, and pepper. He cooked his trout at streamside and, in his words, "brought his catch home inside him."

When he turned twenty-two years of age, he went to work at the Liberty Post Office, and it was there that he met, and was befriended by, Theodore Gordon. Gordon was a frequent visitor to the post office, dropping by to mail many of his fly orders. The two men became good friends, and Roy began visiting Gordon at Neversink a couple of days each week. Gordon introduced the younger man to dry-fly fishing. When not fishing together on the stream, the two spent time at the fly-tying vise, where Steenrod learned how to tie in the Gordon style. Gordon gave Roy many of his flies to use as models, and supplied him with fly-tying materials.

Their close relationship lasted until Theodore Gordon's death in 1915. Roy became the recipient of many of Gordon's personal belongings, including books, fly-tying materials, his vise, and the famous Halford dry flies. The creative proficiency Gordon possessed he shared with Steenrod; and, in passing along his fly-tying knowledge, he could not have selected a more worthy disciple.

Roy went on to develop an excellent dry-fly imitation of his own, and he passed on to many generations what he had learned from the legendary Gordon. In 1916, he created the Hendrickson, one of the most popular and productive dry flies of all time. He first tied the pattern along the banks of Ferdon's Eddy, on the Big Beaverkill, naming it after his longtime fishing companion Albert E. Hendrickson. He and Hendrickson frequented the big river, especially the first two miles downstream of Junction Pool.

Imitationists believe the fly Roy Steenrod developed imitates the mayfly *Ephemerella invaria*, one of the most prolific hatches on the Beaverkill. That he tied a good replica is evidenced by the fact that this hatch is still, today, referred to by the name of the artificial, eighty years after its creation.

Hendrickson tied by Rube Cross.

© Ed Van Put

In addition to his famous Hendrickson, Roy created one other fly of note that was especially popular with local anglers, who fished it with great success. The fly was called Murray's Favorite and was first tied in 1918. He named the pattern after Minos Murray, a New York tailor who was one of his customers. Roy tied flies for many, many years, both as a professional and as an instructor.

He spent a good portion of his life teaching others how to tie flies, particularly young people. In 1939, when the Livingston Manor Central School opened its doors, along the banks of Willowemoc Creek, it offered a six-week course on fishing, possibly the first in the state. Roy Steenrod headed the list of noted instructors, which included fly tier Rube Cross and local experts Wilson Jennings and Jack Vogt. Subjects taught included fly casting, care of tackle, reading water, and conservation.

Perhaps influenced by Theodore Gordon's conservation principles, Roy was, throughout his life, active in conservation. He was a member and past president of the Liberty Rod & Gun Club and the Sullivan County Federation of Sportsmen's Clubs. As such, he was active in trout-stocking programs, fish and game legislation, and various conservation projects. Being especially concerned over public fishing, Roy lobbied for a state public fishing-rights program. He was also one of the first to advocate the instruction of youth in conservation.

It was not surprising to anyone when, at the age of forty-three, Roy abandoned his postal career and turned outdoor professional. In 1926, he became a state Conservation Department game protector, enforcing fish and game laws and protecting trout streams. For twenty-seven years he reigned over a territory that included the Beaverkill, Willowemoc, and Neversink. In addition to his enforcement duties, he taught young people at various Boy Scout reservations around the county and at the DeBruce Conservation Camp, giving instruction in woodcraft, fly casting, and, of course, fly tying. Some of the youngsters he taught at DeBruce are currently state fish and wildlife biologists and conservation officers.

His friend and fellow fly tier Harry Darbee believed Roy Steenrod was the "best-known fly tying instructor in the Catskills":

> He taught at the conservation camp, at Boy Scout meetings, in his home, or anywhere there was a vise handy. He loved young people and he loved to tie. He was still teaching kids even after his nails were splitting, his hands were arthritic, and his sight and hearing were bad.[2]

Harry believed, and stated so many times, that Roy Steenrod was the single person most responsible for passing along the distinct features of the Catskill style.

Roy Steenrod was forced into retirement in 1952, when he reached the age of seventy; yet he continued teaching at DeBruce. Upon his retirement, his friends went out and found the largest

Roy Steenrod at Theodore Gordon's
fly-tying vice.

place available for a dinner, since Roy had become one of Sullivan County's most beloved figures. Local lore has it that because he was such a widely respected individual, half of those in attendance were adversaries he had arrested for fish and game violations.

I met Roy Steenrod the year after I began employment with the Conservation Department. Burton Lindsley, the conservation officer who replaced Steenrod, took me to his home for a visit. Roy was eighty-seven at the time and had stopped fishing because of age and frailty. He graciously signed my copy of *The Complete Fly Fisherman* and gave me a Hairwing Royal Coachman he had tied.

We talked of the Big Beaverkill and what it was like to fish the river in the "old days." It had been years since he had fished there; and perhaps convinced he had seen the best fishing, he asked wistfully, "Are there any more good fishermen on the Beaverkill?"

A short time before his death, Roy wrote to Harry Darbee, requesting a copy of his book *Catskill Flytier*. Sadly, he concluded his letter:

------

[2]Darbee, *Catskill Flytier,* p. 41.

Since I gave up driving my car, have not been able to travel, and miss my visits with you.

Go to see my daughter once in a while, at Geneva, N.Y., and as I ride along the Beaverkill in the bus, it is sad to see, in fact cry a little, when I think of all the happy days I enjoyed on the river.

Roy Steenrod lived a long and fruitful life; he was one of those individuals who readily shared with others those things that gave him pleasure. He died in 1977, at the age of ninety-four.

RUBE CROSS

No individual improved upon the Catskill style of dry fly (created by Theodore Gordon) more than Rube Cross. A native of Neversink, Reuben R. Cross was born on March 16, 1896. He grew up on the family farm on Mutton Hill, at a time when the beautiful Neversink valley and the river running through it were a fisherman's paradise. As a youngster, he developed a love of hunting, fishing, and trapping, and he possessed an eager curiosity about nature, spending much of his early years along trout streams and on forest trails.

Rube began tying trout flies in 1914, shortly after purchasing several dry flies at a local store and not having much success fishing with them. He claimed to have learned from Theodore Gordon, and he certainly could have, since he was in the right place at the right time. He was nineteen years old when Gordon died, in 1915—old enough to have developed a friendship with him and to have been a student of his tying techniques.

Census records reveal that Rube Cross was living on Hollow Road, just outside the village of Neversink, in 1925, and that at twenty-nine years of age he was the "Head of the Household" and his occupation was "Maker (Trout flies)." At the time, he already had an established reputation; Cross flies were recognized as being the very best, models of perfection, trout flies that set the standards his professional peers tried to meet.

In 1930, an informative little book devoted to tying dry flies was written by Dr. Edgar Burke. Titled *American Dry Flies and How to Tie Them,* the book was a guide to tying the more popular dry flies of the day, including instructions on Catskill patterns such as the Quill Gordon, Hendrickson, and Light Cahill. Burke used, as a model of a quality imitation, a dry fly tied by Rube Cross, and he stated that Rube was "one of the outstanding exponents of the Catskill 'school,' and one of the most expert fly tyers living."

A Cross fly had perfectly matched wings; incredibly stiff, evenly wound hackle; a finely tapered body; and a tail of the stiffest hackle fibers available. The fly had a generally sparse appearance and was tied to "float and ride the rough water very much as does the natural insect."

Cross became known as a perfectionist, turning out dry flies with an exactness few could duplicate. He insisted on good, stiff hackle; and his flies had a distinct clean, trim appearance. During the 1930s and '40s, he was the premier fly tier in the country, annually demonstrating his skills across the land in the swankier tackle shops and before huge crowds at the National Sportsman's Show in New York, at the Grand Central Palace.

For several years he tied at Macy's, the renowned giant department store. Scores of shoppers watched, captivated, as this man with the massive hands of a lumberjack created delicate and elegant trout flies. His fingers magically used gossamer thread to bind dainty feathers and frail quills onto a hook—in a manner trout, too, found fascinating.

In 1936, Reuben R. Cross advanced the art of fly tying when Dodd, Mead & Company published his *Tying American Trout Lures*. At a time when most professionals guarded their skills, the gifted Cross revealed to all his methods and many of his secrets. He was the first professional fly tier in America to write a book devoted to the subject of fly tying. For years, *Tying American Trout Lures* had a greater circulation than any other book on fly tying. Experts and neophytes alike were influenced by his advanced techniques of successful fly making.

Rube Cross.

In addition, the book gave early hackle raisers tips on how to crossbreed certain colors and strains of poultry to get that elusive dun hackle, so essential to many of the Catskill patterns. Virtually all Catskill fly tiers found it necessary to raise their own birds. Cooper, Gordon, Christian, Cross, the Darbees, the Dettes, and Art Flick all at one time or another kept chickens—mostly roosters—for dry-fly hackle.

As can be imagined, good roosters were special, and those with the "right stuff" were well taken care of. Tiers often opted to pluck hackles from them rather than putting a bird to rest and removing the whole neck. Rube had such a pet rooster; it was known to sit on his knee, and "every time Rube pulled out a feather it would crow, flap its wings and then settle down and wait for the next pull. It gave every indication of being interested in where its feathers went."[3]

---

[3]Smedley, *Fly Patterns and Their Origins,* p. 28.

Like other professional fly tiers, Rube Cross created a few flies of his own and was instrumental in the development of others. His best-known pattern is the Cross Special, a fly tied in the classic Catskill style. In *Fly Patterns and Their Origins* (1943), by Harold Smedley, Cross is quoted as saying that the Cross Special was a cross between the Gordon Quill and the Light Cahill. He first tied it because the two flies were the best and most popular in the Catskills, and he thought a "cross" between the two flies would be good.

Another pattern Rube Cross is associated with is the Hairwing Royal Coachman. According to A. J. McClane, in *The Practical Fly Fisherman* (1953), Rube substituted white hairwings for the fragile, white mandarin breast feathers typically used on the Fanwing Royal Coachman. This occurred in 1930, when L. Q. Quackenbush of the Beaverkill Trout Club asked him to come up with a more durable pattern.

In the fall of 1938, Rube moved from Neversink to the Beaverkill valley, first staying at the Beaverkill Trout Club and then setting up shop along Shin Creek, in nearby Lew Beach. For years he tied dry flies for the club, maintaining a supply of traditional Catskill patterns in a large box that was divided into various compartments. Rube had a standing order to keep the box well stocked with his famous flies. Club members and guests regularly raided the fly box, leaving a pile of dollar bills beside it for payment. Try as he might, there were times when Rube had difficulty keeping up with demand.

Cross tied flies.

237

In addition to tying, Rube began writing fishing articles, most often on fly tying, for outdoor magazines such as *Field & Stream, Country Life, Outdoor Life,* and *American Fly-Tyer.*

In 1940, he produced his second instructional book on fly tying, titled *Fur, Feathers and Steel.* It explained all of the steps necessary to tie quality flies and featured photographs, taken by Cross, of flies tied by Lee Wulff, Paul Young, Alex Rogan, and Elizabeth Greig, as well as a series showing Harry Darbee tying one of his specialties, a deer-hair-bodied fly.

How good were Cross flies? In his *Any Luck?* (1933), Eugene V. Connett writes, "When we come to consider the best dry fly patterns, I can say without hesitation that the most *killing* fly is the quill Gordon, properly tied—as Reuben Cross ties it."

Connett claimed Cross was "the best professional tier of dry flies in America." These comments were made when Rube was still establishing his reputation; perhaps the highest tribute would come more than forty years later. Writing about Cross in *The Masters of the Nymph* (1979), expert angler and fishing journalist A. J. McClane avowed, "I visited his hayloft shop the following winter [1938] to learn more about tying flies. A huge man, half poet, half mountain lion, he was generous to a fault. His dill-pickle-sized fingers spun the most beautiful flies I will ever see."

When we consider who is making the statement, and how many flies Al McClane must have come across, it makes us realize how exceptional a Cross fly was.

Rube Cross certainly made every effort to pass along his fly-tying skills and knowledge; he wrote two books on the subject, which were eventually republished as one volume, titled *The Complete Fly Tier.* He also taught many people how to tie flies and influenced countless others by demonstrating publicly, before numerous crowds, at tackle shops and sportsman's shows.

As a person, Rube Cross was special. Mention his name, even today, in the mountain communities where he lived, and you find that Rube Cross brings a smile to many a face; that he was well liked; that he was fun to be with; that he was admired and is missed; and, yes, that he was "generous to a fault."

On a summer evening in May 1941, a tragic fire took everything in the world he could call his own. Local headlines blared, "RUBE" CROSS STARTS ALL OVER AS FIRE RAZES HOME; FAMOUS TIER OF FISHING LURES LOSES VALUED COLLECTION OF ANTIQUES, BOOKS, AND FEATHERS IN LEW BEACH BLAZE. A fire of mysterious origin totally destroyed the two-story dwelling Rube was renting. Lost were all of his fly-tying materials, a prized collection of books, Indian artifacts, antiques, and manuscripts. Everything was destroyed, and while there was insurance on the house, there was none on its contents.

Friends, neighbors, and customers came to his aid; other fly tiers donated those materials necessary to put him back in business. Years later, A. J. McClane would write:

The attitude of the purist toward his fly dresser is one of remarkable devotion. When the home of Reub Cross burned down in Lewbeach back in 1941, his frenzied followers took up a collection to put him back in business, for the balding, corrosive, caustic-tongued wit of the Beaverkill tied trout flies like no other man. And there were those who couldn't fish without flies made the Cross way.[4]

Rube Cross stayed in the Beaverkill valley for another year or so, then moved to Rhode Island. It may have been the fire, or the memories of it; or, like many other locals during the war, he may simply have been lured to a defense plant by the high pay. He found work at a wire plant in Pawtucket, and he continued tying professionally and appearing at sportsman's shows.

He did not, however, return to the Catskills, choosing to spend his remaining years in Providence. And though he died there, on November 4, 1958, at the age of sixty-two, his spirit will always be in those mountain communities where he was the standard-bearer, for a while, in the development of floating flies. Theodore Gordon got it started; Reuben Cross, with his remarkable skill and willingness to share, moved American fly tying a giant step closer to where it is today.

W . C . D E T T E

Walter Dette was born in New Jersey on October 24, 1907. When he was thirteen years old, his family moved to the Catskills and settled in the village of Roscoe. The first artificial flies he ever saw belonged to Harry Darbee, who was examining a few wet flies behind a geography book, as the two sat across from each other in the seventh grade.

Harry and Walt became best friends and began fishing together, mostly on feeder streams where brook trout were numerous and eager to take a baited hook, much to the satisfaction of the youthful anglers. A love of trout fishing developed, as did their friendship, which was to last the rest of their lives.

In time, the two boys shifted from fishing small tributaries with worms and grasshoppers to fishing the Big Beaverkill with wet and dry flies. Harry often tagged along with local experts, receiving advice, knowledge, and, on occasion, a few of their favorite flies.

One from whom he learned the skills of fly fishing was Pop Robbins. Harry was befriended by the old man, who looked upon him as a "fishing son." From Pop, he learned about releasing trout and conservation; in Harry's words, "Pop Robbins brought me up a sportsman."

---

[4]McClane, *Fishing With McClane,* p. 109–110.

Walt Dette was satisfied to learn about fly fishing on his own; no one taught him how to cast. He saw men with fly rods practice on the lawn of the Roscoe House, and he watched as they cast their long rods with flies attached, placing them gently up against the far bank of the big river; he learned by watching others.

Walt also developed a keen interest in trout flies. As a nineteen-year-old, he beat out veteran anglers in a contest by naming the largest number of flies in a glass display case at a local tackle-supply store. For his efforts he won a brand-new fly rod.

In 1927, Harry Darbee and Walt Dette decided to go into the business of tying flies professionally. They rented a large room over the movie theater in Roscoe and constructed shelves, cabinets, and a long fly-tying bench along the bay window, which gave them added light. The two young men were joined in their venture by Winifred Ferdon, who was soon to become Mrs. Walter Dette.

Winnie Ferdon was still in her teens, and though she knew little about fly tying, she was knowledgeable about fly fishing. Winnie was born in Roscoe on May 17, 1909. She grew up around fishermen, as her family owned the River View Inn.

Located just downstream of the Forks, the inn property extended to the Beaverkill and included one of the best and largest pools on the river, known as Ferdon's Eddy. The River View catered to angling tourists and was the favorite of A. E. Hendrickson, Corey Ford, Ted Townsend, and many more Beaverkill regulars.

None of the three knew very much about how flies were tied, so they began learning their craft by taking apart the dry flies tied by Rube Cross. Sitting at a vise, behind the large window overlooking Roscoe's main street, Walt painstakingly unwound each turn of thread, while Harry and Winnie took notes; then each in turn would try their hand at tying a fly.

They learned to tie well enough to sell some flies, and they also made extra money wrapping rods. But their little enterprise over the theater did not last, as each pursued other interests. Walt sought employment at the local drugstore, Winnie took a job at the bank, and Harry became a short-order cook, trapped foxes, did some guiding, and dug ginseng. He even left the area, for a time, and became a traveling salesman.

After Winnie and Walt were married, they moved to the River View Inn and helped with its operation. Winnie's father set up a room where they could continue to tie, and he displayed and sold their flies to angling customers. In 1931, the Dettes took over the inn, but the Great Depression was under way, and business was not good enough to prevent them from having to close its doors the following summer.

Employment in the region became more difficult than ever, and Walt and Winnie decided to turn their attention to tying trout flies professionally, on a full-time basis. In 1933 they received a letter from Harry Darbee, inquiring if he could rejoin them in their fly-tying business. This was agreeable, and the three were reunited in the business of fly making.

Their business increased slowly but steadily. They went from a single glass-topped fly case to retail mail orders and large wholesale orders from sporting goods dealers. Business was good; however, the job of turning out dozens of flies daily became a chore that the three found difficult to handle, and they decided to hire someone to sort hackle, to speed up operations.

In the spring of 1934, Pop Robbins recommended Elsie Bivins, the daughter of the woman from whom he rented a furnished room. She quickly became proficient at her job and asked Harry if he would teach her how to tie. A romance blossomed, and soon after becoming a skilled tier herself, she and Harry were married.

Shortly after they were married, Harry ended his partnership with the Dettes, having decided that he and his new bride would share their talents under the name of E. B. & H. A. Darbee.

Following the breakup of their partnership with Harry Darbee, the Dettes produced a catalog, offering customers a choice of one hundred different dry-fly patterns; their business continued under the name of W. C. Dette.

Their reputation as professional tiers was furthered, in 1937, when both Walt and Winnie demonstrated their skills at the National Sportsman's Show, at New York's Grand Central Palace. Each year, the show drew thousands of anglers, many of whom crowded around, standing three and four deep, as the Dettes tied their favorite patterns.

Walt became known as a perfectionist. He was very precise, particularly about the length of hackle he selected. His Catskill-style flies were tied as well, if not better, than Rube Cross's. Walt tied to exact proportions, and so was able to produce one identical fly after another, with a consistency rarely seen from other tiers. A fine example of his work appears in A. J. McClane's *The Practical Fly Fisherman* (1953). The book features color plates of flies tied by Walt Dette, including dry flies, wet flies, nymphs, streamers, and bucktails.

For a few years the Dettes ran their fly shop in a portion of the Esso gas station on Route 17, just outside of Roscoe. They no longer sold fly-tying materials, but they carried tackle for all types of fishing. Business was good enough to hire two or three additional tiers and to stop tying wholesale for dealers. This was the only time that both Walt and Winnie were dependent on fly tying as their sole source of income.

In 1939 Winnie returned to the bank, and a couple of years later Walt found employment in a defense plant in Brooklyn. After the war, he worked as a carpenter, and then for the New York

© Mary Dette Clark

Winnie and Walt Dette, circa 1949.

City Board of Water Supply. While both pursued other careers, they never stopped tying flies professionally.

The Dettes continued tying and selling their flies out of the Esso station until 1955, when they moved their equipment and materials into their home on Cottage Street in Roscoe. They sold retail, from a room at the front of their home, and were busy filling mail orders from all over the country. Most of their walk-in customers were fly fishers who fished the Beaverkill and Willowemoc; and their most popular requests were for Hairwing and Fanwing Royal Coachmen, Hendricksons, Quill Gordons, and Light Cahills.

The Dettes tied in the Catskill tradition, using wood duck flank feathers and large amounts of dun hackle. In order to ensure a plentiful supply of quality hackle, especially blue dun, they raised their own roosters and kept a small flock of chickens at the rear of their home.

Over the years they created and re-created many patterns for their customers, the most popular being the Coffin Fly, which was developed by Walt and Ted Townsend in 1929. The fly was tied to imitate the large green Drake spinner so common on the lower Beaverkill in early June.

While the Dettes' reputation as premier fly makers was established many years ago, they never received the notoriety achieved by other Catskill fly tiers; they tended to shun publicity and the attention that accompanies popularity. In general, their exposure to the media was limited by their own choice.

The Dettes possessed a cynical and disparaging attitude toward outdoor writers and angling authors, though they were, on occasion, cooperative with certain individuals. They had a habit of downplaying their own importance and, at times, fly fishing and fly tying. "I never considered fly tying a great accomplishment," Walt stated in an interview. "It has been a way of making a little extra money."[5]

In spite of such a negative opinion, the Dettes still received recognition in numerous articles and books, because their flies were of such outstanding quality.

E. B. AND H. A. DARBEE

When Harry Darbee decided to leave the Dettes and go into the business of fly tying with his new bride, he and Elsie did so under the name of E. B. & H. A. Darbee. A stipulation in his dissolved partnership agreement with the Dettes stated that if Harry went into the fly-tying business on his own, it could not be in Roscoe. So the Darbees moved to Livingston Manor and began tying along the banks of the Little Beaverkill, on Pearl Street.

Harry Darbee was born in Roscoe on April 7, 1906. That he would choose fly tying as a profession is not surprising, since he was a descendent of a family steeped in angling tradition. His ancestors were among the earliest to settle along the "Great Beaver Kill," in the 1790s, and were the first to cater to the needs of the earliest fishing tourists. Harry's great-uncle was Chester Darbee, a friend and angling companion of the renowned Thad Norris and the son of Mrs. Darbee, of the famous fishing resort that overlooked the junction of the Willowemoc and Beaverkill. The small stream that enters Junction Pool and once flowed through buckwheat fields belonging to Chester Darbee is known today as Darbee Brook.

In addition to fly fishing and fly tying, Harry also maintained a lifetime love of nature and the outdoors, having been influenced in childhood by John Burroughs. When he was a youngster, his family lived for a short time in West Park, not far from Burroughs's home. Harry became friendly with the naturalist and accompanied him on nature walks; he was fascinated with

---

[5]Barry Lewis, "The Art of Flytying," *Catskill-Delaware,* Summer 1986, p. 15.

Burroughs's knowledge of the region's flora and fauna. Harry admired the man throughout his life, and one of his most cherished possessions was a book, titled *American Boy's Book of Bugs, Butterflies and Beetles,* that John Burroughs had given him on his birthday.

While his family lived at West Park, Harry Darbee spent his summers at his grandfather's house in Lew Beach. He caught his first trout in Shin Creek, a stream he always maintained was home to the prettiest wild brown trout in the Catskills. When Harry was ten, the Darbees moved back to Roscoe, and Harry's interest in trout fishing intensified.

Elsie Bivins was born on September 13, 1912, in the town of Neversink, alongside the headwaters of the Willowemoc. She, too, came from a family involved with trout fishing. In 1909 her parents acquired the famous fishing grounds previously owned by Matt Decker. This water was first leased by the old Willowemoc Club, back in the 1870s, and was used as a fishing preserve by Matt Decker in the 1880s and '90s.[6] The Bivins family boarded trout fishermen, and their water was familiar to Theodore Gordon and all who took fly fishing seriously.

Elsie was twenty-one years old when she learned the art of fly tying; little did she know, at the time, that it would become her life's work.

At first, the vast majority of Harry and Elsie's flies were sold wholesale, to dealers, at two-thirds the retail price; they were mostly wet flies and bucktails. The Darbees once filled a single order for eight hundred dozen wet flies, and they often tied a gross of a single fly pattern. This was hard and tedious work, but they gained experience and learned their craft well.

Harry had great hands for tying flies; they were small and fine and well suited to the delicate tasks associated with fly tying. Elsie possessed a sharp eye for color and quality hackle selection, and they both could wing a fly as quickly and expertly as anyone. The Darbees became accomplished professionals, experts with feathers, furs, and fly proportions. They continued improving their skills, becoming among the best of their trade.

As the demand for dry flies increased during the 1930s, so did the price, which influenced the Darbees to specialize in floating flies. They tied in the traditional Catskill style, and said so in their first catalog, published in 1935:

> The dry flies listed in this catalog are the finest flies possible to produce and are
> dressed after the manner made famous by the late Theodore Gordon; who paid espe-

---

[6]In 1937, this stretch of the Willowemoc became the home of the Woman Flyfishers Club, the first women's fishing club. The club became incorporated in 1932 and had eight founding members. Membership grew rapidly, reaching fifty-two by 1939. Today, the Woman Flyfishers Club is located on the West Branch of the Neversink and includes some of the best, and most talented, women fly fishers in the country.

Elsie and Harry Darbee.

cial attention to tying the fly so it would balance on the water in the position of a natural insect.

During his learning years, Harry had "dissected" the flies of Theodore Gordon and was
familiar with their construction. Throughout his life, he maintained a collection of Gordon's flies,
which included thirty to forty original Quill Gordons.

The Darbees began tying dry flies on odd-numbered hooks; instead of the traditional even-
numbered sizes of 10, 12, and 14, they tied on sizes 11, 13, 15. "People knew there was something

different about my flies," Harry says, "but they couldn't quite figure it out. It was a good gimmick."[7]

In addition to the standard Catskill patterns, the Darbees became known for their superior deer-hair-bodied flies. They tied clipped-hair dry patterns, using deer, caribou, bighorn sheep, and antelope. Their flies were uniformly dense and evenly shaped; Harry spun the bodies, Elsie trimmed them, and they both tied on the wings and hackle. They tied so much alike, it was impossible to tell their flies apart.

In 1936 they moved to the upper Beaverkill, becoming resident caretakers on the fishing estate of Henry G. Davis. Davis owned a mile of the stream, now known as Timberdoodle Farm, located immediately downstream of the present Beaverkill Valley Inn.

Their main source of income continued to be professional tying, but Harry would also give casting instructions and do a little guiding. On one occasion, he had the distinction of having as one of his pupils the great American songwriter Irving Berlin. The Berlins were frequent guests of Henry Davis and his wife, the former Consuelo Vanderbilt.

In 1938 Irving Berlin purchased a beautiful streamside property along Shin Creek and desired to learn how to cast a fly rod. He was an eager student, but after several lessons he had not progressed—at least, not to his satisfaction. At the end of one particularly frustrating casting session, Berlin turned to Harry and asked, "How long is it going to take before I can cast like you?" Harry, with typical native wit, replied, "About as long as it would take me to write a song!"

Irving Berlin went on to become a proficient fly caster and a capable fly fisherman. For years he enjoyed fishing along the very picturesque stretch of Shin Creek that flowed alongside his summer home.

The Darbees' reputation as tiers of fine flies continued to grow. Like Rube Cross, they never deviated, even slightly, when tying Catskill patterns. Both were meticulous in their proportions and their selection of colors and hackle for their beautifully tied Hendricksons, Quill Gordons, and Light Cahills. It was not long before fly fishermen began beating a path to their door; and, like Cross, they, too, developed a following of loyal customers who desired dry flies tied by their skillful hands:

> One of our biggest customers was Joseph P. Knapp, chairman of Crowell-Collier
> Publishing Company. He owned 4½ miles of the Beaverkill, leased a stretch of the
> Natashquan in Labrador, and fished all over the world. I remember one day while he

---

[7]McClane, *Fishing With McClane,* p. 114.

was picking up an order of flies, Knapp said, "It takes a lot of flies to make a living. If the time comes when you and Elsie don't have orders, my friends and I will take all you can tie." We thought that was the kindest thing anyone had ever said to us, especially in the depths of the Depression, but we were able to make ends meet without having to take advantage of his offer.[8]

In 1946 the Darbees acquired their own home, a seven-room, two-story wood-framed house located midway between Livingston Manor and Roscoe, and just a rooster's crow from the Willowemoc, at Hazel Bridge Pool.

Harry and Elsie set aside a portion of their home as a fly shop, and it was here that they would spend the next thirty-five years, tying and retailing flies, materials, books, rods, lines, and virtually all of the needs of fly fishermen.

When looking at a Darbee-tied fly, one can see immediately that it will catch fish. The proportions are exact, and the fly is distinctive. The Darbees did not use dyed hackle or bleached or tanned fur; they preferred raw furs, with natural oils left in the hides. The hackles for their Quill Gordons, Red Quills, Hendricksons, and other Catskill patterns came from natural blue dun roosters. Harry was convinced that flies tied with natural dun, with its various tones and hues, reflected light in a unique way and "fished better." From the time they first went into business, the Darbees raised roosters of these elusive colors, which distinguished them from most other tiers.

Harry and Elsie loved what they did; their whole life, every day, revolved around fly tying and fly fishing. In an interview in *Sports Illustrated,* Harry stated:

A perfectly proportioned wet fly tied by Harry Darbee.

© Judy Van Put

To me, fly tying represents a way of life quite as much as a means of livelihood. Tying flies along the banks of a beloved stream away from the bustle and stench of a city, is my idea of the ultimate in occupations. Tying flies for a living has enabled me to enjoy a certain independence of action and thought, not easily come by in these days of mass production and time-clock dominated lives.[9]

---

[8]Darbee, *Catskill Flytier,* p. 33.
[9]Robert H. Boyle, "He Deftly Ties the World's Fanciest Flies," *Sports Illustrated,* 1964, p. 8.

Elsie Darbee was a strong and independent woman who could do virtually anything. She was as skilled at cooking, sewing, and keeping the house as she was at working with a hammer and nails or shooting a pair of raccoons caught raiding the henhouse. She kept her home and business running smoothly. In a house crammed with tackle, fly-tying material, and a steady flow of visitors and customers, she was the one who knew where everything was.

Elsie had to take care of business, as Harry tended to give away more than he sold. Money was just not important to him, and he possessed a special kindness not found in most men. He had a habit of selling items based on what the customer could afford. If he knew someone had little or no money, he gave the item away.

It was said that Harry was a better talker, Elsie a better tier. Those fortunate enough to watch her put perfectly matched wood duck wings on a dry fly saw that she was indeed gifted. Longtime customers sometimes brought her presents of perfume or candy, hoping that their order would be moved closer to the top of a pile that never seemed to get thinner.

Elsie was always at her fly-tying table. She tied most of the orders, leaving Harry time to look after the needs of customers, or to experiment. Harry Darbee created a few flies of his own, and he discovered a unique style of dry fly known as the two-feather fly.

In the late 1930s, he tied a pattern known as Darbee's Green Egg Sac, which developed into a fly called the Shad Fly. This dry fly was a successful imitation of the very prolific caddis hatch of the same name, which appears at about the time shad run up the Delaware.

Harry enjoyed working with deer hair, and his most popular pattern, the Rat-Faced Mc-Dougal, was a high-floating deer-hair-bodied fly. Mentioned in many books on fly fishing and fly tying, the Rat-Faced McDougal was popular for many years with dry-fly enthusiasts.

Another floater, also tied with deer hair, is Darbee's Stonefly, a pattern tied to imitate the large adult stoneflies found on the Delaware. Its popularity peaked after the fly was written about in *Field & Stream,* in an article by A. J. McClane titled "Best Flies for Big Trout."

The two-feather fly was the result of experiments to create an ultralight fly dressing, to imitate the larger mayflies that hatch on the lower Beaverkill, such as March browns and green Drakes. Conventional imitations were tied on large No. 8 or No. 10 hooks, were heavy, and landed hard on the water. Harry wanted to get the lightest possible fly, with the "least steel." He developed a method of making a realistic detached-body fly, which required only one feather for the body, wings, and tail and one other for the hackle.

Harry used a light, short-shanked hook and a flank feather from a mallard, wood duck, or teal. By snipping out the center of the tip of the feather, he fashioned the tail; then, by stroking the fibers forward and adding a drop of rubber cement to hold them in shape, he produced the body, which was then tied to the hook shank. The remaining portion of the feather was used for the wings. A stiff hackle was then added, to make the fly buoyant.

Harry Darbee's two-feather fly was practically weightless. It landed on the water softly, with the same delicateness as a natural. The fly floated on the surface with the grace and beauty of the real mayfly; and because of its elongated body and shape, it possessed the same silhouette as a natural. On the polished surface of the long, flat pools of the lower Beaverkill, it was a killing imitation.

The two-feather fly was popularized in an article in *Field & Stream* by A. J. McClane in October 1960 and was also featured in an English book titled *Fly Tying Problems,* by the noted British fly-tying authority John Veniard.

Surprisingly, the popularity of the fly was short-lived, perhaps because it ran against traditional tying methods. It may, however, resurface in the future, as it possesses many excellent qualities of a good imitation. The fly is lightweight, lifelike, easy to tie, and realistic in shape, and it catches trout in difficult conditions—flat, glassy water.

© Judy Van Put

Two-feather fly tied by Harry Darbee.

Years later, the two-feather fly was illustrated in a book written by Harry Darbee and his friend Mac Francis. *Catskill Flytier* provided insight into the methods and techniques used by the Darbees throughout their professional career. The book told readers about their favorite patterns, their fly-tying and fishing experiences, and their acquaintances.

The Darbees' fly shop was always a social gathering place, for angling tales and trout talk. United by fly fishing, men and women with diverse backgrounds joined in conversation, sharing experiences and stream knowledge with one another. There were clubmen and city firemen, men who drove trucks, and men who chaired the board at Exxon. Bob Boyle, a *Sports Illustrated* editor and writer, once described the scene as follows:

> It serves as a gathering point in or out of season, for anglers, local characters, fishery biologists, curious tourists and wandering oddballs who come to hear Darbee hold forth on all sorts of subjects, often until dawn. The atmosphere is Cannery Row, out of Abercrombie & Fitch.[10]

---

[10]Robert H. Boyle, "He Deftly Ties the World's Fanciest Flies," *Sports Illustrated,* 1964, p. 5.

Their home and shop were busy year-round and, generally, the scene of a constant parade of visitors, most of whom traveled two hours or more to get there. They came to buy flies, materials, books, or tackle; whatever the pretext, they also came to see the Darbees. Harry and Elsie had a large following, and most of their customers were also their friends.

E. B. and H. A. Darbee were to become the most famous husband-and-wife fly-tying team in the country. The Darbees and their flies have been featured in numerous magazine articles and newspaper stories, as well as more than seventy-five books on fishing and fly tying.

36

Fish Management and the Search for Public Fishing

During the 1930s the Beaverkill and its tributaries were still being stocked in the same manner they had been for more than half a century. Applications for trout were still being received from sportsmen, farmers, hunting and fishing clubs, and inn and boardinghouse owners. There was never a charge for these fish; applicants only had to agree to be on hand to receive them and to place the fry or fingerlings in the proper streams.

The system had numerous problems. Many thousands of trout were improperly planted in waters not fitted for their survival, waters that were badly polluted or too warm, and waters that dried up in summer. Many streams were known by more than one name, and there were times when the same stream was stocked repeatedly, resulting in overstocking. To complicate matters further, sportsmen's clubs often purchased trout from private hatcheries and, unknown to the Bureau of Fish Culture, placed them in streams already stocked.

Printed instructions were usually furnished to each applicant, advising them not to plant brown trout in waters inhabited by brook trout and not to place brook trout in warm waters. For the safety of these fry and fingerlings, it was recommended that they not be placed in large pools, where they could be preyed upon by larger fish.

During the 1920s, the New York State Conservation Commission had increased its production of domestic trout by developing a number of new hatcheries throughout the state. The demand for more and more trout, to replenish streams, was being met; but it was growing more costly.

The use of trucks aided the process somewhat, as men experienced in fisheries work, employees of the Conservation Commission, began hauling trout directly from the hatchery to the stream.

Beginning in 1926, comprehensive watershed surveys were conducted throughout New York State. The major objective was to develop an improved stocking policy for hatchery-reared fish, based upon field studies of each body of water. A further goal was to acquire essential information that would lead to better fisheries management. The surveys provided valuable data, a kind of blueprint for a long-term fisheries program. The unit responsible for scientific investigations of the state's watersheds was known as the Bureau of Biological Survey.

The fieldwork included collecting various biological and physical data relative to fish production, such as fish distribution and abundance, water chemistry, pollution, temperature, volume of flow, habitat evaluation, quantitative food studies, and effects of disease. The science of fisheries management was in its infancy, and fortunately, the new Conservation Department was headed by Lithgow Osborne, under whose leadership fisheries programs in New York would make great progress.

Shortly after graduating from Harvard, in 1915, Osborne entered the diplomatic service and served in Germany until diplomatic relations were broken off, in 1917. He was attached to the American Peace Commission in Paris in 1919 and served as assistant secretary general at the Disarmament Conference in 1922. Upon returning to his native Auburn, New York, he became the editor and owner of the *Auburn-Citizen Advertiser* and was active in promoting conservation and reforestation. In 1933 he was appointed conservation commissioner; and, being an ardent fisherman, he took a special interest in the fisheries resources of the state, urging better management.

In 1935, the Delaware and Susquehanna watersheds were surveyed, and fisheries professionals made their first evaluation of the waters of the Beaverkill. Fish collections were made and growth rates studied. The results of overstocking were investigated, as were conditions affecting wild trout populations, the control of undesirable species, and various other aspects of fisheries management.

In reporting on the Beaverkill, the Biological Survey stated:

> This beautiful stream is probably the best known, most heavily fished river as well as the highest producer of any of the State's trout streams. That it maintains production year after year in the face of the very heavy fishing is a significant commentary

on what optimum or near optimum conditions may be expected to do for trout production. Probably maintenance has been greatly aided by the high mileage of posted water where fishing is relatively light, and by consistent heavy stocking. Probably more important than either of these factors are the facts that the greater part of the watershed is still protected by good forest cover, and is underlain by a rock formation favorable to water conservation.[1]

Reporting on the requirements for good trout production, biologists found the following:

Temperatures. Except in the lower 7.5 miles of the stream temperatures of the entire water are suitable for brown and rainbow trout throughout the summer. In the vicinity of Cooks Falls trout are found to concentrate at the mouths of cold tributaries, but the temperature of the river water was not intolerable at the time and the normal feeding range appeared to be still available. The upper 15 miles of the Beaver Kill has temperatures suitable for brook trout throughout the summer.

Cover. While marginal cover is somewhat deficient, forest cover on the watershed as a whole is excellent.

Food. On the basis of insect food present this stream is better than average throughout. In its upper third it is excellent. Forage fish are abundant at least as far up as Lew Beach.

Spawning conditions and tributaries. Most of the tributaries of the Beaver Kill are good nursery streams. Outstanding are Russell Bk., the Willowemoc and Berry Bk. . . . Natural young of both brown and brook trout are found to be common in the Beaver Kill at Lew Beach and young brown trout were common just above the State campsite. Without doubt natural reproduction is very important in maintaining trout fishing in this river.[2]

On the status of the fisheries:

The fact that small brown trout are relatively scarce in the Beaver Kill below Roscoe but common in headwater streams has led many anglers to believe that trout migrate downstream from the spring headwaters as they grow older. . . . The stream is greatly overfished in the open sections between Roscoe and East Branch and the lower stretches are invaded with small-mouthed bass.[3]

---

[1]*Biological Survey of the Delaware-Susquehanna Watershed,* p. 29.
[2]*Biological Survey of the Delaware-Susquehanna Watershed,* p. 30–31.
[3]*Biological Survey of the Delaware-Susquehanna Watershed,* p. 67.

The Biological Survey recommended stocking larger or adult-sized trout in the Beaverkill below Roscoe. This was a change in policy. Records of the previous ten years (1925–34) reveal that the Beaverkill and its tributaries received an average of 48,862 trout per year: 30,516 brown, 17,810 brook, and 536 rainbow trout. At the time, 98.7 percent of all trout stocked, throughout the state, were fry or fingerlings.

The Bureau of Fish Culture actually began changing its stocking methods during the 1934 season, when it increased its production of yearling trout (6 to 9 inches) to 3.5 percent of the total number of trout placed in New York waters. The bureau announced:

> In the past several years it has been the policy of the Bureau to hold many trout through the winter, putting them out in the following spring as yearlings of legal size. That better sport should result for the angler is obvious; and many letters received from sportsmen during 1935 show that this has been the case throughout the State generally.
>
> It is now planned to hold, through their first winter, at least as many fish as existing funds will allow. In this way, and only in this way, can good fishing be maintained for the growing army of fishermen.[4]

This was a dramatic change in policy; instead of stocking for the stream, with fry and fingerlings, the Bureau of Fish Culture began stocking for the rod. Each year, more and more trout were being held through the winter and then stocked as larger-sized yearlings.

In 1938, Commissioner Osborne announced that he was doing away with the old "hit and miss" plan of receiving thousands of applications from all parts of the state, and that a new stocking schedule was being worked out for each county, based on the recommendations of the Biological Survey. In addition, stream stocking was increasingly being switched from fingerlings to yearlings, or larger adult trout.

It was not long, however, before fisheries professionals of the Conservation Department must have recognized that the demand for larger trout would eventually be greater than the supply and additional steps would have to be taken. In the spring of 1940, Commissioner Osborne announced that a new and more scientific program was necessary in order to preserve the standard of fishing on the Beaverkill and other popular New York streams.

---

[4]New York State Conservation Department, annual report, 1935, p. 260.

254

As he had done in the past, the commissioner traveled to Sullivan County to attend the annual dinner of the Liberty Rod & Gun Club; at the affair, he presented an eight-point program to improve fishing and preserve wild trout. He stressed the need to keep more wild trout in the streams and "suggested a radical decrease in the length of the season, the creel limit, and in the hours of fishing (no night fishing)."

The commissioner stated that, in the long run, stocking is the most expensive and unsatisfactory way of producing better fishing. The answer, he said, is "better fish management." His eight-point program was designed to improve fishing and to save "natural trout fishing" and recommended that the department

1. Adjust seasons and creel limits.

2. Slightly increase the amount of stocking.

3. Halt any further increase in the number of yearling and adult trout to be stocked, especially in wild trout streams.

4. Increase the department's supervision of trout stocking.

5. Increase research to determine better stocking practices (which species should be planted and in what quantities) and, above all, to find out what happens to hatchery fish after they are stocked, and why.

6. Continue the purchasing of fishing rights.

7. Continue the program of stream improvement.

8. Increase stream pollution control.

Commissioner Osborne also stated:

> Natural propagation of trout in New York still produces many times the amount of fishing that artificial propagation produces. That is another basic fact which nearly everyone seems to overlook.
>
> More stocking . . . is, unless coordinated with other measures, the least desireable method because its effects are largely temporary. In the long run, stocking of itself . . . is the most expensive and unsatisfactory way of producing better fishing.[5]

---

[5]*Liberty Register,* May 16, 1940, p. 1.

In 1940, the year Commissioner Osborne presented his eight-point plan, the statewide production of yearling trout was 9.1 percent; following his suggestion, it dropped to 7.2 percent the next year. However, Lithgow Osborne resigned his post as commissioner to become a member of the Federal War Strategy Board in 1942. Despite his plan to suspend further increases in the percentage of yearling trout stocked and his claim that stocking was not the answer to good trout fishing, the percentage of yearling trout stocked by state hatcheries soon began to rise—in 1945, it reached 62.8 percent! From 1940 on, the Beaverkill received only yearling and adult trout, and the policy of stocking fry and fingerlings was abandoned.

Two other programs that began under Commissioner Osborne's leadership were the utilization of the Civilian Conservation Corps (C.C.C.) to improve stream habitat along New York's trout waters and the acquisition of public fishing rights.

A federal program, the C.C.C. provided young men with training and employment in public conservation work during the Great Depression. While much of the work involved controlling bank erosion, C.C.C. workers also constructed low dams or pool diggers across streams to create pools and cover for trout. In addition, the work included barrier dams to keep out undesirable species, deflectors, bank cribbing, channel blockers to concentrate split channels, and willow plantings. Important spring runs and feeders were cleared of obstructions, debris, and silt to increase spawning opportunities.

Though considered a new field, stream-improvement structures were developed on the Beaverkill in the 1880's.

Stream improvement was a new field and had only recently been recognized as an important principle of fisheries management. The program was aimed at increasing the number of legal-sized trout in streams. Hundreds of projects and structures were constructed, on miles of trout streams all over New York State. Catskill streams, however, received little attention, as it was believed that they were subject to extreme flooding and erosion. Projects continued through the 1930s, but were halted during World War II.

Public fishing easements were purchased along selected trout streams. In addition to allowing the public the right to fish, they enabled the Conservation Department to do stream improvement, bank stabilization, and tree planting and to develop and improve the streams' fishery resources. The acquisition of public fishing rights became the foundation of the state's fisheries management program.

While the Beaverkill and Willowemoc were not the first streams where these rights were purchased, they played a historic role in the development of the program. By the time automobile travel became popular, all of the best trout waters in the Catskills were closed to public fishing. Private clubs, inns, and boardinghouses posted the upper portions of the Beaverkill, Willowemoc, Neversink, and Rondout.

Following the introduction of brown trout, however, new waters became available, as browns thrived in the warmer, larger, lower river environments—stream sections that had escaped fishing clubs and posting. Brown trout created many additional miles of trout water and, importantly, made them available to all anglers. Because these lower river sections had never been posted, many fishermen believed that they could not be. The tradition of fishing these waters, though, was never entirely legal, as landowners always had the right to exclude others from their property.

This fact became a reality on the Neversink when several miles of the best and most popular stretch of the river were closed. This was water that anglers had always taken for granted, water that was stocked for years by sportsmen, at public expense. The problem first surfaced in 1919, when the front page of the *Liberty Register* announced: "There have been parties around town the past week who are buying up the stream rights from Halls Mills bridge down to, or as near to our covered bridge as they can, says our Neversink correspondent."[6]

A week later the newspaper's editorial declared:

> City residents blessed with money, and desirous of having something good all to
> themselves, are buying up the Neversink River, it is said, with the intent to post it and
> keep it for themselves alone. People will not come here if there is no place to fish. Next
> year if all the streams are posted, the hundreds of fishermen who have been coming
> here will go elsewhere. Let's keep our streams open![7]

By the end of June, the secret was out. Edward R. Hewitt, an avid fly fisherman and wealthy New York City industrialist, had purchased large portions of the lower Neversink.

When the season opened in 1922, anglers were excluded from fishing waters they had fished for generations. Hewitt announced, through local newspapers, that "in the future his fishing

[6]*Liberty Register,* May 23, 1919, p. 1.
[7]*Liberty Register,* May 30, 1919, p. 4.

grounds will be posted and no anglers will be allowed on his property without a permit." Hewitt's announcement that the Neversink would be closed touched off a flurry of angry letters and editorials, and his actions were pivotal in the search for public fishing.

Fearing the eventual closing of all lower river sections, members of twenty rod and gun clubs—representing five thousand area sportsmen from four counties—met to pursue a public fishing program. Sportsmen's concerns over posting were aired in Middletown, early in 1923, with the local effort being spearheaded by the ever-active Liberty Rod & Gun Club and its president, Roy Steenrod.

Reporting on the meeting, the *Sullivan County Democrat* stated, "Mr. Steenrod suggested that the four counties form an alliance, with the idea that sportsmen would be better represented."

This was done, and bylaws were adopted:

> A bill was drawn up at the meeting, to be introduced at this session in Albany, asking that $1,000,000 be set aside for a purchase of streams, lakes and land in this section. If the bill passes, the streams of Sullivan County will be bought and opened up for fishing for all.[8]

The fact that such a request was made by a club from Liberty is not surprising, since some of its members lived along the Neversink and felt its loss through posting more personally. They were equally concerned over other area streams: Could this happen on the Beaverkill? The Willowemoc? Would there be a future for public fishing?

It is not surprising that this particular group made such an appeal to save its trout fishing, since there was definitely more "rod" than "gun" in this club. Its membership included Roy Steenrod, William Chandler, George W. Cooper, and Herman Christian. Aside from their love of fly fishing, these men all shared another common bond. They all knew Theodore Gordon and were influenced by his concern over the future of trout fishing.

The proposed bill was not successful; two years later, the Liberty Rod & Gun Club announced it would attempt to purchase, on its own, land along the Beaverkill, Willowemoc, and Neversink. Seeing the acquisition as a future necessity, the club proposed buying narrow strips of land along these streams, for the purpose of fishing. This idea never became a reality.

The first hint of a state public fishing program surfaced locally in a 1931 editorial of the *Liberty Register*. Citing a shortage of public trout streams near New York City, the editor stated that

---

[8]*Sullivan County Democrat,* February 7, 1923, p. 1.

the Conservation Department was thinking of "leasing streams for public fishing, and two of those were nearby."

In 1933, the subject was discussed in the Conservation Department's report to the legislature:

> Anglers for trout slowly but with ever increasing numbers are being excluded from large sections of our finest streams. Good stream fishing will always be most difficult to maintain by reason of the limited number of suitable streams in each region, the seasonal changes in volume and temperature of water, and the comparative ease with which landowners can post them.
>
> Assuming the State had a far greater supply of funds to carry on. What then? . . . It could buy strips of land on either side and under large sections of our principal trout streams and develop them to carry greater numbers of larger fish.

Finally, in 1935, a program of purchasing permanent fishing easements on the privately owned streams of the state became a reality when the legislature allocated $100,000 from the Conservation Fund for the acquisition of public fishing rights. The allocation was "for the acquisition of narrow strips of land including streams, and rights of way thereto, and the acquisition or lease of fishing rights in streams and rights of way thereto which are desireable to provide public fishing." The aim was to preserve trout fishing for the public and ensure that future generations of anglers would have streams to fish in.

The acquisition from the landowner was for an easement, usually thirty-three or sixty-six feet. The easement allowed anglers the right to travel the stream and banks over those portions purchased, for the purpose of fishing only; swimming, camping, or any other activity except fishing was prohibited.

In a letter to the *Hancock Herald,* Commissioner Osborne revealed that the state had $100,000 to spend on fishing rights but that the purchase of rights on the Beaverkill and Willowemoc would be too costly. The commissioner stated that acquisition had begun on streams in the western part of the state but not in the Catskills, claiming purchases there would be far more expensive than anywhere else.

Two years later, after he had secured additional funds from the legislature, Commissioner Osborne announced that negotiations were under way with landowners along the Beaverkill and Willowemoc. Speaking at the Lenape Hotel in Liberty, at the annual dinner of the Liberty Rod & Gun Club, he gave sportsmen the news they had waited so long to hear. The first public fishing rights easement acquired in the watershed was purchased from the Thomas Keery Company in December 1936.

The Keery Company operated the acid factory at Hazel and owned a long stretch of the Willowemoc. Initially, easements were purchased on four miles of the Willowemoc and two miles of the Beaverkill.

Perhaps eager to sample the new fishing rights his department had recently secured, Commissioner Osborne returned in May for a speaking engagement and two days of trout fishing. Along on the trip was Duncan G. Rankin, supervising forester, who had successfully negotiated the fishing rights along the Willowemoc and Beaverkill.

With Game Protector Roy Steenrod acting as guide, the party fished the newly acquired water at Hazel Bridge Pool, on the Willowemoc. Roy, a skilled fly caster and certainly one of the Catskills' most knowledgeable trout fishermen, saw to it that Commissioner Osborne caught some trout and received a few casting tips as well.

The local press reported that the commissioner told his angling companions that he was greatly pleased with the state's purchase at Hazel and that he was "markedly impressed with the area as a trout fishing center."[9]

Persistent sportsmen and a Conservation Department that looked to the future worked together and developed a program that generations of trout fishers have enjoyed. The program's success along these streams was initially dependent on the cooperation of its landowners and their willingness to sell their fishing rights.

Hazel Bridge Pool.

[9]*Liberty Register,* May 27, 1937, p. 1.

37

Protecting the Resource

Throughout its history, the Beaverkill has been victimized by human disturbances, which have affected its water quality, physical character, scenic beauty, and fisheries resources. The river has withstood the indiscriminate logging and polluting practices of tanneries, sawmills, and acid factories; the encroachments of road builders and gravel removers; and the effluent of slaughter-houses, sewage treatment plants, and highway runoff.

But during the 1930s and '40s, an even greater threat appeared when New York City proposed the construction of water-supply reservoirs on both the Willowemoc and Beaverkill.

The city's right to utilize these, and other streams, for reservoirs was granted in Chapter 724 of the Laws of 1905. Known as the "Catskill Water Act," the law permitted New York City to acquire land in the Catskills for water supply. The city's intent was to locate the cheapest, most accessible source of water; and their plan called for using the entire Catskill region. Each and every major trout stream was targeted to be dammed, their waters diverted through a series of tunnels to New York.

Local residents, politicians, and lawyers spoke out vehemently against the legislation at public hearings; they viewed the act as unconstitutional and a "ruthless and artful scheme."[1]

---

[1]*Ellenville Journal,* December 8, 1905, p. 1.

In 1905, the *Ellenville Journal* bitterly opposed the project and stated so: "No living man is capable of estimating the damage likely to result to the material interests of western Ulster from this foray of the Manhattenese upon our mountain streams."[2]

Its opposition was to no avail, and the city began acquiring, through condemnation, thousands of acres in the Esopus valley to make way for the huge Ashokan Reservoir.

Ashokan has a surface area of 8,315 acres; prior to being flooded, the land, rid of its inhabitants, presented a desolate, ravaged image to Catskill natives who visited the site. Much of the property that was taken had been farms that were originally cleared from the forest, homesteads built by families who never expected to leave. Wrote Elizabeth Burroughs Kelley:

> There were changes even in the mountains, in John's Catskills. A great lake had been added, blotting out landmarks and eradicating whole villages. Shortly before the water had been brought into the area, Julian had driven his family through it—a land of such devastation that it haunted the children for a long time afterward. Not a building had been left standing, every tree had been cut down, every object that could be picked up had been carried away; and then all those acres had been burned over. All that could be seen was blackened, desolate land extending for miles, completely barren like something out of a nightmare.[3]

Shortly after the construction of Ashokan Reservoir, New York City acquired lands along Schoharie Creek, impounding its waters and diverting them through an eighteen-mile tunnel to Esopus Creek and the Ashokan Reservoir. While work was being conducted on the Schoharie, city engineers were in the process of surveying other streams throughout the Catskills, frightening residents into believing their homes and farmlands would be next. During the 1920s, speculation was rampant over which farms, properties, or villages would be taken, and inundated by water.

In 1927, the New York City Board of Estimate approved plans to construct six additional water-supply reservoirs and released a map depicting impoundments on the East Branch of the Delaware, Rondout Creek, Neversink River, Little Delaware River, and, to the shock of many, the Beaverkill and Willowemoc Creek. Local papers reported, "In the Beaverkill, 100 more persons would be forced to vacate their homes in Craigeclair, Beaverkill and Lew Beach. More than 150 residents would be affected by the reservoir in the Willowemoc, which would submerge De Bruce and Willowemoc."[4]

---

[2]*Ellenville Journal,* November 17, 1905, p. 1.
[3]Kelley, *John Burroughs: Naturalist,* p. 216.
[4]*Liberty Register,* August 15, 1929, p. 4.

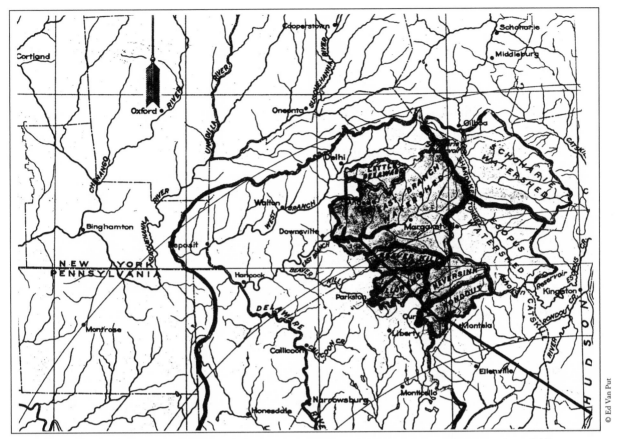

New York City map depicting projected Beaverkill and Willowemoc reservoirs, circa 1927.

It was estimated that the entire reservoir system would be completed by 1939; and 600 million gallons per day would come from the Delaware drainage.

Construction on the Beaverkill and Willowemoc reservoirs was halted temporarily when the state of New Jersey went to the Supreme Court of the United States to prohibit New York State and New York City from diverting the waters of the Delaware or its tributaries. New Jersey contended that withdrawals would seriously affect navigation, waterpower, sanitary conditions, industrial use, agriculture, municipal water supplies, recreation, and the oyster and shad fisheries. Pennsylvania also became a party to the suit.

On May 25, 1931, the Supreme Court decreed that the city was limited to withdrawing 440 million gallons per day. The court also required that a minimum flow be maintained at a point on the Delaware River below Port Jervis and noted that New York would be permitted to petition for more water in the future.

The 440 million gallons per day limited New York City to constructing reservoirs on the Neversink (105 million gallons per day) and the East Branch, at Pepacton (335 million gallons per day). In addition, plans moved forward on Rondout Creek; its waters were not affected by the decision, as they flowed into the Hudson, not the Delaware.

Due to litigation and the Great Depression, construction on the additional reservoirs could not begin until 1937. Plans to construct the Beaverkill and Willowemoc reservoirs were then reviewed, and their construction was to begin in the next five or six years. World War II put a hold on all construction; but in the winter of 1947, Board of Water Supply engineers again turned their attention to the Beaverkill and began making test holes for the dam. In the spring, the *Catskill Mountain News* reported:

> Recently New York City has had engineers at work taking borings in the Beaverkill valley. The report is that these borings have failed to strike bed rock at a depth of 130 feet and that the City plans to extend them down to a depth of 300 feet trying to locate a sound dam foundation. It is reported that it is impractical to build a large dam if a suitable foundation is not found within 130 to 150 feet of the surface of the ground.[5]

This was encouraging news to Beaverkill anglers, who in no way wanted to see their favorite waters destroyed by New York City.

In January 1949, Conservation Commissioner Perry Duryea was the guest speaker at the annual Liberty Rod & Gun Club dinner. Following the commissioner's speech, members voted to adopt a "resolution to memorialize the State Legislature to amend the existing law in such a way as to prevent New York City from taking, for water purposes, the Beaverkill River." Club members were not optimistic that this would have an effect on the city's plans to dam the stream, but they wanted to go on record with their opposition.

Another powerful club that lobbied against building a dam on the Beaverkill was the Beaverkill-Willowemoc Rod and Gun Club, a sportsmen's conservation organization with a membership of well over a thousand—the largest in Sullivan County. Harry Darbee was, at various times, president, conservation chairman, and editor of its informative newsletter, *Voice of the Beamoc*. His wife, Elsie, served as secretary and treasurer.

The Beamoc, as the club became known, lobbied hard for legislation prohibiting any municipality from building a dam for water-supply purposes on the Beaverkill or Willowemoc. The bill was aimed at preventing New York City from completing its plan to use these waters for reservoirs.

---

[5]*Catskill Mountain News,* April 30, 1948, p. 6.

Present at a Beamoc field day at Roscoe, in 1952, are Ellis Newman, Harry Darbee, Joan Salvato (Wulff), Bill Taylor, and Betty Bonavita.

The Beaverkill faithful rejoiced when later in the year it was learned that New York City had revised its plans, abandoning its interest in the Beaverkill and Willowemoc and turning its attention instead to the West Branch of the Delaware River.

Hearings were held by the Water Power and Control Commission (of which Commissioner Duryea was a member) at Delhi, and many objections were filed against the proposal. It was at this hearing that trout fishermen first learned of the city's change in plans regarding the Beaverkill:

> Representatives of the City of New York officially stated that the City is no longer interested in the development of the Little Delaware, the Beaverkill or the Willowemoc as sources of water supply.
>
> In view of the above official statements, sportsmen are assured that if the proposed Cannonsville dam is eventually approved, the interests of fishermen will be protected. And they can rejoice, in the fact that the Little Delaware, the Beaverkill and the Willowemoc will be preserved for trout fishing.[6]

---

[6]*Conservationist,* April–May 1950, p. 35.

In November, the Water Power and Control Commission granted approval for Cannonsville Reservoir, contingent upon the United States Supreme Court's modification of the 440-million-gallons-per-day restriction. (In June 1954, this amount was increased to 800 million gallons per day.)

Why the city turned its attention to the West Branch is uncertain. It may have been more practical to operate one large reservoir than three lesser ones; or, as reported, the city may have been discouraged by the failure to locate a suitable bedrock site for a dam on the Beaverkill. It is believed that growing opposition from organized sportsmen also played a part in this decision.

Perhaps it was all of these reasons, and more. But credit must be given to those angling conservationists who cared about the Beaverkill and became unified in their efforts to protect and preserve the stream. Their opposition to the construction of a dam and reservoir was the first major confrontation on the Beaverkill in which public interests were represented by organized sportsmen. Modern anglers were learning that there was strength in numbers, and that they had a voice, when registering their concerns with politicians and government officials.

No one ever worked harder at protecting and preserving the Beaverkill than Harry and Elsie Darbee. They fought against anything that threatened stream habitat, water quality, or the Beaverkill's trout populations. They joined and helped form several conservation organizations, wrote numerous letters, and lobbied state offices and politicians for stricter environmental legislation.

Harry Darbee had a special dislike for road builders. In the mountainous region of the Catskills, roads tend to parallel the stream courses, often too closely. They encroach on waterways, causing stream degradation, erosion, loss of shade trees, and a general destruction of habitat.

In the 1950s, Harry campaigned against the abuses that highway departments inflicted on trout streams. At meetings of Rotary clubs, conservation groups, and hunting and fishing organizations he presented a slide program titled *What's Happening to Our Streams?* The slides depicted specific abuses occurring along the Beaverkill and Willowemoc, such as gravel removal, bulldozing for flood control, and the dumping and filling of earth and rubble into watercourses. These activities were generally accepted by local people, who often saw them as reasonable and necessary, and who viewed Harry Darbee as something of a radical or extremist.

In 1955, Harry and Elsie Darbee tackled the problem of the open dumps and landfills found along the Beaverkill. At the time, there was an increasing use of stream banks for dumping; there were no less than fourteen sites along the lower river. Not only were local highway departments depositing "thousands of tons of soil,"[7] but area residents, too, were dumping household garbage, unwanted tires, furniture, and appliances by the truckload.

---

[7] *Liberty Register,* January 5, 1956, p. 1.

Garbage dump at Elk Brook along the Beaverkill.

Garbage dump at Hazel Bridge Pool along the
Willowemoc Creek. The angler is Harry Darbee.

Photographs were taken and sent to
the Conservation Department. Harry used
the power of the press, cajoling his out-
door-writer friends to publicize the problem. Red Smith reported on the deplorable
conditions in his weekly column in the
New York Herald Tribune; and Sparse Grey
Hackle wrote an inflammatory article, titled "The Scandal of the Desecrated
Shrine," for *Sports Illustrated.*

The Darbees traveled to Albany and
visited lawmakers. Through their efforts
and those of other Beamoc members, legislation was proposed; and in the spring of
1956, Governor Averell Harriman signed
a bill making it unlawful to dump "earth,
soil, refuse or other solid substances except
snow and ice in any stream or tributaries
therein which is inhabited by trout."

Dumping practices were halted; trash was removed in some areas of the Beaverkill and covered in others.

One year later, the Darbees engaged in a campaign to halt the spraying of DDT in the Catskills. Airplanes, spraying for gypsy moths, had a habit of not shutting off the valves that dispensed their lethal poisons when flying over rivers and streams. The Darbees wrote letters of opposition to newspapers and organized volunteer scientists and specialists to monitor operations along the Neversink, where the spraying was then taking place. The spraying caused the death of massive numbers of aquatic insects, which, as they fell back onto the water, were eaten; in turn, the trout that had eaten the insects turned belly-up. Through the Darbees' efforts, including the documentation of the fish kills resulting from the environmental effects of DDT, spraying practices were altered and eventually curtailed in the Catskills.

When automobile travel came to the Beaverkill, in the early 1900s, the lower river was paralleled by a narrow, two-lane roadway with twists and turns and steep gradients. The road was located on only one side and contained no bridges. Its impact on the river was minimal, though it did encroach along the river's banks and make the Beaverkill more easily accessible to increased fishing pressure and environmental abuses.

An artistic angler painted a fly on this highway sign.

The need for a new highway became inevitable as automobile and truck traffic steadily increased, especially after the region was no longer serviced by the railroad. In the late 1950s, the state's Department of Public Works unveiled plans to construct a major four-lane expressway (Route 17) along the lower Willowemoc and Beaverkill, all the way to East Branch and, beyond, to Binghamton.

Fishermen from across the state found it inconceivable that a modern, high-speed highway was charted to run through, and along, New York's most historic trout stream, within sight and sound of the Beaverkill's most famous pools.

The expressway would closely follow the rivers, crossing them no less than nine times and destroying the aesthetics that generations of trout fishers had come to revere. Those anglers seeking the peacefulness and tranquility often associated with the riffling waters of a trout stream would now find their solitude destroyed by the deafening din of speeding traffic and the echoing of diesels racing through the valley floor.

Members of the Beamoc saw the construction of the expressway as the ruination of the Beaverkill. A storm of protest began to build in opposition to the plan; and Harry Darbee, as chairman of the conservation committee, became the leading spokesman, spearheading a massive campaign. Fishermen from across the country were angered that the Beaverkill would be despoiled by rechannelization, bridge piers, and concrete retaining walls.

The Darbees had many other concerns about the impact that the highway would have on the Beaverkill's future. Harry believed that the river would be polluted by highway runoff, such as the salt, chemicals, and sand spread on the roadway in winter. He felt that rainwater runoff from the asphalt pavement and paved drainage sluices would be speeded to the river, raising water temperatures, and that major construction could ruin important springs entering the lower Beaverkill, which were vital to trout survival in times when low flows led to warm water temperatures.

Harry thought that contractors would be insensitive to the stream, and one of his greatest concerns was for the aquatic insect population, a mainstay of the lower river. The Beaverkill was famous for its abundant mayfly hatches, and aquatic insects contributed enormously to the food supply of the river's brown trout population.

In the past, automobiles traveling the old road had destroyed countless numbers of mayflies and other aquatic insects, plastering them against windshields, hoods, and radiators. This problem intensified whenever it rained, as many mating mayflies mistook the wet roadway for the river and deposited their eggs on the pavement. One passing vehicle would drive over thousands of flies. With the construction of four high-speed lanes, the additional traffic crisscrossing and paralleling both sides of the Beaverkill, Harry's concern seemed valid.

The fight between highway proponents and conservationist-anglers lasted several years. Following initial meetings with members of the Beamoc, the Department of Public Works consented to alter their plans and not divert or rechannel sections of the Beaverkill and Willowemoc. They also agreed not to construct concrete retaining walls along stream banks. It was announced that these changes were made to appease fishermen—and that the concessions would add several million dollars to the cost of the highway construction.

Another meeting was held at the Antrim Lodge, during the winter of 1962, and was attended by members of the Beamoc, the Conservation Department, and state officials from the Department of Public Works. The Conservation Department was represented by Dr. Harold G. Wilm, commissioner, and Dr. C. W. Greene, chief of the Bureau of Fish.

The *Liberty Register* reported that Commissioner Wilm was the guest speaker, and that he faced a hostile audience. Many in attendance believed that his department should publicly declare its opposition to the project and force highway engineers to find an alternate route. Commissioner Wilm informed anglers that the expressway was necessary and could not be located in a different area, primarily "because construction of other segments had placed the general location of this one at a point of no return." (Both east and west of the Beaverkill, the highway had already been completed.)

The Beamoc had requested that the expressway be built at a higher elevation, away from the rivers. It was informed that this was too expensive; costs would be prohibitive. Commissioner Wilm stated that he sincerely believed "revised plans came as close to a reasonable solution as possible, with a minimum of stream disturbance."

Hi Wright, an outdoor writer for the *Liberty Register,* summed up the feelings of many when he wrote:

> The Beamoc fight may appear to be a losing one, but I, for one, wish to salute Harry Darbee and his associates for carrying it on. To quit in discouragement just because you have lost a battle to entrenched interests serves only to entrench those interests a little deeper.[8]

Beamoc members believed that their concerns were not being taken seriously by state officials; those at the Department of Public Works complained that needless delays continued to drive up the costs of highway construction. The Beamoc decided to petition Governor Nelson Rockefeller, asking him to personally intervene and not allow these famous rivers to be destroyed. With the Darbees at the forefront, more than one hundred thousand signatures were collected on a petition protesting the route of construction.

When it became apparent, in 1964, that the expressway would follow the route chosen by the Department of Public Works, Harry Darbee urged the Conservation Department to conduct preconstruction studies of aquatic insects. In addition, he asked that temperature records be kept and the depth of existing pools be ascertained, to document the effects that highway construction would have on the Beaverkill.

Knowing that he had lost the battle to relocate the highway from the valley floor, Harry wrote, "The cost of our highway program should not include loss of our sports fisheries and the aesthetic values of undefiled and undamaged streams. There is a price on progress; it should be no greater than necessary."[9]

---

[8]*Liberty Register,* July 5, 1962, p. 5.
[9]*Liberty Register,* February 20, 1964, p. 1.

Dual highway bridges frequently crisscross the lower Beaverkill.

Friends of the Darbees knew that Harry and Elsie sacrificed a great deal of effort, time, and expense in trying to preserve a river they both loved; and while the loss of this battle sapped much of Harry's fighting spirit and optimism, he never stopped trying to convince others not to take trout streams for granted.

In the spring of 1964, Harry Darbee received the Salmo Award from the Theodore Gordon Fly Fishers for his "leadership in the battle to prevent the famous Beaverkill and Willowemoc trout streams from being ruined by highway construction."

Shortly after the expressway was completed, Conservation Commissioner Harold Wilm stunned everyone when he stated that "highway building had ruined the Beaverkill and Willowemoc trout streams." In a well-publicized news story that was carried by the wire services, the *Binghamton Evening Press* reported, ROCKY AIDE CHARGES STATE TROUT STREAMS RAVAGED. The article related the following conversation: " 'Will they [the trout streams] come back, Harold?' the Governor asked. 'We don't think so,' Dr. Wilm replied."[10]

---

[10]*Liberty Register,* November 25, 1965, p. 2.

Commissioner Wilm had previously stated that bridge construction over the streams would cause only short-lived damage that would be corrected by the freshets of the following spring. Many had assumed that the Department of Public Works had finalized its plan in response to the "studies and affirmation" of the Conservation Department and were, therefore, puzzled by the turnabout of Commissioner Wilm.

Leaders in many of the conservation efforts to protect the Beaverkill, Harry and Elsie Darbee became mentors to generations of anglers. They shared their knowledge of the Beaverkill with all who stopped by, and both of them dispensed fishing information—where to go, which flies were hatching, and which flies were "catching."

Many came because the Darbees were teachers; Elsie would demonstrate to anyone how she winged a dry fly, and Harry would warn of the dangers of DDT. Interspersed with his wisdom on how to catch trout, he would preach that rivers and streams had to be protected and could not be taken for granted. Dam builders, gravel removers, sewer plants, and road builders were the enemy, and the Darbees fought everybody and anybody who would spoil or threaten the rivers they loved.

Harry and Elsie lobbied for lower creel limits and no-kill water and harassed state and local officials into doing their jobs by enforcing regulations that stopped the degradation of trout streams.

Elsie Darbee died in 1980, at the age of sixty-eight. Three years later, Harry passed away. They are buried, side by side, in the small cemetery in Lew Beach. It is the final resting place for a number of fly-fishing veterans, who lie in rest near their beloved Beaverkill.

The Darbees are missed by many. On more than one occasion, I have stopped to visit their grave site and found a trout fly placed on their headstone, as if to pay homage to their memory.

$Addendum$

The expressway did not "ruin" the Beaverkill, as Conservation Commissioner Wilm had stated, though it did have a major impact on the river's environment.

The final segment of Route 17, between Livingston Manor and Roscoe, was completed in 1966, and during this time much of the Willowemoc valley between the two villages was ravaged. Scores of earth-moving machines were busy scalping the steep hillsides of protective vegetation, excavating and filling the floodplains. Earth, sand, and silt found their way into the rivers, at times causing great turbidity.

Temporary and permanent bridges were constructed every couple of miles up and down the Beaverkill and Willowemoc, and huge amounts of earth were mined from hastily developed gravel pits, too near the waterways. Even thirty years later, they still detract from the integrity of the rivers. Along the old highway, new bridges constructed with box culverts or concrete aprons made passage upstream difficult for mature spawning fish.

The highway was not the end of good trout fishing, though to a great many veteran Beaverkill anglers the lower river would never be the same aesthetically. Some were heartbroken over the fact that they had lost the battle to keep the highway out of the valley floor. They remembered the river as it used to be, and found the incessant drone of high-speed traffic so offensive and unpleasant that they stopped fishing the Beaverkill and went elsewhere.

However, just as the river was losing some of its faithful, it began to recruit a new following of seemingly dedicated anglers who adopted a no-kill philosophy.

Beaverkill trout fishing had been in a state of decline during the 1950s. It was claimed that there were fewer large fish (over 12 inches) and that the number of wild trout being caught was smaller than in previous years. Fisheries surveys conducted in the 1950s supported this general belief, though the reasons were not obvious.

Some attributed the decline to a series of dry years, which caused low flows and high water temperatures; they believed that the larger trout were exposed to increased predation when they gathered in spring holes and off cooler tributary mouths. Others pointed to the post–World War II popularity of the spinning rod.

Previously, anglers who fished with bait often used a fly rod. Because of the difficulty of casting, they had to wade the stream, learn where the trout were, get close to the fish, and run the risk of spooking them or putting them down. But now, the new spinning rods enabled fishermen to cast the lightest of lures or bait across the river without even entering the water. Spin fishermen could cover large stretches of the Beaverkill in a short time, with very little effort or knowledge of the river and its trout.

In 1964, the Conservation Department conducted a creel census on the lower Beaverkill to monitor angler success, catch composition, and fishing pressure. The study was intended to provide a basis for future management and to evaluate the effects of the expressway construction on the Beaverkill fishery.

Fish collections were made at the end of the season by electrofishing, and the data collected from the study was analyzed by fisheries biologist Russell D. Fieldhouse. The findings revealed a very small population of wild trout (only 2.5 percent of trout caught by anglers were of wild origin); and of the 15,881 trout caught in 1964, 91.8 percent had been stocked that same year. In addition, few trout over 12 inches in length were collected.

Russ Fieldhouse believed that the five-trout-per-day creel limit then imposed was of little value in restricting the catch of wild trout, and he made the courageous decision to place two miles of the Big Beaverkill under a fish-for-fun special regulation. This proposal was not popular with the general population of anglers, but it did receive support from some fly fishermen. The regulation required anglers to release all trout back to the water unharmed.

Sign depicting special fishing regulations.

Originally known as a fish-for-fun and, later, no-kill area, the stretch of water ran downstream from the head of Barnhart's Pool to the old railroad bridge. Initially the use of bait was permitted, as it was believed that this concession made the law more acceptable to those opposed to the regulation, and it was assumed that not many bait fishermen would want to fish where they had to return their catch. Even though the use of bait was allowed, the trout fishing improved dramatically.

Fisheries professionals within the Conservation Department recognized the success of the regulation immediately, though it continued to be unpopular with many local residents and organized sportsmen in the area. They viewed the no-kill regulation as an infringement on their rights. Local judges let conservation officers know that they would not be happy to have violators brought before them as, in their opinion, a person went trout fishing to catch, keep, and eat fish.

A few years after its success on the Beaverkill, fisheries biologist William H. Kelly instituted a catch-and-release regulation on a section of the lower Willowemoc. An ardent and expert fly fisher, Bill Kelly had experienced firsthand the success of the Beaverkill no-kill water, and he was determined to expand the concept. Despite local opposition, he lobbied sportsmen, landowners, and civic groups successfully and initiated the regulation on the Willowemoc in 1969.

This no-kill water, too, became highly successful and popular. It was recognized, though, that those anglers using bait often defied the law and kept trout; so at the start of the 1971 season the use of bait was prohibited, and anglers were limited to artificial lures only.

Trout measuring 12 to 15 inches became increasingly common in both the Beaverkill and the Willowemoc; and catching a dozen such trout in an afternoon or evening was routine. Catches of twenty or thirty fish, and even more by skilled fly fishers, became frequent to no-kill regulars. During the peak mayfly hatching periods of late April, May, and June, the fishing was excellent; and a great many fly fishers began comparing it to that of previous generations, when the Big Beaverkill held many trout in the 1- and 2-pound range.

By the mid-1970s the amount of no-kill water available on both rivers was expanded to more than eight miles, and a small army of devoted fly rodders could be found along its waters seven days a week. The license plates of vehicles parked along the river revealed that while most were from adjoining states, many visiting anglers traveled across the country to fish the no-kill water.

While construction of Route 17 was a significant environmental disturbance to the Beaverkill, the watershed, through reforestation, is better protected today than at any time in its history. Lands once cleared for agriculture and those denuded by the wood chemical industry (lands that some people thought would never yield timber again) have changed to second-growth woodlands and mature hardwood forests.

Trees are the Catskills' most abundant natural resource; they flourish, mostly due to moderate temperature and the large amount of rainfall. In the words of historian Alf Evers, "Just as some parts of the world are desert country or grass country, so the Catskills are tree country."

Bald Mountain, aptly named, as it appeared in the 1890's, with hardly a tree standing.

Same view today, illustrating the reforestation of the once-cleared lands.

Addendum

Early settlers had attempted to eke out a living from the thin mountainside soils by clearing even the most remote hollows and glens. Hillside farms were everywhere, their patchwork of emerald fields made more obvious by the dark gray stone fences that outlined their boundaries.

While farmers did clear many sections of the forest, their activities in general had a minor effect on the watershed. And while the removal of the hemlocks by tanners did affect the Beaverkill and its fisheries, the greatest impact came from the wood chemical industry, which employed the destructive practice of clear-cutting vast areas of hardwoods.

By the time the wood chemical industry peaked, many of the farms in the region were being abandoned. The Catskills were never compatible with farming; the land was generally too steep and too stony. The high mountains and narrow valleys made morning and evening shadows long, and it was said that "the sun rises two hours late and sets two hours early." The decline in agriculture reduced the number of people living in the area, and when the wood chemical industry departed, the population decreased even further.

Today the region is lightly populated. In some parts of the watershed there were once many more residents than there are at present. The upper Beaverkill flows through the town of Hardenbergh (its citizens are divided by a mountain range separating the Beaverkill from Dry Brook and Mill Brook). In 1875, the population of Hardenbergh was 671; in 1995 it is 204, with less than 60 living in the Beaverkill valley.

Most of the watershed flows through the town of Rockland, which includes the main population centers of Livingston Manor and Roscoe. The last census taken revealed that the population had decreased from 4,216 in 1960 to 4,096 in 1990. Since 1905, the population of Rockland (90.48 square miles) has increased by only 382 residents.

On the lower Beaverkill, Route 17 passes over what was formerly the community of Elk Brook, an acid factory village, which had contained forty buildings and, in 1921, about two hundred people.

The fact that the area has remained lightly inhabited contributes to the scenic landscape; however, one important element of the successful reforestation of the Beaverkill watershed has been the creation of the Catskill Forest Preserve.

The preserve was created by an act of the legislature in 1885, and initially the lands forming the foundation of the preserve were those acquired through mortgage foreclosures and tax sales, often areas stripped of their timber. Over the years many of the old, abandoned farms and lands cleared by the acid industry became part of the forest preserve.

From 1890 to the present, new lands were added primarily through bond acts approved by the legislature. Beginning in 1895, these lands were protected by the state constitution, which ensures they will be kept as forever-wild forest; their timber may not be sold, removed, or destroyed.

All but the last 6.3 miles of the Beaverkill flows through the Catskill Forest Preserve, and the watershed receives a great deal of permanent protection from state-owned lands lying inside these boundaries. Since 1973 more than 10,000 acres of the drainage area have been acquired and added to the forest preserve. Today, more than 54,000 acres, or nearly 30 percent of the Beaverkill watershed, are state-owned, forever-wild forest.

Further protection of the Beaverkill has also come from the private conservation efforts of Larry Rockefeller. While visiting friends along the upper Beaverkill, Larry admired the exceptional natural beauty of the area so much that he purchased a hilltop dairy farm and became a resident of the Beaverkill valley. As an environmental lawyer with the Natural Resources Defense Council, he became aware that changes were occurring in the area, and as the son of the well-known conservationist Laurance Rockefeller, he had an inherent desire to protect the scenic beauty and critical habitat of the Beaverkill.

While the private fishing clubs that bordered the Beaverkill were historically good stewards of the land, changes in the valley began to occur when large parcels were acquired by developers intent on apportioning them into numerous small lots, turning the unspoiled landscape into thoughtless subdivisions.

In 1978, Larry Rockefeller made a personal commitment to preserve the land through planned development, a project he saw as "the most economical way to recycle the land back as closely as possible to what it had been a century ago."[1]

He began purchasing land throughout the upper Beaverkill, assembling small parcels and old farms into larger tracts, eventually dividing these into homesites. Each site was carefully chosen; houses were placed as inconspicuously as possible, out of view of one another.

Sensitive to the ecology and the stream environment, Larry imposed conservation easements and environmental covenants on the property, restricting its use. His project has been lauded by environmentalists, who see his efforts as "protecting the land and the interests of the people who are buying it."[2]

One of Larry's early purchases included the Bonnie View, the last of the old Beaverkill fishing resorts. This streamside inn's popularity with trout fishermen dates back to the horse-and-carriage days, having opened in 1895, when the wet fly was still the most common method of fly fishing.

[1,2]*New York Times,* October 11, 1987, p. R9.

Today, the upper Beaverkill Valley still remains densely forested.

At the time of his purchase, the building was in a serious state of disrepair. Larry made major renovations, tastefully remodeling the interior while retaining the theme and decor of a country inn. The outside appearance was restored to that of its original construction, and the name was changed to the Beaverkill Valley Inn. This upper Beaverkill resort remains open to the public.

To date, Larry Rockefeller has expended a great deal of time and money to secure the protection of an additional 11,000 acres from the exploitation of uncontrolled development and land speculators.

While efforts were being made both publicly and privately to preserve the sensitive environment of the Beaverkill, an endeavor was under way to preserve the history of fly fishing as well.

A few years before she passed away, the late Catskill fly tier Elsie Darbee began promoting the idea of establishing a museum devoted to the history of fly fishing in the Catskills. In 1978, a small number of local men and women began meeting to perpetuate the idea, and Elsie served as their first president, until her death in 1980. The following year the group became incorporated and known as the Catskill Fly Fishing Center; a board of directors was elected, and Dr. Alan Fried of Livingston Manor became president.

Under Dr. Fried's leadership the Center made great strides toward fulfilling Elsie's vision. At first it found a temporary home, displaying artifacts and memorabilia in the old Roscoe movie theater, the same building where Walt and Winnie Dette and Harry Darbee had begun their fly-tying careers so many years before. Shortly, through donations and membership contributions, the Catskill Fly Fishing Center acquired a permanent site along the Willowemoc between Livingston Manor and Roscoe.

The property included an old farmhouse, a barn, and thirty-five acres, as well as a half mile of stream frontage. The farmhouse was renovated into an office and temporary museum, and money was raised for a vehicular bridge to connect the site with the main roadway.

Immediately after the acquisition a fund was started to build a professional museum large enough to house a research library, archival storage, and a display area for the many artifacts the Center began to accumulate.

In September 1984, the Catskill Fly Fishing Center received significant support when former president and first lady Jimmy and Rosalynn Carter accepted its invitation to come and fish for five days and promote the Center's building fund. The Carters stayed at the Beaverkill Valley Inn. Hardly had their luggage been placed in their room when President Carter was on the stream. With an entourage of Secret Service agents eyeing his every cast, he successfully plied his skills on a number of Beaverkill brown trout. The president quickly revealed that he had the ability to read water, place his fly where he wanted to, and, when it was accepted by the trout, react with the quickness that separated the expert from the average fly fisher.

In the days ahead, Mrs. Carter also proved she had a talent for fly fishing, as she more than held her own on the Beaverkill and took a wily rainbow or two from the Delaware River, under high-water conditions veteran anglers would have found difficult.

Being an avid fly fisherman, President Carter concurred with the Center's goal of preserving the heritage of fly fishing in the Catskills. He gave freely of his time, making a number of public appearances and attending a formal fund-raising dinner. The affair was extremely successful and kicked off the Center's effort to raise funds for a modern museum building.

One year after the Carters' visit, Paul Volcker, an avid and capable fly fisherman, contributed his notoriety to aiding the Center. As chairman of the board of the Federal Reserve, he attracted a number of people to attend a fund-raising event at the Beaverkill Valley Inn.

Both benefits were very successful in providing important seed money for the Center's building fund. In the years following these events, money was raised through various methods, including dinners and donations. After ten years of fund-raising, the Catskill Fly Fishing Center began constructing its new museum.

On May 28, 1995, the dream had become a reality when the Center opened the doors to the new building. At a ribbon-cutting ceremony conducted by Elsie Darbee's daughter, Judie, the public was introduced to a climate-controlled, state-of-the-art, four-thousand-square-foot modern museum. Plans call for a research library of fly-fishing books and videos, environmental information concerning area streams and rivers, and an area for fly tying and rod building.

The facility currently features exhibits showing artifacts from anglers and fly tiers who made the Catskills famous. Visitors can see how much hackle Art Flick placed on a Red Quill, what a Theodore Gordon dry fly looked like, and how Lee Wulff tied flies in his hands.

Addendum

On one particular weekend, when the Beaverkill contained even more than its usual number of fly fishers, it was visited by Lee and Joan Wulff. The year was 1977, and the Wulffs were guests at the Eastern Conclave of the Federation of Fly Fishermen at the nearby Campbell Inn.

Lee and Joan enjoyed international reputations as superb anglers; their skills with a fly rod were legendary, the envy of all who were familiar with their exploits. Lee was known as a great innovator and developer of tackle and fly-fishing techniques, Joan as a world-class fly caster and national casting champion. The Wulffs distinguished themselves by challenging fresh- and saltwater game fish with light tackle, broadening and pioneering the range and versatility of the fly rod.

The Wulffs traveled along the no-kill water of the Beaverkill, stopping at different pools to observe the fishing activity. Everywhere they stopped, trout were rising; and many anglers were either playing or landing fish. Lee had often fished the Beaverkill in the late 1920s and '30s, and to him "it was just like coming home again."[3]

Henry Lee Wulff was born in Valdez, Alaska, in 1905. When he was ten his family moved back to the United States, first to Brooklyn, then to San Diego. He graduated from Stanford University with a degree in civil engineering, but he decided to pursue a career in art and went to Paris in 1926 to further his studies. After a year overseas, he returned to New York and found employment in an advertising agency.

A born fisherman, Lee spent every weekend fishing the Adirondacks, the Battenkill, or the nearby waters of the Catskills. Being pent up in the city all week, he greatly enjoyed wading straight up the middle of the swift-flowing, boulder-strewn Esopus, "just for the sheer physical pleasure and exercise."

Lee fished at every opportunity and took a hardworking, intense approach to his fishing. He was applying his fishing skills to the Beaverkill at a time when many of America's most prominent fly fishermen and angling writers were fishing the river. And while some men retired from their fishing early, to reminisce the day's sport at Keener's Pool or one of the other popular fishing hotel bars, Lee would remain on the water, learning the habits of the trout of the lower Beaverkill.

Lee Wulff studied the mayflies along the streams he fished, especially the Hendrickson on the Beaverkill, and *Isonychia* on the Ausable River in the Adirondacks. Dissatisfied with the thinly dressed imitations then in use, he desired floating flies with "fatter bodies." He wanted a slate gray pattern with a "reasonably solid silhouette," and in the winter of 1929–30 he created the Gray Wulff. To match the spinner (coffin fly) of the green Drake he found on both rivers, he tied the White Wulff. Lee tied thicker-bodied flies and used bucktail for wings and tails, developing a

---

[3]Kubik, "Lee Wulff," *Kaatskill Life,* Winter 1990, p. 49.

281

high-floating, durable dry fly. He first tried these flies on the Esopus, then on the Beaverkill—and they were successful right from the start. He also created the Royal Wulff "to give utility to the Fanwing Royal Coachman," changing the pattern to white bucktail wings and a brown bucktail tail. Today, Wulff-style dry flies are known and used all over the world, not only for trout but for salmon as well.

During the 1930s Lee Wulff decided to abandon the business world and become a freelance outdoor writer and filmmaker. He began fishing with a camera around his neck and quickly became a talented writer, photographer, and illustrator.

Soon he was contributing articles to many magazines, including *Field & Stream, Outdoor Life, Esquire,* and *Sports Afield*. He published the first of several books in 1937; by 1950, Lee Wulff had become one of America's foremost outdoor writers. In 1938 he produced his first film, and during the 1960s and '70s he produced and was featured in a great many fishing films for television, including the first network angling films on CBS's *Sports Spectacular* and ABC's *American Sportsman*.

In 1977, at the time of the Wulffs' visit to the Beaverkill, they were searching for a location to start a fly-fishing school. They had traveled the country and seen many of the best fishing locations. While there were many aspects to consider, one that was important was the mileage of no-kill water along the Beaverkill. As a longtime proponent of catch and release, Lee was greatly impressed with the Beaverkill's successful regulation promoting this philosophy. The Wulffs moved to the area in 1978 and established their now-famous fly-fishing school on the upper Beaverkill the following year. Both Lee and Joan participated in every phase of their school, demonstrating, lecturing, teaching, and passing on their knowledge of fly fishing to their students; the school became an immediate success.

For more than forty years, Lee piloted his own aircraft, a single-engine Piper Super Cub, which he kept tied down in the meadow adjoining the school ponds and classroom. Flying made Lee happy, and often when the weather allowed and he was between lectures, he would get in the airplane, taxi down the grassy field, take off, and fly over the river and valley he loved. His flights were never very long, as he always put in a full day teaching at the school. Even at age eighty-six, Lee showed no signs of slowing down, and often spoke of and planned for the future, as if he would always be here.

On April 28, 1991, he taxied his airplane down the meadow airstrip and lifted off, beginning a routine recertification test for his pilot's license. Tragically, he never returned; his life ended when he had a heart attack, which resulted in a plane crash.

Several weeks after his death, close friends and family members gathered along the banks of the Beaverkill to remember this man who had led such an extraordinary life. They took turns distributing his ashes into the stream's swirling waters, uniting forever the legend that was Lee Wulff with the legend that is the Beaverkill.

Bibliography

PUBLIC RECORDS

Delaware, Greene, Sullivan, and Ulster County Clerk's Offices: deed and mortgage books; miscellaneous books (Sullivan County); maps placed on record, often bound in books, but earliest found in deed books.
New York State Census Records, Delaware and Sullivan Counties.
Delaware, Greene, Sullivan, and Ulster County surrogates records, wills, and probate records.
Field Books: Hardenbergh Patent Great Lot 6—1809; Delaware County Clerk's Office, Delhi, N.Y.

PUBLIC LIBRARIES

Adriance Memorial Library, Poughkeepsie, N.Y.
Cannon Free Library, Delhi, N.Y.
Ellenville Public Library, Ellenville, N.Y.
Kingston Area Library, Kingston, N.Y.
Liberty Public Library, Liberty, N.Y.
Livingston Manor Free Public Library, Livingston Manor, N.Y.
Louise Adelia Read Memorial Library, Hancock, N.Y.
Mann Library, Cornell University, Ithaca, N.Y.
McDonald De Witt Library, Ulster County Community College, Stone Ridge, N.Y.
Mudd Library, Yale University, New Haven, C.T.
New York Public Library, New York, N.Y.
New York State Library, Albany, N.Y.
Newburgh Free Library, Newburgh, N.Y.
Orange County Community College, Middletown, N.Y.
Roscoe Library, Roscoe, N.Y.

Stamford Village Library, Stamford, N.Y.
William B. Ogden Free Library, Walton, N.Y.

N E W S P A P E R S

The years indicate the period researched. The location is where the research was done.

Andes Recorder (1867–92), Delaware County Historical Society, Delhi, N.Y.

Bloomville Mirror (1853–74), Stamford Village Library, Stamford, N.Y.

Catskill Mountain News (1902–55), Offices of the *Catskill Mountain News,* Margaretville, N.Y.

Delaware Gazette (1819–1903), Cannon Free Library, Delhi, N.Y.

Ellenville Journal (1849–1916), Ellenville Public Library, Ellenville, N.Y.

Hancock Herald (1874–97), Louise Adelia Read Memorial Library, Hancock, N.Y.

Kingston Argus (1873–1905), Kingston Area Library, Kingston, N.Y.

Kingston Craftsman (1820–22), Kingston Area Library, Kingston, N.Y.

Kingston Democratic Journal (1849–64), Kingston Area Library, Kingston, N.Y.

Kingston Press (1863–74), Kingston Area Library, Kingston, N.Y.

Kingston Weekly Freeman & Journal (1868–99), Kingston Area Library, Kingston, N.Y.

Kingston Weekly Leader (1887–1904), Kingston Area Library, Kingston, N.Y.

Liberty Register (1878–1967), Liberty Public Library, Liberty, N.Y.

Livingston Manor Times (1922–60), Dr. Paul D'Amico, Livingston Manor, N.Y.

Narrowsburg Democrat (1914), Offices of the *Sullivan County Democrat,* Callicoon, N.Y.

New York Times (1851–1950), Orange County Community College, Middletown, N.Y.

The People's Press (1857–63), Kingston Area Library, Kingston, N.Y.

Pine Hill Sentinel (1885–1908), Ulster County Community College, Stone Ridge, N.Y.

Political Reformer (1839–40), Kingston Area Library, Kingston, N.Y.

Rondout Courier (1848–69), Kingston Area Library, Kingston, N.Y.

Rondout Daily Freeman (1871), Kingston Area Library, Kingston, N.Y.

Rondout Weekly Freeman (1871–72), Kingston Area Library, Kingston, N.Y.

Roscoe-Rockland Review & Sullivan County Review (1895–1941), Roscoe Central School, Roscoe, N.Y.

Stamford Mirror (1874–86), Stamford Village Library, Stamford, N.Y.

Sullivan County Democrat (1907–56), Offices of the *Sullivan County Democrat,* Callicoon, N.Y.

Sullivan County Record (1950–56), Offices of the *Sullivan County Democrat,* Callicoon, N.Y.

Ulster Palladium (1830–33), Kingston Area Library, Kingston, N.Y.

Ulster Republican (1833–61), Kingston Area Library, Kingston, N.Y.

Ulster Sentinel (1826–30), Kingston Area Library, Kingston, N.Y.

Walton Blade (1856–57), William B. Ogden Free Library, Walton, N.Y.

Walton Chronicle (1877–88), William B. Ogden Free Library, Walton, N.Y.

Walton Journal (1857–59), William B. Ogden Free Library, Walton, N.Y.

Walton Reporter (1885–1941), William B. Ogden Free Library, Walton, N.Y.

Walton Weekly Chronicle (1869–78), William B. Ogden Free Library, Walton, N.Y.

BOOKS, MAGAZINES, AND ARTICLES

American Angler, The. Edited by William C. Harris. New York, N.Y. A weekly journal devoted to fishing—brook, river, lake—and sea-fish culture. 1881–95.

American Angler, The. Edited by Enos Post. New York, N.Y. 1916–21.

American Fly-Tyer. Fitchburg, Mass. April, May, June 1941.

American Turf Register and Sporting Magazine. Baltimore, Md. The first of its kind in the United States; featured material on shooting, hunting, fishing, and other outdoor sports. 1829–44.

Barrus, Clara. *John Burroughs: Boy and Man*. Garden City, N.Y.: Doubleday, Page & Co., 1920.

————. *The Life and Letters of John Burroughs*. 1925. New York: Russell & Russell, 1968.

Bayer, Henry G. *The Belgians First Settlers in New York and in the Middle States*. New York: The Devin-Adair Co., 1925.

Biological Survey of the Delaware-Susquehanna Watershed. New York State Conservation Department Report. New York: J. B. Lyon Co., 1935.

Bradley, William A. *Fly-Fishing Reminiscences of My Early Years at the Beaverkill Trout Club*. New York: Private printing, 1927.

Brink, Benjamin Myer, ed. *Olde Ulster*. 10 vols. Kingston, N.Y.: Published by Benjamin Myer Brink, 1905–14.

Brinton, Daniel G. *The Lenape and Their Legends*. Philadelphia: D. G. Brinton, 1885.

Brown, Eleanor. *The Forest Preserve*. New York: Adirondack Mountain Club, 1985.

Brown, John J. *The American Angler's Guide*. 1845. New York: D. Appleton & Co., 1876.

Burke, Edgar, M.D. *American Dry Flies and How to Tie Them*. New York: Derrydale Press, 1930.

Burroughs, John. *In the Catskills*. 1871. New York: Houghton Mifflin Co., 1910.

————. *Locusts and Wild Honey*. 1879. Boston and New York: Houghton Mifflin Co., 1907.

————. *Wake-Robin*. Boston and New York: Houghton Mifflin Co., 1871.

Camp, Samuel G. *Fishing with Floating Flies*. 1913. New York: The Macmillan Co., 1923.

Clearwater, A. T. *History of Ulster County*. Kingston, N.Y.: W. J. Van Deusen, 1907.

Connett, Eugene V. *Any Luck?* 1933. Garden City, N.Y.: Garden City Publishing Co., Inc., 1937.

Conservationist. New York State Conservation Department, 1946–60.

Cross, Reuben R. *The Complete Fly Tier*. Rockville Centre, N.Y.: Freshet Press, 1971.

Darbee, Harry. *Fishermen's Tricks, Tips and Hints*. New York: J. Lowell Pratt & Co., 1967.

Darbee, Harry, with Mac Francis. *Catskill Flytier*. Philadelphia and New York: J. B. Lippincott Co., 1977.

Delaware River Drainage Basin. New York State Department of Health and New York State Conservation Department, 1960.

DeLisser, R. Lionel. *Picturesque Ulster*. Kingston, N.Y.: The Styles & Bruyn Publishing Co., 1896.

DeNio, Pierre. *The Winding Delaware*. Equinunk, Pa.: Equinunk Historical Society, 1984.

Eggert, Richard, "The Theodore Gordon Heritage, III: The Legacy." *Fly Fisherman* December 1969.

Evers, Alf. *The Catskills: From Wilderness to Woodstock*. Garden City, N.Y.: Doubleday, 1972.

———. "Indians of the Catskills." *Catskill Center News* Fall 1988.

Foote, John Taintor. *Anglers All*. New York: Appleton-Century-Crofts, Inc., 1947.

Ford, Corey. "The Best-Loved Trout Stream of Them All." *True* 1952.

Field & Stream. Published monthly. New York. 1898–1980.

Forest and Stream. Edited from 1873–80 by Charles Hallock. A journal of outdoor life, travel, nature study, shooting, fishing, and yachting. New York. 1873–1914 weekly, 1915–30 monthly.

Francis, Austin M. *Catskill Rivers*. New York: Nick Lyons Books, 1983.

Freese, John W. "Catskill Hatchery at De Bruce." *Conservationist* Feb.–Mar. 1949.

Fretz, Warren. "Old Methods Of Taking Fish." *Bucks County Historical Society*. Vol. 5., 1921.

Fried, Marc B. *The Early History of Kingston and Ulster County, New York*. Kingston, N.Y.: Ulster County Historical Society, 1975.

Gerow, Joshua R. *Alder Lake*. Liberty, N.Y.: Fuelane Press, 1953.

Gill, Emlyn M. *Practical Dry-Fly Fishing*. New York: Charles Scribner's Sons, 1912.

Gingrich, Arnold. *The Fishing in Print*. New York: Winchester Press, 1974.

———. *The Joys of Trout*. New York: Crown Publishers, Inc., 1973.

———. *The Well-Tempered Angler*. New York: Alfred A. Knopf, 1965.

Goodspeed, Charles E. *Angling in America*. Boston: Houghton Mifflin Co., 1939.

Gordon, Theodore, and a Company of Anglers. Edited by Arnold Gingrich. *American Trout Fishing*. New York: Alfred A. Knopf, 1966.

Graham's Magazine, Casket, Gentleman's Magazine. Published in Philadelphia. 1827–56.

Hackle, Sparse Grey. *Fishless Days, Angling Nights.* New York: Crown Publishers, Inc., 1971.

———. "A Friend of Theodore Gordon's: An Interview with Roy Steenrod." *Anglers' Club Bulletin* June 1955.

———. "The Scandal of the Desecrated Shrine." *Sports Illustrated* February 27, 1956.

———. "Theodore Gordon and Herman Christian." *Anglers' Club Bulletin* June 1950.

Haring, H. A. *Our Catskill Mountains.* New York: G. P. Putnam's Sons, 1931.

Harper's New Monthly Magazine. 1850–74.

Heacox, Cecil E. "The Catskill Flytyers." *Outdoor Life* May 1972.

———. *The Compleat Brown Trout.* 1974. Clinton, N.J.: Amwell Press, 1983.

Hedrick, Joan D. *Harriet Beecher Stowe.* New York: Oxford University Press, 1994.

Hills, John Waller. *A History of Fly Fishing for Trout.* 1921. Rockville Centre, N.Y.: Freshet Press, 1971.

History of Delaware County, N.Y., 1797–1880. New York: W. W. Munsell & Co., 1932.

Hodge, Frederick Webb, ed. *Handbook of American Indians North of Mexico.* Pageant Books Inc., 1959. Republished Grosse Pointe: Scholarly Press, 1968.

Holden, George Parker. *Streamcraft.* Cincinnati: Stewart & Kidd Co., 1919.

Ingraham, Henry A. *American Trout Streams.* New York: Derrydale Press, 1926.

Irwin, R. Stephen. *Hunters of the Eastern Forest.* Surrey, British Columbia: Hancock House Publishers Ltd., 1984.

Ives, Marguerite. *Seventeen Famous Outdoorsmen.* Chicago: The Canterbury Press, 1929.

Jennings, Preston J. *A Book of Trout Flies.* 1935. New York: Crown Publishers, Inc., 1970.

Judd, David W. "Beecher's Clearing." *American Agriculturist* September 1881.

Kelley, Elizabeth Burroughs. *John Burroughs: Naturalist.* West Park, N.Y.: Riverby Books, 1959.

Knox, Thomas W. *Life and Work of Henry Ward Beecher.* Hartford, Conn.: Park Publishing Co., 1887.

Koller, Lawrence R. *Taking Larger Trout.* Boston: Little, Brown and Co., 1950.

Kovalik, Dr. Thomas. *Ned Buntline: King of the Dime Novels.* Charlotteville, N.Y.: SamHar Press, 1986.

Kubik, Dorothy. "Lee Wulff." *Kaatskill Life* Winter 1990.

Kudish, Michael, Ph.D. *Catskills Soil and Forest History.* Hobart, N.Y.: The Catskill Center for Conservation, 1979.

Kudish, Michael. "Vegetational History of the Catskill High Peaks." Unpublished doctoral thesis. Syracuse University, 1972.

La Branche, George M. L. *The Dry Fly and Fast Water*. New York: Charles Scribner's Sons, 1914.

———. "The Evolution of a Dry Fly Fisherman." *Recreation* July 1904.

Leggett, John D., Jr. "The Quill Gordon Water." *The Anglers' Club Bulletin* Spring–Summer 1990.

Leiser, Eric. *The Dettes*. Fishkill, N.Y.: Willowkill Press, 1992.

Lewis, Barry. "The Art of Flytying." *Catskill-Delaware* (Callicoon, N.Y.) Summer 1986.

Longstreth, T. Morris. *The Catskills*. 1918. New York: The Century Co., 1921.

Mack, Arthur C. *Enjoying the Catskills*. New York: Funk & Wagnalls, 1950.

Malone, Dumas, ed. *Dictionary of American Biography*. New York: Charles Scribner's Sons, 1932.

Marbury, Mary Orvis. *Favorite Flies and Their Histories*. 1892. Secaucus, N.J.: The Wellfleet Press, 1988.

Martin, Roscoe C. *Water for New York*. Syracuse, N.Y.: Syracuse University Press, 1960.

Mather, Fred. *My Angling Friends*. New York: Forest and Stream Publishing Co., 1901.

Mayes, Mary Ann. *Early Indians of Delaware County: The Lenni Lenape*. Fleischmanns, N.Y.: Purple Mountain Press, 1976.

McClane, A. J. "A Basic Fly Box." *Field & Stream* August 1958.

———. "Best Flies for Big Trout." *Field & Stream* June 1964.

———. "Brown Trout." *Field & Stream* December 1971.

———. *The Compleat McClane*. New York: Truman Talley Books/E. P. Dutton, 1988.

———. "The Dry Fly on Fast Water." *Field & Stream* January 1974.

———. *Fishng With McClane*. Ed. George Reiger. Englewood Cliffs, N.J.: Prentice-Hall, Inc., 1975.

———. *McClane's Angling World*. New York: Truman Talley Books/E. P. Dutton, 1986.

———. *The Practical Fly Fisherman*. Englewood Cliffs, N.J.: Prentice-Hall, Inc., 1953.

———. "The Rainbow." *Field & Stream* November 1971.

McDonald, John, ed. *The Complete Fly Fisherman*. New York: Charles Scribner's Sons, 1947.

———. *Quill Gordon*. New York: Alfred A. Knopf, 1972.

McIntosh, Robert P. *The Forests of the Catskill Mountains*. Cornwallville, N.Y.: Hope Farm Press, 1977.

McLean, Jay. "School for Sportsmen." *Field & Stream* July 1958.

Migel, J. Michael. *The Stream Conservation Handbook*. New York: Crown Publishers, Inc., 1974.

———, and Leonard M. Wright Jr. *The Masters on the Nymph*. 1979. New York: Lyons & Burford, Publishers, 1985.

Monaghan, Jay. *The Great Rascal*. Boston: Little, Brown & Co., 1952.

Monroe, John D. *Chapters in the History of Delaware County, N.Y.* Delaware County Historical Association, 1949.

Munger, William P., ed. *Historical Atlas of New York State*. Phoenix, N.Y.: Frank E. Richards, 1941.

Murray, David, ed. *Centennial History of Delaware County, N.Y., 1797–1897*. Delhi, N.Y.: William Clark, 1898.

Myers, Frank Daniel, III. *The Wood Chemical Industry in the Delaware Valley*. Middletown, N.Y.: Prior King Press, 1986.

New York State Fisheries Commission. Annual reports, 1869–95.

New York State Fisheries, Game and Forest Commission. Annual reports, 1895–1910.

New York State Conservation Department. Annual reports, 1911–50.

Norris, Thaddeus. *The American Angler's Book*. Philadelphia: E. H. Butler & Co., 1864.

Orvis, Charles F., and A. Nelson Cheney. *Fishing with the Fly*. 1883. Rutland, Vt.: Charles E. Tuttle & Co. Inc., 1968.

Pond, Fred E. *Life and Adventures of Ned Buntline*. New York: The Cadmus Book Shop, 1919.

Quinlan, James Eldridge. *History of Sullivan County*. Liberty, N.Y.: G. M. Beebe & W. T. Morgans, 1873.

Rhead, Louis. *American Trout Stream Insects*. New York: Frederick A. Stokes Co., 1916.

———. *Fisherman's Lures and Game-Fish Food*. New York: Charles Scribner's Sons, 1920.

———, ed. *The Speckled Brook Trout*. New York: R. H. Russell, 1902.

Rich, John Lyon. *Glacial Geology of the Catskills*. New York State Museum Bulletin No. 299. 1935.

Ritchie, Dr. William A. *Indian History of New York State, Part III: The Algonkian Tribes*. The University of the State of New York. (Pamphlet.)

———. "The Indian in His Environment." *Conservationist* Dec.–Jan. 1955–56.

The Rod and Gun and American Sportsman. 1875–77.

Roosevelt, Robert Barnwell. *Game Fish of the Northern States of America and British Provinces*. New York: G. W. Carleton, 1862.

Roscoe-Rockland Bicentennial, 1789–1989. Souvenir booklet. 1989.

Ruttenber, E. M. *Indian Geographical Names*. New York: State Historical Association, 1906.

———. *The Indian Tribes of Hudson's River*. 1872. Port Washington, N.Y.: Kennikat Press, 1971.

Schaldach, William J. *Coverts and Casts*. 1943. Rockville Centre, N.Y.: Freshet Press, 1970.

———. *Currents and Eddies*. New York: A. S. Barnes & Co., 1944.

———. "Net Results." *Field & Stream* February 1946.

———. *The Wind on Your Cheek*. Rockville Centre, N.Y.: Freshet Press, 1972.

Scholz, Lynn. "Louis Rhead's First Career." *The American Fly Fisher*. Vol. 12, No. 1, 1985.

Schwiebert, Ernest G. *Matching the Hatch*. New York: The Macmillan Co., 1955.

Seagears, Clayt. "For New York Waters." *Conservationist* April–May 1951.

———. "Homespun Hackles." *Conservationist* June–July 1947.

Senectutus. "Fifty-four Years on the Beaverkill." *The Angler's Club Bulletin* February 1943.

Shanks, William F. G. "Fish-Culture in America." *Harper's New Monthly Magazine* November 1868.

Shooting and Fishing. A weekly journal of the rifle, gun, and rod. Boston. Nov. 1, 1888– Oct. 8, 1891.

Smedley, Harold. *Fly Patterns and Their Origins*. Muskegon, Mich.: Westshore Pub., 1943.

Smith, Red. *Red Smith on Fishing*. Garden City, N.Y.: Doubleday & Co. Inc., 1963.

Soil Survey of Sullivan County. Soil Conservation Service. 1989.

The Spirit of the Times. Edited by William T. Porter. A weekly chronicle of the turf, agriculture, field sports, literature, and the stage. New York. 1831–61.

Street, Alfred B. "A Day's Fishing in the Callikoon." *Graham's Magazine* October 1845.

Sturgis, William Bayard. *Fly Tying*. New York: Charles Scribner's Sons, 1940.

Summer Homes on the Midland. New York: New York & Oswego Midland Railroad, 1878.

Sylvester, Nathaniel Bartlett. *History of Ulster County*. Philadelphia: Everts & Peck, 1880.

Teale, Edwin. "Reuben R. Cross: Dry Flies from a Kitchen Workshop." *Outdoor Life* December 1934.

Terres, John K. *The Audubon Society Encyclopedia of North American Birds*. New York: Alfred A. Knopf, 1980.

Tiffany, Lena O. B. *Pioneers of the Beaverkill Valley*. Laurens, N.Y.: Village Printer, 1976.

Turf, Field and Farm. New York. 1872; July 4, 1873–December 31, 1875; July 7, 1882–December 29, 1882; 1886; January 7, 1887–June 24, 1887.

Van Siclen, George W., ed. *An American Edition of the Treatyse of Fysshyinge wyth an Angle*. By Dame Juliana Berner. Private printing, 1875.

Van Valkenburgh, Norman J. *Land Acquisition for New York State*. Arkville, N.Y.: The Catskill Center, 1985.

Wakefield, Manville. *To the Mountains by Rail*. Grahamsville, N.Y.: Wakefair Press, 1970.

Wetzel, Charles M. *American Fishing Books*. 1950. Stone Harbor, N.J.: Meadow Run Press, 1990.

Whipple, Gurth. *Fifty Years of Conservation in New York State, 1885–1935*. Albany, N.Y.: J. B. Lyon Co., 1935.

Willis, Joseph F. *The Pioneer*. Livingston Manor, N.Y.: Livingston Manor Central School Board of Education, 1939.

The Woman Flyfishers Club. Fortieth Anniversary booklet. 1972.

Weslager, C. A. *The Delaware Indians* New Brunswick, N.J.: Rutgers University Press, 1972.

Wood, Leslie C. *Holt! T'Other Way*. Middletown, N.Y.: L. C. Wood, 1950.

———. *Rafting on the Delaware River*. Livingston Manor, N.Y.: *Livingston Manor Times*, 1934.

Wright, Leonard M., Jr. *The Fly Fisher's Reader*. New York: Simon & Schuster, Inc., 1990.

Wulff, Lee. *Trout on a Fly*. New York: Nick Lyons Books, 1986.

Year Book of the Holland Society of New York. New York: Knickerbocker Press, 1886–87, 1904.

Index

Note: Page numbers in *italics* refer to material in illustrations or captions.

Index